THE RECKONING

How the Democrats and the Left Betrayed Women and Girls

KARA DANSKY

BOMBARDIER
BOOKS

Published by Bombardier Books
An Imprint of Post Hill Press
ISBN: 979-8-88845-082-6
ISBN (eBook): 979-8-88845-083-3

The Reckoning:
How the Democrats and the Left Betrayed Women and Girls

Cover Design by Jim Villaflores

Post Hill Press
New York • Nashville
posthillpress.com

Published in the United States of America
1 2 3 4 5 6 7 8 9 10

TABLE OF CONTENTS

~ To TERFs Everywhere ~

Laila Joan
1st TERFS
2004

I am fighting what I see as a powerful, insidious, misogynistic movement, that has gained huge purchase in very influential areas of society. I do not see this particular movement as either benign or powerless, so I'm afraid I stand with the women who are fighting to be heard against threats of loss of livelihood and threats to their safety.

—J.K. Rowling, March 2023

In just 5–10 years, my side of the political aisle went from 'gender is something we made up to control people's behavior' to 'gender is one of the few things that defines who you are as a person' and nobody who went along with that massive change realizes how weird it is.
—"Russell," anonymous X (formerly Twitter) user, May 2023[1]

[1] Throughout this book, I will refer to the social media forum that used to be called "Twitter" simply as "X."

Bartender: "Um, sorry, ma'am there's no porn allowed at the bar."
Man in dress, looking at phone: "It's okay, I'm transgender."
Bartender: "Oh, I had no idea. Do whatever you want, all the time."
—*Family Guy* episode

PREFACE

A NOTE TO AMERICAN DEMOCRATIC WOMEN

American Democratic women, can we have a word, please?

I grew up in a small town in southeastern Ohio called Athens, home to Ohio University. The town has a population of about 10,000, which roughly triples when the university is in session. Athens tends to run Democratic—every presidential election, Athens County shows up as bright blue in a sea of red—though of course some political conservatives live there. There's a shop in Athens called Artifacts Gallery. My friends and I frequently shopped there as teenagers. It sells fun knick-knacks, funky earrings, and cool T-shirts. Its current owner is a woman named Amy Mangano. One day in 2022, Mangano decorated the shop front with a bunch of posters carrying messages that were all very pro-woman, pro-gay, and pro-free speech. In response, the community largely turned on her, calling for boycotts and protests. These calls were not coming from conservatives; they were coming from university students and progressives. Why? Why on earth would a bunch of university students and political progressives target a female small business owner who was spreading messages that were unambiguously pro-woman, pro-gay, and pro-free speech, traditionally progressive causes?

The best way to explain it is that the Democratic Party, the left-leaning media, and the entire leftist political and cultural establishment, have all betrayed and abandoned women and girls at the altar of "gender identity" or "trans." By the "entire leftist political and cultural establishment," I include traditionally progressive organizations like the American Civil Liberties Union (or ACLU, where I once worked) and celebrities like Jamie Lee Curtis and Charlize Theron who constantly go on about their "transgender children." Women (and men) on the left who speak about this are usually ignored, silenced, punished, and/or threatened with cancelation and sometimes violence. I say this as a life-long Democrat and a progressive feminist who strongly supports abortion rights and rights for lesbians and gay men. I registered to vote as a Democrat in 1990 and the only time since then that I have not been a Democrat was a brief period in the 2000s when I was registered Green. I re-registered as a Democrat to vote in the 2008 Democratic presidential primary and have remained a Democrat ever since. I am also a radical feminist who has been following the "transgender" movement since 2014. During that time, I have learned a few things.

When I say that Democrats have betrayed women and girls, I mean that Democrats in power (along with the cultural left) have allowed men and boys to compete on sports teams intended for women and girls, taking honors and awards that belong to women and girls; permitted convicted male felons to be housed in women's prisons with vulnerable women; and encouraged policies that permit men to invade women's intimate spaces like bathrooms, locker rooms, changing rooms, and spas. This all falls disproportionately on black women and lesbians, both traditionally reliable Democratic voting blocks. They have promoted laws and policies that permit a corrupt medical establishment to feed puberty-blocking hormones, opposite-sex hormones, and surgeries to children and young people, causing sterility, illness, and other harm, including permanent loss of sexual and reproductive function.

The deeply unfortunate truth is that Democratic politicians (including many women) and the mainstream organized progressive movement, including historically feminist organizations, have entirely abandoned us and our society's children to the "transgender" lobby and the for-profit "trans" medical establishment. An example: The National Park Service has essentially redecorated Women's Rights National Historical Park in Seneca Falls, New York, the birthplace of American women's suffrage, with "trans progress" flags and signs suggesting that sex isn't real and that we don't exist as a sex class.

With some notable exceptions, the mainstream media has largely covered this up, which is why many of us don't understand it is happening. A lot of American Democratic women are concerned about these issues but are uncomfortable talking about them because all opposition to "trans" seems to be coming from conservatives. That is understandable, but it's not true. I hear from rank-and-file Democrats (including progressives and feminists) every day who say they are fed up with party leadership because of what they are doing on this issue. American liberal and progressive women (and the men who care about them) have every reason and right to be concerned about this issue and to talk about it with our voices and, if necessary, with our votes.

It is, of course, only Congressional Republicans who are taking steps to protect women's spaces and sports and to stop the sterilization and mutilation of healthy young people at the federal level (though some Democrats are taking similar steps at the state level) and only conservative media outlets are having even slightly honest conversations about these things. *But that's because Congressional Democrats and liberal media outlets have allowed that to happen by refusing to step up on behalf of women and girls.* If a single Congressional Democrat would take it upon herself to say, "Men are not women and should not have access to women's bathrooms, locker rooms, sports, or prisons," we would not be in this position.

If you are worried about speaking out because you are concerned you will appear homophobic, don't be. Feminists and gay rights activists have been complaining for years now that the "trans" movement is *itself* homophobic. We argue that "gender identity" constitutes "transing the gay away." By denying the material reality of sex, it denies the reality of same-sex attraction. For Pride month 2023, the mayor of London declared, "Pride in London has helped to change our society. It's part of the reason London is renowned across the globe as a beacon of inclusion and diversity. I'm pleased that this year's campaign will be in support of the capital's trans and non-binary community." He didn't have a word to say about support for lesbians or gay men. The mayor of London is not even pretending that Pride is about gay rights anymore. Shortly after the mayor made that announcement, a group called Pride London starting blocking lesbians and gay men who complained on X about their exclusion from Pride. One U.K. lesbian remarked, "London Pride is determined to block all of the gay men and lesbians and welcome only the gender confused. Nothing gay about pride marches anymore. Pride is a traitor to sexuality, specifically same-sex attraction." American Democratic women, if you think of yourself as a supporter of gay rights, which I do, we need to pay very close attention to what is going on here. There's no reason to think something similar can't happen in the U.S.

In fact, something similar *has* happened in the U.S. In 2018, a lesbian radical feminist (and a Democrat) named Julia Beck was serving on the Baltimore "LGBTQ Commission," under the direction of the Democratic mayor Catherine Pugh. Also serving on the commission was Ava Pipitone, a man who claimed to be a woman and the president of Baltimore's Transgender Alliance. Beck eventually became a co-chair of the commission's Law and Policy Committee. A few months after the first commission meeting, Beck participated in the local Pride march, carrying signs that said things like "LESBIAN NOT QUEER." Pipitone did not like this at all and he challenged her at a later meeting. Beck brought up the case of Karen White (a man who was at the time being housed in a U.K. women's prison on the basis of his woman identity and went on to rape two women in the prison). Beck said that she would not refer to White as "she." Eventually, the Law and Policy Committee voted her off it on the grounds that her refusal to recognize men's "gender identities" rendered her a "transphobe." In 2022, Pipitone simply dropped the entire ruse and stopped claiming to be a woman. To the best of my knowledge, no one has ever apologized to Beck for the committee's treatment of her.

"Gender identity" also disproportionately harms black women—one of the Democrats' largest voting blocks—and in many ways, uniquely. For example, it ignores the increased risks of violence that black women face throughout society, denigrates black women into harmful stereotypes of what it means to be a woman, and erases language that black women use to describe their experiences of living in a society that is both profoundly sexist and racist.

Women are not supposed to talk about any of this, and feminists who do so anyway are punished. Donna Hughes is a professor at the University of Rhode Island, where she holds the Eleanor M. and Oscar M. Carlson Endowed Chair in Women's Studies. She serves as the Director of Graduate Studies in the Gender and Women's Studies Program. Her main research area is in prostitution and human trafficking. She also has a Ph.D. in genetics. In February 2021, she published an article on the feminist website *4W* titled "Fantasy Worlds on the Political Right and Left: QAnon and Trans-Sex Beliefs." In it, she called "trans" a "fantasy," and compared it to QAnon. She said, "The trans-sex fantasy, the belief that a person can change his or her sex, either from male to female or from female to male, is spreading largely unquestioned among the political left." In response, the university's Gender and Sexuality Center director publicly referred to Hughes's comments as "beyond the pale" and said that she was "heartbroken," and the university put out a statement condemning Hughes. Students demanded that she undergo "implicit bias and micro-aggression awareness training" and launched a campaign to have her formally disciplined.

Callie Burt is a sociologist and criminologist in the Andrew Young School of Policy Studies at Georgia State University, with a Ph.D. in sociology. She once served on the editorial board of a journal called *Feminist Criminology*. In June 2020, she published a peer-reviewed article in the journal that recognized the distinction between sex and gender. She opposed the prioritization of "gender identity" over sex. She was then removed from the journal's editorial board based on accusations of "transphobia." Similar things are happening to female academics all over the world. Anna Kalvig taught at Norway's University of Stavanger for twenty-five years, but after being vilified for defending women's sex-based rights, she resigned, stating, "For several years, I have been the target of a smear campaign because I claim that objective, material evidence must also take precedence in the area of gender, when we draw up rules, arrangements and legislation and when we demand protection from existing legislation."

The establishment left will tell you that "trans people have always existed throughout history" and that there has been a "decades-long movement to protect trans rights." Neither assertion is true, but it is a phenomenon that has come to be known as "trans-washing," that is, historical revisionism to paint historical figures and/or organizations as "trans," when the individuals were more than likely lesbian or gay, and the organizations were more than likely gay rights groups. For example, a play premiered at Shakespeare's Globe Theater in 2022 titled *I, Joan*, in which a Joan of Arc character is portrayed as "trans" and "non-binary." In one line, she says, "I'm not a girl. I do not fit that word." But Joan of Arc was certainly female, and there is evidence that she was likely a lesbian. The playwright is a woman named Charlie Josephine who refers to herself as "transgender, queer and non-binary."

In June 2023, New York Democratic state senator Brad Hoylman-Sigal posted, "On June 28, 1968, a crowd of mostly trans women of color rose up against state-sponsored bigotry at Stonewall Inn. 54 years later LGBTQ NYers continue to fight back, enacting our nation-leading legislation to protect trans youth & their families seeking gender-affirming care." This is not true. The Stonewall rebellion was started by a lesbian and fought by lesbians and gay men at a time when the concept of "trans women of color" did not yet exist. Democrats and progressive organizations simply have to make us think that "trans" is a decades-long civil rights struggle to justify their efforts to allow men to invade women's spaces and poison children with dangerous hormones. Organizations like the ACLU and GLAAD have spent the past few years completely re-writing history in the U.S. to portray decades' worth of advocacy on behalf of lesbians and gay men as part of a decades-long "trans rights" movement. Trans-washing is the complete rewriting of gay rights history and movement-building, and it is blatantly homophobic.

In May 2023, there was boycott of Target, and America went a bit crazy. The *New York Post* declared, "Target loses $9B in week following boycott calls over LGBTQ-friendly kids clothing." *Time Magazine* ran this headline: "Queer Activists Criticize Target for Removing LGBTQ+ Merchandise After a Conservative Backlash." In an episode of *The View*, Whoopi Goldberg called the entire episode a "war on gay people." But what was really going on here? No one really objected to gay people or to gay pride. Today, people across the political spectrum generally accept homosexuality as a healthy and normal aspect of human society. A 2021 Gallup poll found that 70 percent of the U.S. population supports same-sex marriage, including 83 percent of Democrats and 55 percent of Republicans. Even among Republicans who oppose same-sex marriage, most do not really care what same-sex couples do in their bedrooms; they object to gay marriage for religious reasons, but they do not really care that some people are same-sex attracted. There are even some [many!] gay and lesbian Republicans!

What Target did that really angered people was put Pride merchandise, including a women's style bathing suit that included an internal fold for "tucking," front and center in their stores. "Tucking," for anyone who does not know, refers to hiding the fact of a penis. This was a women's style bathing suit that men and boys can wear while hiding their penises. This was being marketed not to adult men in a sex shop; it was being marketed to men and boys front and center in Target—one of the largest chains that caters to families with children. That's what sparked the boycott; not a hatred of gay people. All the media outlets that reported this incident as being about "LGBTQ" people were just lying.

In the spring of 2022, a woman contacted me to say that she was very concerned about a student named Lia Thomas competing on the University of Pennsylvania women's swimming team. Her daughter was a swimmer on a different Ivy League team. The previous fall, she was looking at the season's roster and saw a senior named Lia Thomas on the Penn team. That surprised her, because she had never seen a Lia Thomas on the Penn women's team. Where had Lia come from? Was Lia a transfer student? That seemed the likeliest explanation, but it also seemed odd because college students do not typically transfer as seniors. She looked into the matter and learned that "Lia" was a man named Will who had previously competed (and regularly lost) on the Penn men's team. She did a little more digging and learned what many of us have known for several years—all over the country (and the world), men are competing on women's sports teams on the basis of their supposed "female gender identity" and taking honors that are supposed to be reserved for women. She learned that the very category "women and girls" is being erased. She also learned that women who object to this are labeled "transphobic," or sometimes "fascist" or "Nazi," even when we are progressive Democrats.

This woman knew that *Glamour Magazine* had named Caitlyn (formerly Bruce) Jenner "Woman of the Year" in 2015 and that *Vanity Fair* had put him on its cover (all of which she thought was pretty weird, but didn't stress too much about), but she had no idea how pervasive this had become. She lamented, "I am progressive on women's rights. I have voted for Democrats because of women's issues, and I have always believed we could count on Democrats not to abandon women! How could this happen without me even knowing about it?!" That woman's name is Kim Jones and today she is a co-founder of ICONS, the Independent Council on Women's Sports, which fights to keep women's sports for women. There are countless Democratic women like her all over the country.

In 2017, I went on *Tucker Carlson Tonight* to talk about this issue. I had never seen the show before because I don't watch *Fox News*, although, of course, I knew who Carlson was. I explained that I am a leftist radical feminist and that the Women's Liberation Front (WoLF), of which I then served as board chair, was suing the Obama administration over its 2016 policy of redefining sex to include "gender identity" under Title IX. Although my decision was generally supported by radical feminists who understood the threats that "gender identity" pose to women and girls, it was not appreciated by many of my friends and allies on the political left who think that Tucker Carlson is basically the devil incarnate. What they didn't understand is that I would have preferred to go on the *Rachel Maddow*, *Anderson Cooper*, or any other left-leaning political shows, but none of them would have me. Even now, none of them will speak openly or honestly about the Democrats' betrayal of women and girls.

I have also found myself making some very interesting friends over the years—conservative women who, like me, are disgusted by how our entire society seems to think it is acceptable for men to be allowed to say they are women and take over everything we have spent the past fifty years fighting for. Even though many of these women are staunchly anti-abortion (although some are not), they also want many of the same things progressive women want—professional leadership positions, more authority within their families, and the right to safety and autonomy. These are some very smart and politically savvy women and I'm glad to know them.

These women understand that if they vote Republican, they have first-wave feminists to thank for their right to do so. They understand that all women (regardless of political affiliation) who have benefited from rape crisis centers, domestic violence shelters, and laws protecting married women's property have second-wave feminists to thank. I make no apologies for working with conservative women over the years to protect women and girls as a sex class. This would not have been necessary if the American political left had stood up against the onslaught of the "trans" movement to protect women and girls from its attacks on us. But it didn't. So now, liberal and progressive women, regardless of whether we consider ourselves feminists, need to be open to working with conservative women to protect women and girls. Men on the left aren't going to save us.

But, but, but...what about abortion? I know. I get it. I have been in favor of abortion rights since I wrote a letter to Tip O'Neill in eighth grade, asking him to scrap the Hyde Amendment (which prohibits the expenditure of Medicaid funds on abortion). I did abortion clinic defense in college, where I locked arms with women (and some men) who were protecting access to clinics from anti-abortion demonstrators. In law school,

I volunteered at the National Abortion and Reproductive Rights Action League (which now champions the rights of men with woman identities over women themselves). My support for abortion has never wavered and it never will. But please understand that the Democrats cannot be counted on to protect abortion rights. President Barack Obama is on record in 2009 saying that protecting abortion rights was not a legislative priority for his administration. The Democrats in Congress had fifty years to codify *Roe v. Wade* into law and they didn't do it.

What's more, abortion rights supporters on the left (including some women) are *handing* Republicans the talking point that "abortion is not a women's rights issue." Feminists have *always* maintained that abortion is a women's rights issue. Yet, in 2022, anti-abortion Republican Senator Josh Hawley sparred with University of California at Berkeley law professor Khiara M. Bridges over whether it is. During a hearing on a proposal to codify *Roe* into law, Bridges had referred to "people with a capacity for pregnancy." Hawley asked, "Would that be women?" Her response was that "many cis women have the capacity for pregnancy. Many cis women do not have the capacity for pregnancy. There are also trans men who are capable of pregnancy as well as nonbinary people who are capable of pregnancy."[2] This presented the perfect opportunity for Hawley to retort, "So this isn't really a women's rights issue?" She had no answer other than to accuse him of "transphobia."

Something similar happened in June 2023 when Kelley Robinson, president of the Human Rights Campaign (HRC), testified before the Senate Judiciary Committee about the Protection of Women and Girls in Sports Act. Republican Senator Ted Cruz asked her the question, "Is there a difference between men and women," and she had no answer. She

---

[2] People who adhere to "gender identity" ideology will tell you that the term "cis women" means something like "women whose gender identity aligns with their birth sex," or "women whose gender identity matches the sex they were assigned at birth." It is meant to differentiate women (the female kind) from men who claim to be women. It asserts that the word "women" refers to an overarching category of human beings that includes female women (cis) and male women (trans). Feminists reject this pejorative term completely.

immediately pivoted to inquire as to whether he was asking her a question about "transgender," and he reiterated that it was a simple question: "Is there a difference between men and women?" She *still* fell short of a response. This is the president of one of the largest so-called "progressive" organizations in the United States not knowing whether there is a difference between men and women and thereby making Senator Cruz seem like the reasonable one in the room.

In fighting for abortion rights, feminists often chant slogans like "no uterus, no opinion." The point we are making is that men, who will never face the choice of whether to terminate a pregnancy, should have no say in the abortion debate. Seth Dillon is an anti-abortion conservative and a comedian, and the chief executive of the satire magazine *The Babylon Bee*. In 2022, after the decision overturning *Roe* was leaked, he posted, "You can't say 'no uterus, no opinion' anymore. You gave that up when you said trans women are women." He wasn't wrong. The category of people who are colloquially referred to as "trans women" are men. Not a single "trans woman" (man) has a uterus. If, as many on the left like to insist, "trans women are women," then every single one of them should have the right to an opinion about abortion, notwithstanding the absence of a uterus. Because of women who regularly claim that "trans women are women," the left has given Republicans the talking point "You can't say 'no uterus, no opinion' anymore." The left literally handed the right these arguments to make in their advocacy *against* abortion. At the end of the day, we cannot protect women's right to abortion if we cannot name women as a sex class. The right knows this, and they will not stop using the left's nonsensical arguments against us. The left, in other words, is *helping* the right further erode abortion rights.

There's a group called Parents with Inconvenient Truths about Trans (PITT) who write about their struggles navigating situations in which their children (sometimes minors, sometimes young adults) are confused about their sex. These are parents who are desperate to help their children survive a damaging and dangerous industry that encourages "transition" at every step. Their stories are agonizing and they say things like,

"I'm very liberal and accept my children's sexual orientation, however I don't believe in the notion that my son is actually a woman/girl." PITT published the results of a survey in May 2023 reporting that parents who responded to the survey skewed female, highly educated, upper income, and politically liberal or independent. These parents are hardly right-wing homophobes; they lean left and they are doing everything they can to save their kids from "trans."

The insistence on adhering to this regressive and sexist ideology sometimes comes in the form of mandatory "preferred pronouns." Readers may have heard about "preferred pronouns" in their places of employment or possibly because Vice President Kamala Harris announced her "preferred pronouns" (she/her, in case that wasn't obvious) during a town hall event when she was a candidate for the presidency. So-called "preferred pronouns" are a nod to the idea that sex isn't real and/or that people can be the opposite sex (or some mysterious third sex that doesn't exist). Some employers mandate them in email signatures and/or Zoom names. The city of Dallas Texas mandates that city employees use people's "preferred pronouns" or risk termination, even if they disagree with them. This is probably unconstitutional; one federal court has already ruled that public entities may not mandate that employees use "preferred pronouns." But the authoritarian nature of "gender identity" knows no bounds.

Women who speak out about this are being silenced all over the world. For the most part, leftist feminists in the U.S. cannot get a platform in U.S. media. Kellie-Jay Keen is a women's rights activist in the U.K. who has traveled the world holding events called "Let Women Speak." In Australia, a female artist named Pearl was ousted from an art festival because she had spoken at one of these events. In Ireland, you can be imprisoned for up to five years for speaking out about "gender identity." In August 2023, an Irish pop singer named Roísín Murphy posted some comments on a private Facebook post that was critical of puberty blockers and her recording company stopped promoting her upcoming album. Lawmakers in the Dominican Republic have proposed penalties of up to thirty years for "misgendering." Luckily, in the U.S., we have the First Amendment, which protects us from being penalized for so-called "hate speech," but in the past several years, governments all over the world have been passing laws to penalize people for the alleged crime of "misgendering." And even though Americans can't be imprisoned for it, we can be, and often are, kicked off social media platforms, no-platformed in the media, socially ostracized, and terminated from our jobs.

I have never in my life experienced the type of woman-hatred, vitriol, or fury that comes from "trans" activism. I frequently speak up for the rights of women and girls as a sex class and am told that I am "transphobic," that I need to kill myself or "die in a fire." People (mostly men, but also plenty of women) who champion "trans" show up to women's rights rallies armed with bats and batons, threatening to kill women. This has happened time and again, all over the U.S. and in other countries like the U.K., France, Germany, Italy, the Netherlands, Australia, and New Zealand. The pushback against women and girls can be vicious and, often, disgusting. In England, "trans" activists have dumped large bottles of urine at the Equality and Human Rights Commission building in London because that agency had issued guidance concerning the importance of maintaining single-sex spaces. In August 2023 in Portland, Oregon, a man named Vivian allegedly smashed and defecated in the car of a seventeen-year-old girl and later told police that he did it because the girl was "transphobic." I have attended many pro-abortion rallies where anti-abortion protesters have screamed that I am a "witch" and a "baby killer" and that I am "going to hell." Not one of them has ever actually threatened to kill me, though. I can't say the same for "trans" activists, who have.

In early 2023, I was contacted by a reporter from the U.K. paper *The Daily Mail* who wanted to run a story about this violence that is being inflicted on women and girls who speak about the threats that "gender identity" and "trans" pose to women and girls as a sex class. He eventually published a piece exposing the violence of what he dubbed "trantifa" (combining "trans" and "antifa"). Trantifa is a perfect descriptor. These men with "gender identities" are fascists who call themselves "antifascists." As J.K. Rowling has posted, in today's society, "War is Peace. Freedom is

Slavery. Ignorance is Strength. The Penised Individual Who Raped You Is a Woman." And now, fascists are antifascists. Trantifa's hatred of women is unparalleled, in my experience.

In February 2020, I spoke at a WoLF event at the Seattle Public Library titled, "Fighting the New Misogyny: A Feminist Critique of 'Gender Identity.'" A mob of hundreds of trantifa gathered outside the library, chanting and screaming that we are "TERFs" (i.e., "trans exclusionary radical feminists," or leftist feminist women who know that sex is real). After the event, the speakers had to be escorted out of the building by library security and then by city police officers to our car. Once we reached our car, trantifa activists pounded on the hood and roof of the car with their fists while chanting "FUCK TERFs!"

At one rally in California in 2022, a trantifa man threw a raw egg directly at my head. It hit me and cracked, and raw egg streamed down my face, neck, and chest. Others hit women in the face with pies. At one rally in Tacoma, Washington, in 2022, a trantifa man crushed a woman's hand, breaking her bones; this caused her to sustain permanent and irreparable injury. At a rally in New Zealand, Kellie-Jay Keen was nearly crushed to death and a twenty-year-old trantifa man repeatedly punched a seventy-year-old woman in the face, giving her a black eye. It later came out that one of the police officers who was supposed to be there to protect Keen and her supporters was a man who claims to have a woman identity. After she spoke at the University of San Francisco, trantifa barricaded swimmer Riley Gaines (who competed against Lia (Will) Thomas in the 2022 NCAA championships) in a room for three hours and demanded a ransom for her release. Her crime was speaking out against the inclusion of male athletes in women's sports.

The situation has become so dire globally that the U.N. Special Rapporteur on Violence Against Women issued a statement condemning this violence in early 2023. By the summer of 2023, Lia (Will) Thomas was openly advocating for trantifa violence on Instagram. At London Pride, a man called Sarah Jane (Alan) Baker said, "If you see a TERF, punch them in the fucking face!" and the crowd cheered. Baker had previously been convicted of kidnapping, burglary, unlawful imprisonment, and intentionally causing great bodily harm, and spent decades in prison, so his threats of violence seem quite credible. The London police initially failed to arrest him, but they eventually did. Trantifa responded to the arrest with calls to "Free Sarah Jane!" as though inciting violence against women makes him some sort of human rights hero. He eventually managed to persuade a judge that his statement was a "joke," and he faced no consequences for his actions.

In August 2022, I taped an episode of the *Dr. Phil* show, along with radical feminist and lesbian Ruth Barrett, who self-published a book in 2016 called *Female Erasure: What You Need to Know About Gender Politics' War on Women, the Female Sex, and Human Rights*. The reason that she self-published is that she could not find a single publisher willing to discuss the subject. On the opposite side of the debate were one woman who had recently given birth to a baby and insisted on referring to herself as a "non-binary dad" and one man who wore a flowery dress, curly wig, and copious amounts of makeup, all designed to mask his male sex. Both were extremely aggressive toward me and Ruth and insisted that sex isn't real, or that if it is, it is less important than their "gender identities." The man (called Chandi) demanded to be called a woman and I told him that he couldn't because he's male. Dr. Phil tried hard to get me to refer to him as a "transgender woman," but I refused. Dr. Phil asked me if "transwomen" can be included in the women's movement and I said that *men* aren't included in the women's movement because I think it is critically important that women retain language that pertains specifically to us as a sex class. A complete stranger approached me in September 2023 to tell me that she had seen the episode; she said she agreed with me and thanked me for what I said. The episode aired in April 2023 and I encourage Democratic women to watch it. See what you think. Form your own opinions.

TERFs and our male allies use the phrase "peak trans" to mean the moment when liberals and progressives who have been going along with the "transgender" charade wake up and say, "Wait a minute, something isn't right here." Once liberals and progressives dig into the issue a little bit, we can see that the entire edifice is an authoritarian, sexist, homophobic nightmare that is harming women and children. Once you see it, you can't unsee it. That moment is "peak trans."

The U.S. chapter of Women's Declaration International (WDI USA, of which I serve as president) held its second annual convention in San Francisco in September 2023. A few weeks before the convention, we learned that there was a campaign to get us cancelled. The hotel informed us that they had received a barrage of phone calls and email messages calling us a "hate group" and demanding that our contract be cancelled. Feminists are used to this; it happens all the time, all over the world. But the hotel held firm because they could see that we are clearly not a "hate group." In fact, they appeared to agree with our message. We were in close contact with hotel security, which was, in turn, in contact with the San Francisco Police Department. On the second day of the convention, trantifa turned up to protest us. They were loud, hostile, and completely annoying to us, hotel staff, security, and regular hotel guests. They yelled, screamed, chanted, and banged on pots and pans. They tried to infiltrate the hotel, and hotel security ended up having to lock all the doors other than the main entrance and stand in a line at the main entrance to expel trantifa while welcoming legitimate hotel guests. The day after the convention, we had an event at City Hall where we stood up for lesbians' rights. Trantifa turned up again to yell and scream, fight with the police, and get in the way of average people who were just there to conduct business or have wedding pictures taken on the steps of City Hall. We think that over the course of a few days in San Francisco, trantifa managed to peak trans countless San Franciscans with their horrible, violent, juvenile behavior.

In August 2023, the rock legend Alice Cooper did an interview with the online music magazine *Stereogum*. Cooper has clearly peak transed. He said, "I'm understanding that there are cases of transgender [children], but I'm afraid that it's also a fad. I find it wrong when you've got a six-year-old kid who has no idea. He just wants to play and you're confusing him [by] telling him, 'Yeah, you're a boy, but you could be a girl if you want to be.'" He also addressed the topic of men invading women's spaces, saying "A guy can walk into a woman's bathroom at any time and just say, 'I just feel like I'm a woman today,' and have the time of his life in there. Unfortunately, this is now a very real concern for many women. Predatory men have been given a green light to enter women's private spaces, and women who push back will be branded as bigots. Where do you draw this line?" One intention with this book is that more and more liberal and progressive women (and the men who care about them) will reach "peak trans." Come on in, the water's warm. If Alice Cooper can do it, so can you.

American Democratic liberal and progressive women: We need to insist that our lawmakers represent our interests. We need to explain this to them in no uncertain terms. They have sold us out and if they don't change course, they will be held accountable. Many leftist progressive women in the U.K. are stating publicly that they will not vote for the Labour Party or the Green Party until it stops throwing women and girls under the bus at the altar of "gender identity." Progressive feminists all over the world are doing the same with respect to their own so-called "progressive" parties. I won't tell anyone who to vote for, but I can say this: unless Democrats change course immediately and publicly hold themselves accountable for what they have done to women and girls as a sex class, I have no plans to vote for them in 2024. And I am not alone.[3]

---

[3] I hesitated before publishing this book. A lot of people, including many friends and family members, are going to be very unhappy with me for doing it and a few will probably cancel me from their lives. It is not at all unusual for TERFs to be cancelled by their friends and family members, but I'm willing to take that risk because this is so important. One day while I was working on an early version of the initial manuscript of the book, this email landed in my inbox: "Hello, I am a scientist and executive, recently retired and moved to [REDACTED]. My family has been totally destroyed by trans. I want to be active and combat this vicious political movement. How can I help?" The truth about all this needs to be told. If the Democratic Party establishment won't tell the truth, and if no one else will hold them to account, then someone has to do it.

PART 1

THE NEED FOR A RECKONING

In every life, there comes a day of reckoning—a time when unsettled scores demand retribution, and our own lies and transgressions are finally laid bare.
–Emily Thorne (a fictional character in the television series *Revenge*)

CHAPTER 1

THE BETRAYAL OF DEMOCRATIC PARTY LEADERSHIP

Democratic Party leadership and other leftist institutions have *knowingly* sold out women and girls in America. Most people don't know it, but some of the fiercest opposition to "gender identity" all over the world comes from people who consider themselves as being (or having been) on the political left. The reason that most people don't know this is that our party leaders and the media consistently ignore us and actively suppress our views.

"Gender identity" (or "transgender") is not real in any actual material sense, but readers wouldn't know that from listening to Democratic leadership or the legacy media. As I explained in my previous book, *The Abolition of Sex: How the "Transgender" Agenda Harms Women and Girls*, it is a made-up concept that is designed to obscure the reality of sex. It has largely succeeded in doing so globally. When people say someone "is transgender," what they usually mean is that the person claims to have a "gender identity" that is opposite to their actual sex. Sometimes they mean that a person is "non-binary," or "neither male nor female." There is, however, no credible scientific evidence to support the idea that any of that is possible. Every single human being on the face of the planet, all eight billion of us, is either female or male. This is true for every single person who claims to have a "gender identity" and it is true no matter what clothes or how much eyeliner we may wear.

It's fine if someone wants to adopt an identity; someone can have an identity as a unicorn or as a turtle, I guess. Plenty of kids in the seventies and eighties had an identity as punk or goth, and we all survived with our sex intact (including the boys who wore eyeliner!). The problem comes when that person forces everyone else to comply with demands that the identity in question supersedes reality, and that is what is happening throughout society today. I spent a portion of the early eighties wishing that I was Madonna and a portion of the late eighties persuaded that I was the reincarnation of Janis Joplin. At no point did I insist that anyone go along with these silly teenaged fantasies. As one British X user recently commented, "When my son was 3, he thought he was a Royal Guard. He marched everywhere, only wore a red t-shirt, black trousers, and a black hat with a feather taped on the side. We thought it was cute. We did not affirm him and drop him off at Buckingham Palace."

Are there people who sincerely believe that they are the opposite sex? I'm sure of it. I have read story after story of people who say that they suffer tremendous stress at the thought of their sexed bodies. Most of them seem to be young women (though there are young men who suffer from it too). Dr. Lisa Littman brought nationwide attention to the phenomenon of "rapid onset gender dysphoria" in young people in her 2018 study, "Parent Reports of Adolescents and Young Adults Perceived to Show Signs of a Rapid Onset of Gender Dysphoria." Abigail Shrier delved deeply into the topic of "gender dysphoria" among young women in the 2020 book *Irreversible Damage: The Transgender Craze Seducing our Daughters*. I don't doubt the sincerity of these people at all. The thing is, no matter how sincere (or how severe) the belief that a person is the opposite sex, no one is, or can be made to be, the opposite sex. All these people have been sold the lie that they can change sex and I have tremendous sympathy for them.

There is another category of people who claim to "be transgender" who are not sincere at all. These are adult men who are sexually aroused at the thought of themselves as female. They are called "autogynephiles." To be crude about it, these are straight (or sometimes gay) men who get off by wearing stereotypical women's clothing, often lacy or silky lingerie. They are often heavily into pornography (including a version of porn called "sissy porn," which involves getting off on imagining oneself as a woman and being sexually and violently degraded). By enshrining "gender identity" in the law and throughout society, the Democrats and the cultural left have given such men access to women's spaces like bathrooms, locker rooms, changing rooms, prisons, and domestic violence shelters.

However, even though "gender identity" is neither real in any material sense nor grounded in biology, it *is* a very powerful political movement that is backed by an enormous industry. This movement is extremely regressive because it is grounded in sexist stereotypes about what women and men should look and act like (e.g., if you are a person who likes pink and glitter you must be a girl). "Trans" proponents often argue that a young boy who likes to dress up in his mom's clothes is actually a girl and should therefore be given life-altering hormones to stop his puberty and make him look more like a girl. The movement is also sexist (something the left used to consider a bad thing but apparently no longer does) in that it erases women and girls as a coherent category of people and allows men to invade our spaces and activities. It insists that women refer to ourselves as "uterus havers" or "menstruators" or "birthing bodies," as though women are chattel. It is also homophobic in that it denies the reality of sex and insists that some people with penises (i.e., "trans women") can be lesbians (I have spoken with several lesbians who have been told that they are "transphobic" if they are not interested in dating "trans women," i.e., men). This is no different from fifties-style homophobia.

Finally, the movement is authoritarian because dissent is not permitted (numerous women and men all over the world have been fired from their jobs and/or removed from conferences and other events because they stand up for the material reality of sex). I have experienced this first-hand. Today, people are being forced, legally and socially, to accept the lies of "gender identity," to the detriment of everybody, but especially to that of women and girls. Democratic Party leadership is largely responsible for sacrificing women and girls at the altar of "gender identity" in the U.S., although they are not the only perpetrators. I say all of this as a lifelong leftist radical feminist activist Democrat. Or, if you like, a TERF.

For anyone who doesn't know, the acronym TERF can stand for (depending on who you ask) "Trans Exclusionary Radical Feminist," "Telling Everyone Real Facts," or "Tired of Explaining Reality to Fu*kwits," among other descriptors. Regardless, an authentic TERF is a radical feminist political leftist woman who recognizes the material reality of sex and who isn't afraid to stand up for the sex-based rights of women and girls against the onslaught of misogyny that comes in the form of so-called "gender identity." When TERFs try to talk about these things, we are often labeled "right wing," or sometimes "fascists" or "bigots." In March 2023, I attended a women's rights demonstration hosted by WDI USA. Those of us in attendance held a banner saying that a woman is an adult human female and gave speeches. A man dropped by to tell us that we are "fascist bitches." We're not. We're leftists. We are mostly Democrats, and those of us who are not Democrats are mostly former Democrats who fled the party because of this issue. Some of us consider ourselves to be left of the Democratic Party ideologically but we stay in the party for our own political reasons. Others are much more centrist. So it is with a profound sense of betrayal to acknowledge that our own political tribe has thrown women and girls completely under the bus at the altar of "trans."

Many women (and plenty of men) who think of ourselves as being on the political left in the U.S. have been complaining to Democratic Party officials for years about how the enshrinement of "gender identity" in U.S. law and throughout society harms women and children. We complain that the redefinition of sex to include "gender identity" will result in all public accommodations (including bathrooms, locker rooms, changing rooms, and the like) being open to men who claim to have "female gender identities." We complain about the housing of men who claim to have "female gender identities" in women's prisons and how those men often go on to sexually assault and/or impregnate female inmates. We complain that so-called "gender affirming" care (which often results in sterility, disease, and premature death) for minors constitutes child abuse. We complain that "gender identity" is insulting to the lesbians and gay men who fought hard for societal acceptance of same-sex attraction. They have steadfastly ignored us.

I hear from countless rank-and-file Democrats every day who tell me that they wrote to their Democratic lawmakers complaining about the enshrinement of "gender identity" in the law. The response from these lawmakers is usually along the lines of "I support the LGBTQ community" (occasionally they'll add a + symbol). What these Democratic leaders refuse to acknowledge is that we rank-and-file Democrats absolutely support the rights of lesbians, gay men, and bisexual people. Our objection is to the T and the Q (and the occasional +) and how they represent an obscuring of the material reality of sex, and the ramifications of that for women and girls, and for lesbian, gay, and bisexual people *themselves*. Our concerns have fallen on deaf ears.

However, Democratic Party leaders and their media puppets *are* starting to realize how unpopular and controversial "gender identity" is. They know that Americans across the political spectrum support female-only sports and spaces like bathrooms and locker rooms. They also know that Americans across the political spectrum know how babies are made and that sex is real. The unpopularity of "gender identity" can be demonstrated through 2023 polling that proves it. According to these polls, the vast majority of Americans understand that the following phrase is false: "Transgender women are biological women." Even 65 percent of people who call themselves "very liberal" and 80 percent of people who call themselves "liberal" know that phrase is false. As a proud Gen X progressive, I'm happy to see that fully 85 percent of Gen Xers know that phrase is false. Another 2023 poll shows that more Americans now say that gender (they mean sex) is binary than did in 2021. What's more, the increase is especially pronounced among young adults. In 2021, 43 percent of Gen Z thought that it was binary and by 2023, the number had increased to 57 percent. That's a fourteen-point increase over the last two years. By early

2023, the entire "trans" edifice began to unravel globally precisely because average everyday people could see with their eyes what us TERFs have known all along: that "trans" is a vicious lie driven by a cruel and exploitative industry. The "gender identity" house of cards is crumbling and the Democrats in power know it.

In May 2023, a Republican lawmaker in Indiana named Ryan Webb, who is a straight white man, announced that he had decided to "come out as a lesbian woman of color" and his announcement went global. The left essentially lost its mind because it had no idea what to do with Webb's announcement. As Webb explained during testimony, the left had "made the rules" that allow all of us to claim to be whatever we say we are and then demand that everyone else play along. They accused him of "mocking trans people," but really he was mocking the credulity of the liberals who go along with this charade. Although Democratic TERFs disagree with Webb on probably most things, many of us cheered him on.

Meanwhile, traditional "leftist" groups like the ACLU, HRC, Amnesty International, the National Organization for Women (NOW), the Lambda Legal Defense Fund, the National Center for Lesbian Rights (NCLR), and Planned Parenthood routinely and savagely throw women under the bus by working to ensure that men who claim to be women are permitted to compete in women's sports, be housed in women's prisons, and invade women's spaces. Planned Parenthood (which I used to support) has become one of the grossest offenders—it routinely hands out puberty blockers and cross-sex hormones to minors without a prescription and with almost no counseling or therapy. Groups like these, which claim to be "progressive," work hard to ensure that parents who want to protect their children from life-altering hormonal and surgical procedures are punished. I worked at the ACLU on criminal justice policy from 2012–2014 and even before then, I spent decades as a "card-carrying member." I was proud of the ACLU's legacy of protecting civil rights and civil liberties. I now know that the ACLU has become nothing other than a money-grubbing shill for the woman-hating and reality-denying movement that is "trans."

I'll explain below why I know that Democratic leaders *know* how dangerous "gender identity" is for women and children but have been relentlessly pushing it anyway. They *know* that "gender identity" is a regressive, authoritarian, sexist, and homophobic behemoth that destroys everything in its path. Unfortunately, the institutions that society would normally count on to hold them accountable for this (the media and Republicans especially) are either unable or unwilling to do so. *I am gravely concerned that as Democratic leaders' awareness of how unpopular "gender identity" is among the American electorate grows, they will simply start pretending that they never supported it in the first place.* "What? Who, me? I never supported the invasion of women-only spaces by men or the sterilization and mutilation of children!" they will say. "I never denied that sex is real or that it matters," they will claim. We cannot let that happen. Too many women have been raped in prison by men who claim to be women; too many female athletes have lost titles to men who claim to be women; too many women and girls have been exposed to erect penises in women's spaces by men who claim to be women; too many women have been subjected to violence and cancelation; and too many children have been harmed by "gender-affirming care" for them to be able to get away with it.

* * * * *

On May 13, 2016, President Obama's Departments of Justice and Education issued a joint "Dear Colleague" letter to schools all over the country, proclaiming for the first known time that Title IX's prohibition on sex discrimination in education "encompasses discrimination based on a student's gender identity, including discrimination based on a student's transgender status." A few months later, WoLF sued the administration. In its complaint, WoLF stated that the administration's "unilateral decree that women are not, as has been understood since the dawn of time, people who are biologically female, but anyone who, for any reason or no reason at all, choose to so describe themselves at any given time, is an arbitrary and breathtakingly irresponsible action that denies every female's biological and social reality." The crux of WoLF's legal argument was that in addition to violating various provisions of the Administrative Procedure Act, the Dear Colleague letter violated the Fourteenth Amendment's fundamental right to bodily privacy for women and girls. We *told* them.

Incidentally, one of the named defendants in the lawsuit was Vanita Gupta, who was then serving as the Principal Deputy Assistant Attorney General for Civil Rights and who signed the Dear Colleague letter in that capacity. I know Vanita. I worked with her directly when she was the director of the ACLU's Center for Justice and when I was the center's senior counsel. Our offices were next to each other in the ACLU's Washington D.C. office. As far as I know, throughout the entire time we worked together, Vanita knew exactly what a woman is and supported women's rights. At the time, she staunchly supported the ACLU's National Prison Project on its work to halt the barbaric practice of shackling incarcerated pregnant women and girls during childbirth, and I cannot believe that she was confused about what the phrase "pregnant women and girls" means. And yet there she was in 2016, putting her name on a Dear Colleague letter that redefined sex to mean "gender identity," thereby denying that the sex "female" is even a coherent category.

As mentioned, I went on *Tucker Carlson Tonight* in February 2017 to discuss the WoLF lawsuit. I made it very clear that I am a leftist radical feminist and that we on the left have our own reasons for fighting "gender identity." I went on the same show at least eight or nine times since then to talk about this issue—sometimes sports, sometimes prisons, sometimes something else—and I always made it clear that my analysis is coming from the left. I am aware that Democratic lawmakers are generally not in the habit of watching *Fox News*, but I also find it very difficult to believe that in all that time, over all of those years, *no one* told anyone with influence in the Democratic Party that there are Democrats who are deeply disturbed about what the party is doing on this issue. WoLF's lawsuit was eventually dismissed without objection after the 2016 presidential election and the incoming administration withdrew the Dear Colleague letter.

I voted for President Obama in the 2008 Democratic presidential primary election, the 2008 general election, the 2012 primary, and the 2012 general, long before I knew anything about "gender identity." I did not know when I cast those votes that Obama's political career was fueled in part by money from the Pritzker family, including Penny Pritzker, who would eventually land a job as Obama's commerce secretary. Pritzker met President Obama in Chicago in the late nineties and raised money for his U.S. Senate campaign. She served as his campaign finance chair during the 2008 presidential election, where she oversaw his fundraising efforts. After he was elected, he appointed her to the President's Council for Jobs and Competitiveness. In 2013, he appointed her to be the Secretary of Commerce, and she was confirmed by the Senate that June. Pritzker is the sister of Illinois governor J.B. Pritzker and a cousin of a man named Jennifer (James) Pritzker. President Obama endorsed J.B. Pritzker in his 2022 gubernatorial reelection campaign. The Pritzker family is one of the wealthiest in America, worth nearly $34 billion. "Jennifer" served in the military and is now generally known to be "the first openly transgender billionaire." Through his Tawani Foundation, he routinely gives money to leftist organizations to promote "trans," such as a $100,000 grant in 2021 to the ACLU to promote "trans" in one state alone.

At least as early as 2016, the Obama administration was put on notice—by leftist radical feminists—that redefining sex to include the nebulous concept of "gender identity" was dangerous for women and girls. They didn't care because they were paid not to.

In January 2019, the conservative think tank The Heritage Foundation hosted an event titled "The Inequality of the Equality Act: Concerns from the Left." The panelists were myself, Julia Beck, and Jennifer Chavez (all members of WoLF), and Hacsi Horvath (a man who spent some years claiming to be a woman and now fully embraces the fact that he is a man). We are all on the political left. None of us particularly wanted to do an event at The Heritage Foundation, having spent all of our lives detesting its aims, but the hard truth was that none of the more mainstream or left-leaning think tanks in Washington would host us. We asked them and they declined. But The Heritage Foundation agreed to do it, and they were completely candid about the fact that we were leftists and feminists and that we had legitimate concerns about the bill that we were there to discuss (the Equality Act). At no point did The Heritage Foundation try to paint us as "right wing," because they knew we weren't.

My appearance on that panel would eventually cost me my nearly twenty-year-career in criminal justice law and policy reform and my membership in the so-called "progressive criminal justice reform community." From roughly 2001 until 2019, I was very active in efforts to end mass incarceration, rein in police militarization, improve the immigration system, decriminalize simple drug possession, and reform sentencing policy. The reason that my appearance on the Heritage panel would eventually cost me my career is that at the time I was working at a D.C.-based criminal justice agency. A stranger posted an image of me on the panel, tagging a member of the D.C. City Council, wanting to know why a TERF was serving at the agency, even though my participation on the panel was during non-work hours and nothing I said during the panel had anything to do with my work at the agency. That council member spoke with my boss about it and told her to "fix the problem." My boss would later receive email message after email message complaining about me, from anonymous sources, wondering why there was a TERF serving at the agency. Over the course of 2019, my job there became untenable and I had a choice: keep my job and shut up about women's rights or quit. So I quit.

Even before that, I had lost income earned for work related to criminal justice reform because of my status as a TERF. From 2015 until 2018, I worked as an independent consultant engaged in research and writing projects for "progressive" criminal justice non-profits. During 2017 and 2018, I was working on a project to improve the criminal justice outcomes of immigrants at the U.S.–Mexico border. One day, my contractor called me to tell me that she was pulling me from the project because someone at the ACLU of Texas had told her that my presence on the project was "toxic" because I'm a TERF. My contractor told me that although she didn't want to pull me from the project, she felt she had no choice.

My contractor wasn't wrong to worry that my presence on the project was "toxic." Today, there is no way that any criminal justice reform organization that claims to have leftist credentials would hire me. In contemporary society, outspoken TERFs aren't allowed to have jobs in the so-called "progressive left" or sometimes, any jobs at all. I have had women (usually left-leaning feminists) contact me to tell me that they agree with me but that they can't speak out due to fear of losing their jobs (at software companies, banks, libraries, you name it). These women have understandable concerns—they have mortgages, children, school loans, and car payments to worry about. Because I do not have any of those things, I decided a long time ago that I was willing to "take one for the team."

The Equality Act (the bill under discussion during the Heritage event) was first introduced in Congress in 2015. It would redefine the word "sex" to include the phrase "gender identity" throughout the entire U.S. Civil Rights Act (including places of public accommodation like bathrooms and locker rooms). It would define "gender identity" to mean "the gender-related identity, appearance, mannerisms, or other gender-related characteristics of an individual, regardless of the individual's designated sex at birth." Feminists understand the implications of this. We understand that it would mean eliminating all female-only spaces all over the country. Our purpose at the 2019 Heritage event was to make our feminist leftist case for opposing it. I cannot prove that any Democrats took note of our panel presentations, but I do know that several Republican members of Congress were present. I would be surprised if not a single one of them took our message to their Democratic colleagues in Congress.

For various reasons, I happen to have indirect access to some fairly high-level Democrats, most notably Vice President Harris and Senator Warren. I have met Vice President Harris on three occasions: at an event sponsored by the Stanford University Black Students' Association when she was the District Attorney of San Francisco and I was the executive director of the Stanford Criminal Justice Center at Stanford Law School; in an elevator at an event about the plight of incarcerated women that was taking place at a journalism museum in Washington, D.C. when she was a senator from California; and at a fundraiser for her 2020 presidential campaign. All three encounters were very brief, and she would have no reason to remember meeting me at any of them.

I worked closely with her sister Maya Harris during Hillary Clinton's 2016 presidential run. I was part of a team, led by Maya, to help Clinton craft her positions and policies on criminal justice topics. Maya and I met once in person at Clinton's Brooklyn, New York campaign headquarters and corresponded frequently by email and phone. Senator Warren's husband, Bruce Mann, was my property law professor during my first year of law school at the University of Pennsylvania. I very much valued his teaching style and I would email him from time to time after law school. For example, I emailed him when Senator Warren was first elected to the Senate and asked him to send her my congratulations. That was in 2012, while I was working at the ACLU and two years before I knew anything about "gender identity."

On May 26, 2019, I emailed Professor Mann and asked him to share the contents of my message with Senator Warren. That email laid out the entire Democratic progressive case against enshrining "gender identity" in the law including, especially, the argument that including "trans" along with "lesbian, gay, and bisexual," is homophobic and regressive. I asked him to ask the Senator to talk about "lesbian and gay rights" rather than "LGBT rights" because including the T is essentially force-teaming "gender identity" with sexual orientation, which harms lesbians and gay men. I explained that "gender identity" erases women and girls. I sent him a written version of testimony that lesbian radical feminist Julia Beck had read to the House Judiciary Committee the previous month, explaining the threats that "gender identity" poses to the human rights of women and girls.

He responded, thanking me for sending the materials and saying that he looked forward to reading them. He did not promise to share the information with Senator Warren, and I have no way of knowing whether he did so. If he did, however, Senator Warren was on notice as of May 2019, before she announced her intention to run for president in the 2020 election, about the dangers of enshrining "gender identity" in the law. But also, if Professor Mann shared the contents of my message with Senator Warren, she ignored my plea to stop force-teaming the T with the LGB. In October 2019, just a few months after I sent my email to her husband, she published a presidential campaign promise to "secure LGBTQ+ rights and equality." Her pronouncement was filled with nonsensical slogans like: "We need a President who will lift up the voices of every gay, lesbian, bisexual, transgender, non-binary, queer, Two-Spirit, and intersex person" and "We can't just wait for Congress to act. In my first 100 days as president, I will use every legal tool we have to make sure that LGBTQ+ people can live free from discrimination."

I sent a nearly identical email message to Maya, the vice president's sister. She never responded. When I learned that she had joined the Arcus Foundation's board of directors in 2017, I understood why. The Arcus Foundation has donated over $60 million to various "queer" projects over the years. In March 2021, Jon Stryker, the founder and director of the Arcus Foundation, gave the ACLU a $15 million donation to push its "gender identity" agenda. Maya most likely did not share my email message with her sister because her presence on the board of Arcus makes her all-in on "gender identity." If she did, however, the woman who would go on to become the vice president of the United States was on notice as of May 2019 that "gender identity" is bad for women and children. Again, the reason the Democrats in power have done nothing to stop it is because they and their friends are paid not to.

Julia Beck's April 2019 testimony on the Equality Act (attached to my email messages to Professor Mann and Maya Harris) included these statements: "The Equality Act is a human rights violation. Every person in this country will lose our right to single sex sports, shelters, grants, and loans. We will be unable to provide or deny intimate services to people of the opposite sex. We will no longer be able to distinguish between women and men. The concept of gender identity suggests that there's an essentially female personality or feeling that a person can have, but no such thing as a female body. Making gender identity the law will in fact mandate a belief in a 'female penis' or 'female testes.' I thank the Republicans who invited me here, and I urge my fellow Democrats to *wake up*. Please acknowledge biological reality." I watched the entire hearing live on C-SPAN. All of the male Democrats on the committee glared at her the entire time. Not a single female Democrat on the committee would even look her in the eye. The committee proceeded to pass the measure, with 100 percent of Democrats in support.

If the Democratic Party leadership did not get the memo that "gender identity" is dangerous for women and girls in 2016 when WoLF filed its lawsuit, it must have gotten the memo by 2019, after WoLF members explained it at the Heritage event, Julia Beck testified about it before the House Judiciary Committee, and I sent my email messages to family members of now Vice President Harris and Senator Warren.

The same bill eventually passed in the House in February 2021 (including 100 percent of Democrats) and from there it went to the Senate. It was sent to the Senate Judiciary Committee, which quickly scheduled a hearing in March 2021. Shortly before that hearing, I submitted written testimony on behalf of the U.S. chapter of what was then the Women's Human Rights Campaign USA (WHRC USA) and is now WDI USA. The testimony went into detail about the leftist feminist concerns we had with the Equality Act. It explained that the country has not had the national conversation that we need to have about the far-reaching implications of redefining sex to include so-called "gender identity"; that men aren't women even if they say they are; and that children are being harmed at the altar of "gender identity." I received written confirmation that every single member of the committee, including every Democrat, received it. Every single Democrat on the committee voted to pass the bill anyway.[4]

That same month, WHRC sent a letter to Majority Leader Charles Schumer that was signed by thousands of women all over the world. It said: "Although the enactment of the Equality Act would only affect

---

[4] They were Chair Dick Durbin, and senators Sheldon Whitehouse, Chris Coons, Patrick Leahy, Jon Ossoff, Cory Booker, Richard Blumenthal, Amy Klobuchar, Dianne Feinstein, Alex Padilla, Mazie K. Hirono.

U.S. women directly, we are terrified of the impact that such enactment is likely to have globally. Our governments look to your government for leadership, expertise, and guidance. Already, we are seeing the word sex being redefined to include 'gender identity' in laws throughout the U.K., the European Union, Australia, Canada, and New Zealand. These laws have had devastating impacts on the lives of women and girls, including the rapes of vulnerable women in prison, the inclusion of men in women's spaces such as locker rooms and changing rooms, and the inclusion of men in women's sports. This situation will only get worse if this law passes in the U.S., and similar laws are likely to extend to other geographic areas as well." We did not send that letter into an internet void. We sent it directly to the private email address of one of his staffers, with whom we had previously communicated via Zoom. That staffer confirmed she had received the letter and said she would share it with the senator. To date, Majority Leader Schumer has not brought the Equality Act to the floor of the Senate for a vote, suggesting to me that he knows (and that other Senate Democrats know) how harmful and unpopular it is.

I personally know a woman who is married to a former Democratic member of Congress. In January 2022, she helped WDI USA deliver a copy of my book *The Abolition of Sex* to every single member of Congress. She told me that Democratic members of Congress (women, in particular) are discussing this privately, among themselves behind closed doors. She is not hopeful that any of them will have the guts to take a public stance against the abolition of sex or the abuse that women and children suffer because of it. I have no way of knowing whether any Democratic members of Congress read the book we sent, but I do know that we made our best effort to get the information into their hands. I also know that the woman I'm speaking of has had private in-person conversations with a handful of Democratic female members of Congress about it.

Part of the reason I am convinced that Democratic Party leaders know what is happening concerns the apparent death of the Equality Act in 2022, even though it was resurrected in 2023. Majority Leader Schumer appears to have been silent about the bill since January 2022. As far as I can tell, the last time he said a word about it publicly was in January 2022, when he talked about it at a joint meeting of the groups Freedom for All Americans, New Pride Agenda, and The NYC LGBT Center. I have not been able to find a single reference to any public statement that Senator Schumer has made about the bill since then, *including in 2023 after a small group of Democrats reintroduced it*. Senator Schumer needs to answer for this. He needs to explain to the nation—his female constituents in particular—why he worked so hard to advance the bill for several years and now seems to be backing away from it. He cannot be allowed to memory-hole his previous support for throwing women and girls under the bus.

In the summer of 2022, the Department of Education issued proposed amendments to the Title IX regulations that would redefine sex to include "gender identity" for all Title IX purposes and imposed a comment deadline of September 12. By the deadline, the proposed amendments had received over 200,000 public comments, the most ever to have been received in the department's history. On September 12, a group of Senate Democrats sent a letter to the department expressing support for redefining sex to include "gender identity" for Title IX purposes, which is not surprising in today's political climate. What is perhaps surprising is that only nineteen Senate Democrats signed the letter, which means that thirty-one *did not*. There were fifty Democratic senators in the U.S. Senate in 2022, and fewer than half of them signed that letter.

My view is that even in 2021, the Democrats in the Senate would have been in lock-step with each other in support of the department's proposed amendments to redefine sex out of existence. By September 2022, fewer than half of them were. It is also significant to me that the letter was submitted at the last minute, on the literal last day that the proposed amendments were open for comment. This suggests that the Democrats who signed the letter worked very hard to persuade more of their colleagues to sign it before the deadline and that they were unable to do so. If thirty-one Senate Democrats are unwilling to express public support for the Education Department's attempt to redefine sex to include "gender identity" for Title IX purposes, is it possible that some number of Senate Democrats are similarly unwilling to express public support for the U.S. Congress to redefine sex to include "gender identity" for all civil rights purposes?

We know that Democratic leaders have gotten the memo by now, because Hillary Clinton talked about the issue in June 2022 in a *Financial Times* article, heading into the November 2022 midterms. A reporter asked her, "Democrats seem to be going out of their way to lose elections by elevating activist causes, notably the transgender debate, which are relevant only to a small minority. What sense does it make to depict J.K. Rowling as a fascist?" She responded: "We are standing on the precipice of losing our democracy, and everything that everybody else cares about then goes out the window. Look, the most important thing is to win the next election. The alternative is so frightening that whatever does not help you win should not be a priority."

Clinton could easily have virtue signaled about the importance of protecting "gender identity" in the law or about the supposed "marginalization of trans people." She didn't. This is significant. Democratic insider politicos are surely talking among themselves. If Clinton thinks that "transgender" is bad for the Democrats electorally, surely others at the top think this too. A friend who knows Clinton personally once told me in confidence that the reason Clinton doesn't think she can speak out about any of it is that the U.S. State Department began allowing people to change their sex on their passports without requiring surgery under her watch as Secretary of State.

During Pride month 2023, much ado was made of the fact that the White House held a garden party on the South Lawn, at which a man named Rose Montoya flashed his fake breasts and made a video of the occasion, which went viral. To its credit, the White House later banned him ("her," if you believe the media) from attending future White House events, calling his behavior "inappropriate and disrespectful," which it was. One aspect of the incident that didn't make the news was that in her remarks during the event, First Lady Jill Biden thanked the Gill Foundation who "helped make the day possible," and President Biden thanked his "dear friend Tim Gill." The Gill Foundation, founded by Tim Gill, claims to be "one of the nation's leading funders of efforts to secure full equality for lesbian, gay, bisexual, transgender, and queer (LGBTQ) people." It has invested more than $400 million in "programs and nonprofit organizations around the nation, substantially contributing to many of the country's watershed victories for LGBTQ equality." He is regularly referred to as a "megadonor" in the media and in Democratic circles. *Rolling Stone* calls him "the nation's most powerful force for LGBTQ rights." Gill is heavily invested in artificial intelligence and stands to benefit tremendously by persuading all of American society that sex isn't real because sex is an integral part of who we are as human beings. So he's paying the White House to advance the narrative that sex doesn't exist.

Many people predicted a "red wave" during the November 2022 midterms; that did not happen, in part because the Supreme Court inspired a lot of Democratic voters to vote Democrat by overturning *Roe v. Wade* in June 2022. I strongly suspect that had the Supreme Court not done that, a lot more Democrats would either have voted Republican in the midterms or sat out the election completely. My aim here is not to get Democrats to lose at the ballot box. My hope, instead, is that Democratic leaders will take a good hard look in the mirror, start taking this seriously, and own up to what they have done to women and children at the altar of "gender identity."

The Democrats are not alone. As angry as I am at my own party leaders, I am just as angry at several other institutions. But the bottom line is this. Democratic Party leaders have betrayed and abandoned women and girls by abolishing the category of sex in the law and throughout society. Feminists have a saying: We cannot protect women and girls on the basis of sex if we cannot acknowledge what sex is. That is exactly what the Democrats have been doing—pretending that the category of sex either does not exist or that it is less important than the nebulous, nonsensical, and unscientific category of "gender identity." What's even worse, countless leftist feminist women have been disenfranchised by "gender identity." Many of us who fit into that category refuse to vote Republican, for various reasons, but the Democrats have made it impossible for us to vote for them either. Because of the U.S.'s two-party system and the vagaries of our electoral structures, this means that many of us just don't feel comfortable exercising our 19th Amendment rights at all, which feels like an insult to the twentieth-century women who fought and died so that we could vote.

In October 2021, a story broke about the Loudoun County (Virginia) Public School District allowing boys to use the girls' bathroom on the basis of their "female gender identity." A boy had sexually assaulted a girl in the bathroom and the district's response was simply to move him to a new school, where he sexually assaulted *another* girl. Parents complained, and eventually it came out that the board of the original school knew about the initial assault and did nothing about it. At the time, my friend, the Irish comedy writer Graham Linehan, published a Substack piece about it called "America wakes up to a nightmare: A scandal the Left will be unable to ignore." But so far, Graham has been wrong: the American left *has* ignored it. We need to make Graham right and create the conditions in which it will be impossible for the American left to keep ignoring the scandal of "gender identity."

In September 2023, California governor Gavin Newsom vetoed a bill that would have given preference to a parent who "affirms" a child's "gender" in a custody dispute. He did not do this because he has had a change of heart regarding matters of sex and gender; Newsom has been rubber-stamping bills that enshrine "gender identity" in California law for years now. He did it because he is running for president and he can see which way the political winds are shifting. He wants Americans to forget everything he has done to enshrine "gender identity" in the law because he knows how unpopular it is. Other Democratic Party leaders are going to tell us that they didn't know. That they couldn't have known. That the science has changed in ways they couldn't have anticipated. Don't believe them. Don't let them get away with it. They knew. They have known all along.

PART 2

THE VICTIMS

Always the innocent are the first victims, so it
has been for ages past, so it is now.
–J.K. Rowling, *Harry Potter and the Sorcerer's Stone*

CHAPTER 2

WOMEN AND GIRLS AS A SEX CLASS

Women and girls are being erased as a sex class and trampled on by men and boys as a sex class at the hands of the political left. This was supposed to have been resolved by #MeToo in 2017, but it wasn't. Instead, we live in a society where men are permitted to abuse women if they claim to have a woman identity. They are allowed to be housed in women's prisons, enter women's bathrooms and locker rooms, take over women's sports, and claim to be lesbians if they say they are "transgender." Women are expected to refer to themselves as "birthing persons," "menstruators," or "uterus-havers." Some have gone so far as to tell women that we should refer to a vagina as a "bonus hole"—a term that was allegedly developed with "expert organizations who work with the LGBT community" to avoid offending "non-binary" people. The CDC tells us that "transgender and nonbinary-gendered individuals may give birth and breastfeed or feed at the chest (chestfeed)" and that "some families may have other preferred terminology for how they feed their babies such as nursing, chestfeeding, or bodyfeeding." As though nursing women are nothing but "bodyfeeders."

The Smithsonian Institution recently announced that it would have a new Museum of American Women. One of its inductees is a man named Monica Helms (born Robert Hogge), who designed the "trans Pride flag," forced his wife to participate in his fetishistic cross-dressing, and once worked in a porn store. In 2023, *USA Today* named Leigh Finke as one of its Women of the Year. Finke is a man who claims to have a woman identity and serves in the Minnesota state legislature as a member of the Minnesota Democratic-Farmer-Labor Party. Things have become so dreadful for women and girls as a sex class that Columbia University recently awarded a man named Andrea (Andrew) Long Chu a Pulitzer Prize in literary criticism for his commentary at *New York Magazine*. Chu published a book in 2019 called *Females*, in which he argued that anyone can be female and that being sexually penetrated defines womanhood. He said, "Getting fucked makes you female because fucked is what a female is." He also described himself as once being "a sad, pretentious boy, furious about rape, hopelessly addicted to pornography." He states openly that his obsession with porn (specifically, "sissy porn") is what ultimately led him to "be transgender." He added: "At the center of sissy porn lies the asshole, a kind of universal vagina through which femaleness can always be accessed."

Men are invading women's prisons, women's sports, and women's intimate spaces like bathrooms, locker rooms, and changing rooms in the U.S. and all over the world, on the basis of their so-called "female gender identity." Black women and lesbians are disproportionately harmed. They are being permitted to do this because of laws and policies that left-leaning parties, including the Democrats, have enacted and traditionally progressive organizations have championed. Women and girls, and the material reality of sex, are the victims.

Female Inmates

The "Nelson Mandela Rules" (the U.N. Standard Minimum Rules for the Treatment of Prisoners) set forth Mr. Mandela's views regarding the best practices for the humane treatment of prisoners. Rule 11(a) states: "The different categories of prisoners shall be kept in separate institutions or parts of institutions, taking account of their sex, age, criminal record, the legal reason for their detention and the necessities of their treatment; thus

[m]en and women shall so far as possible be detained in separate institutions; in an institution which receives both men and women, the whole of the premises allocated to women shall be entirely separate." Rule 52(1) states: "Intrusive searches shall be conducted in private and by trained staff of the same sex as the prisoner."

No jurisdiction in the U.S. is bound by any of these standards, but they exist as a matter of official U.N. policy and they came from (and are named for) a global icon who was an expert in the humane treatment of prisoners, having spent twenty-seven years in prison himself. Notwithstanding these standards, jurisdictions all over the U.S. are in flagrant violation of them because of laws and policies enacted by Democratic lawmakers and pushed by the U.S. establishment left. Incarcerated women are one of the most vulnerable demographics in the United States. It is estimated that 70 percent of incarcerated women have struggled with some form of drug or alcohol addiction. Half have experienced some form of sexual abuse, typically at the hands of men. Locking women in cells with violent and sexually abusive men may be one of the cruelest aspects of "gender identity's" vicious assault on women and girls.

The Federal Prison System

On January 13, 2022, the U.S. Bureau of Prisons (BOP, an agency within the Justice Department) published its new "Transgender Offender Manual" (replacing previous versions). One person providing advice to the BOP during the drafting of the manual was Sasha Buchert, an attorney at Lambda Legal. Buchert's biography on the Lambda Legal website states: "Sasha Buchert was the first openly transgender person to be appointed to an Oregon state board, and from 2012–13, she served as the chair of the Oregon State Hospital Advisory Board." What this is saying is that Buchert is male and claims to be a woman (i.e., "is transgender"). Anyone can find interviews that Buchert has conducted online and see that Buchert is obviously male. To the best of my knowledge, the BOP did not consult with any feminist organizations (the ones that care about the safety and dignity of female inmates) in drafting its new policy.

The BOP uses a data system called SENTRY to track inmates. One of the data points collected is sex, and the agency's Policy on Inmate Security Designation and Custody Classification specifically instructs staff to enter either M or F (male or female). The Bureau of Prisons, in other words, knows that sex is real.[5] However, the "transgender" policy allows inmates to receive a "transgender" designation, where "transgender" means: "the state of one's gender identity not matching one's sex assigned at birth." This is accomplished via a Case Management Activity (CMA) form that "assigns" the inmate as "transgender." SENTRY is then updated accordingly. Decisions about where to house male inmates who claim to have "female gender identities" are made on a case-by-case basis.

All of this is overseen by a branch of the BOP called the Women and Special Population Branch. At least as late as 2016, this branch was called the Female Offender Branch and its purpose was to tend to the needs of female prisoners. At some point between 2016 and 2021, it was renamed, where "special population" evidently refers to men with "gender identities." So much for the needs of female prisoners. Once an inmate receives a "transgender" designation on a CMA, all matters concerning his placement and programming are overseen by a Transgender Executive Committee (TEC). The TEC is "the agency's official decision-making body on all issues affecting the transgender population."

The January 2022 policy manual put BOP staff on notice that "[s]taff interacting with inmates who have a CMA assignment of transgender, shall either use the authorized gender-neutral communication with inmates (e.g., by the legal last name or 'Inmate' last name) or the pronouns associated with the inmate's identified gender. Deliberately and repeatedly mis-gendering an inmate is not permitted." So evidently, all BOP staff have

[5] Incidentally, the federal government also knows that sex is real when it serves other purposes for it to do so, for example the military draft. The U.S. Selective Service has a policy in place that states: "Individuals who are born male and changed their gender to female are still required to register. Individuals who are born female and changed their gender to male are not required to register." The Selective Service understands, for obvious reasons, that men are male and that women are female.

to now dance around men's "preferred pronouns" while they are attempting to do their job of actually managing the prison. I have never managed a prison, but I can imagine that there are risks involved. Fears of "misgendering" people should not be one of them. I would think that correctional officers would much prefer to concentrate on concerns about smuggling, inmate and officer safety, and making sure everything runs on time than on referring to a male inmate as "Susan" or "she." This is a lot of bureaucracy for the BOP to accommodate the demands of men with "gender identities" at the expense of women. According to BOP data received by the group Keep Prisons Single Sex, as of November 2022, there were 1,143 men claiming to be women in the federal prison system, of whom 45.9 percent have a history of a sex offense. By August 2023, there were 1,295, of whom 47 percent have a history of a sex offense.

In December 2022, a man named Donna (Peter) Langan received "gender affirming" surgery at taxpayer expense while in BOP custody—the first to do so. Langan was convicted in 1997 of robbing two banks using firearms and a destructive device. His purpose in robbing banks was to funnel cash to a neo-Nazi group called the "Aryan Republican Army," of which he was a member. He had been transferred to a federal women's prison in Texas a few years before receiving the surgery.

In February 2023, Robert William Perry II was sentenced to life in federal prison after being convicted of the aggravated sexual abuse of a seven-year-old girl. He had coerced the girl into performing sex acts in exchange for candy, toys, and the opportunity to play video games in a part of his house where he regularly watched pornography. According to the child's testimony (when she was eleven), he would order her to strip naked and kneel on the floor and force his penis into her throat causing her to choke. He would also touch and lick her genitals. He would then give her Jolly Ranchers or Starburst candies. She testified that this happened regularly after school. Shortly after being sentenced to life in prison, the Department of Justice announced that Perry is a woman and began referring to him using "she" and "her" pronouns.

The 2022 BOP policy does not go as far as Sasha Buchert would like it to. When asked to comment, he stated: "I am hopeful that the spirit of the policy is clear, that they transfer people appropriately, and that they will provide [health]care, but you know, we'll be watching like a hawk." What Buchert was really saying was that he would prefer to see a policy in place that allows any male inmate to transfer to a facility designated for women simply on the basis of a self-declared "female gender identity" and that all inmates should have access to any medical care that allows them to masquerade as the opposite sex (as opposed to doing these things on a case-by-case basis). The BOP policy doesn't go that far yet, but under the Biden administration, Buchert just might get his wish.

The State Prison Systems

In 2020, the majority-Democratic California legislature passed and Democratic governor Gavin Newsom signed a measure called SB 132, "The Transgender Respect, Agency, and Dignity Act." It went into effect in January 2021. It requires the state Department of Corrections and Rehabilitation to ask each inmate to state her or his "gender identity," as well as her or his "gender pronoun and honorific." It also permits inmates to update this information as they choose. It prohibits staff from failing to "consistently use the gender pronoun and honorific" inmates choose and mandates that intimate searches be conducted according to an inmate's "gender identity" (so female correctional officers are required to conduct intimate searches on male inmates if a male inmate claims to have a woman identity). Finally, it requires the department to house inmates "in a correctional facility designated for men or women based on the individual's preference."

By mid-2021, hundreds of men had applied to be housed in either the Central California Women's Facility (CCWF) or the California Institution for Women (CIW)—the two primary facilities where female prisoners are housed in the state, and dozens of those applications were granted. One-third of the applicants had been imprisoned for a sex offense. These men argue either that they "are transgender" (i.e., they claim to have a woman identity) or that they are "non-binary" (a nonsensical way of claiming not to be a member of either sex class). No hormones or surgery is required. The bill was sponsored by state Senator Scott Wiener, a Democrat who has worked relentlessly to abuse female inmates and prostituted women throughout the state, and to make California a safe haven for children seeking puberty blocking and/or wrong-sex hormones.

In November 2021, WoLF filed a complaint on behalf of four incarcerated women in federal court, arguing that this law violates the First, Eighth, and Fourteenth Amendments to the Constitution. The plaintiffs are Janine Chandler, Krystal Gonzales, Tomiekia Johnson, and Nadia Romero. According to WoLF, these women and thousands of others have been subjected to a loss of privacy and opportunities for rehabilitative programming; psychological anguish; constitutional rights violations, and intimidation, sexual harassment, physical assaults, and sexual assaults as a result of being housed with men, some of whom allegedly discontinued estrogen treatment so they could keep getting erections. The ACLU moved to intervene on behalf of four incarcerated men who want to be housed in the women's prisons and that motion was granted in 2023. So now the ACLU is representing these men who want to be housed in the women's prison so they can torment female inmates. All because of a law pushed by state senate Democrat Scott Wiener and Democrat governor Gavin Newsom.

Plaintiff Tomiekia Johnson said in 2023, "I told my male roommate a thousand times I can see his penis and the whole package through his panties. He walks around in a bra and panties, not properly dressed." A woman named Mimi Le provided a sworn declaration to WoLF to be included in the case, where she stated that she was one of several eyewitnesses to an alleged sexual assault committed by a male inmate against a woman. The woman had been assaulted by a man named Jonathan Robertson—a man who claims to have a woman identity and goes by the name Syiaah Skylit. In February 2023, WoLF submitted court documents requesting that the state provide information about how many incarcerated women had requested birth control and how many had become pregnant by a male inmate. There is only one reason why such questions are even necessary: the "transgender women" who are being housed in the women's prisons are men. There is no type of woman who can get another woman pregnant.

A man named Jessica (Jason) Hann is being housed in the California women's prison on the basis of his "female gender identity." Hann had previously been convicted of murdering his infant son and daughter. He murdered his infant son by head trauma in 1999 and his ten-week-old daughter, Montana, in 2001. The little girl's body had been found in an advanced state of decomposition and stuffed in a Tupperware onboard an RV trailer once owned by Hann after the vehicle had been repossessed and sent to auction.

Amie Ichikawa is a former inmate and founder of Woman II Woman, a nonprofit organization that advocates for the rights of incarcerated women. She is frequently in communication with the women who are incarcerated in the California women's prison. She tells the story of her friend Cathleen, who has complained about a man with a woman identity (who is also a self-proclaimed satanist) being transferred from the men's prison. Cathleen complains that he has violated her privacy many times by entering the toilet when she was in the stall. She says that she was and still is "scared to death of this man," who is reportedly 6'5 and described as "a big dangerous man who was convicted of murder 40 years ago and killed another inmate while he was in the men's prison."

Cathleen had been granted parole, but after she and other women complained about the presence of this man, she was issued a "serious rule violation" for doing so, delaying her release. Her attorneys advised her to write a letter apologizing to the man and "owning her part in the harm she caused." She was required to say in the letter, "Today, I have done the work to understand more deeply what your identity means and I have more knowledge about the issues you face as a transgender woman." She was further told to "reflect on the negative impact her actions had on the transgender community as a whole and to commit to using correct gender pronouns." They suggested that she express a "willingness to use her cis-gendered privilege to create a reverse ripple effect in support of the transferred inmates from the men's prison." Cathleen reports that the entire experience has amounted to nothing other than "psychological terror." This is all thanks to California state senator Scott Weiner and other California Democrats, including the governor.

In 2022, a man named Dana Rivers (born David Warfield) was convicted of murdering a lesbian couple (Patricia Wright and Charlotte Reed—he shot Charlotte to death and then stabbed her dead body over forty times) and their teenage son Benny. Before and throughout the trial and sentencing, he was housed at the Santa Rita Jail in Alameda County, California, which classified him as female. In 2023, he was sentenced to multiple terms of life in prison without the possibility of parole. In issuing the sentence, the judge said, "It's a horrible thing to sentence someone to die in prison, and I don't take that lightly. But this is the most depraved crime I ever handled in the criminal justice system in 22 years. Frankly, you deserve to spend the rest of your life in prison." Rivers was sent to the Central California Women's Facility two days later. To no one's surprise, women have since reported that he is harassing them inside the facility.

In August 2023, a man named Steven Raymundo (who calls himself Isabella Kurumi Asuka Raymundo) was accused of the brutal stabbing murder of a homeless woman named Patricia Roper outside a Fresno post office, and the stabbing was caught on a surveillance camera. In December 2022, he had posted on social media, "I'm so happy my first surgery will be my vaginoplasty whoo hoo I get my pussy I can't wait to look and touch it" and "Talking to my surgeon about my vaginoplasty and facial feminization I'm so excited I can't wait to get my vagina—meow—I'm super excited!!!" Under California law, if he is convicted, he will have the right to be held in the California women's prison on the basis of his woman identity.

This situation is hardly limited to California. In 2023 alone, at a jail near Cincinnati, Ohio, a woman reported that she awoke in her cell one morning to find a man raping her and holding his hand over her mouth. She reported that the rapist was "a biological male who identifies as a female and is believed to be in some stage of gender transition." In Kansas, a man named Thomas Lamb who was convicted of the brutal murder of one woman and the kidnapping of another was transferred to the state women's prison in Topeka after he adopted a woman identity and started calling himself Michelle. In Montana, a man named Jeffrey Mann, who now goes by the name of Serena Alana Mann, was convicted of violently assaulting his physically and mentally disabled girlfriend and given a suspended sentence of five years (having to serve five consecutive days in jail each year). He had previously been convicted of assaulting a stranger with a crowbar during a road rage incident. The Montana Department of Corrections classifies him as female. In Washington, a man named Khael Aguilar-McNamee—who was convicted of attempting to kidnap a 5-year-old boy and admits to being sexually attracted to children—was sent to the women's prison directly from his holding cell in the county jail, which means that he never spent any time at all in the men's prison and would not have received any hormones or surgery.

Also in 2023, a man named Christina Lusk won a settlement with the state of Minnesota. While incarcerated in a men's facility on drug-related charges, he sued to be transferred to the women's prison on the basis of his claimed woman identity. Under the terms of the settlement, the state agreed to transfer him to the women's prison, use taxpayer dollars to fund his new fake vagina, and pay him $495,000 in legal fees and damages. The state of New Jersey designated a man named Marina (Matthew) Volz as female on official prison records the same year. Volz is a pornographer who had been convicted of sexually abusing and exploiting his seven-year-old daughter and sentenced to twenty-five years on charges of human trafficking, aggravated sexual assault, conspiracy, and endangering the welfare of a child. During his trial, prosecutors had described his conduct as involving "sadistic sexual abuse" and as a "vortex of darkness." At sentencing, the judge referred to his behavior as "heinous, cruel, and depraved." He was quietly transferred to the women's prison even though prison records still recorded him as male. As of 2023, the state officially considers him to be female.

That very same women's prison in New Jersey houses a female inmate named Kokila Hiatt, who reached out to the feminist publication *Reduxx* to report her experiences of being housed with male inmates who claim to have a woman identity. Hiatt states, "I have been incarcerated since 2010, but nothing could have prepared me for the incoming tidal wave of a group of these males into the prison. I was completely unaware that us women would ever be housed with men, and, what's more, I was left shocked at the myriad of ways the New Jersey Department of Corrections was prepared to facilitate and defend their access to our traditionally female-only space.... For complaining about them, I have received backlash from the transgender males here. Their tactics ranged from verbal harassment and threats of violence to multiple allegations causing me to be investigated by the prison. One of those allegations resulted in me being placed in a lock-down unit for three days. I am not the only female inmate who has experienced consequences, other women have been harassed and bullied too."

The situation in New Jersey (at the Edna Mahan Correctional Facility for Women) is all the result of a settlement reached between the state corrections department and the ACLU in 2021, allowing men to be housed according to their supposed "gender identities," which was entered into under the administration of Democratic governor Phil Murphy.

In Washington state, a man named Brett David Sonia, who also goes by the name Brooke Lyn Sonia, was convicted in 2005 and 2006 of dozens of charges related to the sexual exploitation of a young girl. A man named Donna Perry was convicted of murdering three women within a four-month timeframe and once claimed to a cellmate that his total kill count was nine women. Both are housed in the Washington women's prison. Previously, a man who goes by the name Princess Zoee Marie Andromeda Love was transferred to the same prison after being convicted of raping a twelve-year-old girl. While there, he raped a woman who is developmentally disabled and a survivor of sexual abuse.

In 1993, a man named Joel Thomas Nichols entered the home of an eleven-year-old girl by pretending to be a telephone repairman while her parents were away. He cornered the girl, forced her to the floor, and ordered her to put on a pair of underwear that he had brought with him. He then cut the underwear off her and tried to penetrate her vaginally, but she cried out so he turned her over and raped her anally. He then ordered her to shower, and then raped her vaginally and anally again. The next year, he tried to kidnap a nine-year-old girl from a park, but three girls who were nearby intervened to protect her. During the attack, the nine-year-old scratched him, leaving his blood underneath her fingernails, and the police were ultimately able to track him down. He was convicted and sentenced to thirty years in prison. As of 2023, he was claiming to be a woman and going by the name Jolene Charisma Starr, and he was transferred to the Washington state women's prison.

Also housed in the Washington state women's prison is a man named Christopher Scott Williams, initially convicted of sexually abusing a nine-year-old girl. According to *Reduxx*, Williams was held in closed custody after being caught offering sex toys for sale to female inmates. His cellmate allegedly filed a report against him after becoming increasingly uncomfortable with the presence of sex toys in their shared cell.

As of writing, the Washington women's prison houses at least eleven male inmates who claim to have woman identities, all of whom have been convicted of violent and/or sex crimes against women or girls. This is all happening under a state administrative policy that was adopted in 2020 and updated in 2022, all under the administration of Democratic governor Jay Inslee. One of them who goes by the name Nonnie Marcella Lotusflower (born Nathan Goninan) was convicted of second-degree manslaughter for killing a seventeen-year-old girl named Jessica Franklin in 2007. He strangled her to death and left her body under an underpass in Bellingham, Washington. In 2017, the ACLU successfully sued to have him transferred to the women's prison. In 2022, the prison facilitated his breast augmentation surgery (at taxpayer expense) and in 2023, the prison gave him a bra from Victoria's Secret (which is not an approved vendor for inmate apparel).

In 2016, a Maine man named Andrew Balcer was upset that his family allegedly did not support his "gender identity," so he killed them. One month shy of his eighteenth birthday, on Halloween night, he woke his mother up and stabbed her in the back nine times, killing her. He then went on to murder his father and the pet chihuahua Lily. By 2022, Maine was housing him in the state women's prison on the basis of his woman identity. He calls himself Andrea.

In 2002, a man named Perry Cerf was convicted of raping and murdering a woman named Flor Andrade—an Ecuadorian immigrant who was likely a victim of sex trafficking. Cerf was found wearing Andrade's clothes and using her ID. He eventually led police to Andrade's body. She was naked and bound and had been dumped in a ravine. While awaiting trial, Cerf wrote a letter to *The New York Daily News* confessing to the crime and boasting of drinking Andrade's blood. He said that he drank her blood so that he could "allow this person to live vicariously" through him. Today, Cerf calls himself Michelle Angelina and is housed in New Jersey's women's prison. Also in New Jersey, it was reported in 2022 that two female inmates had been impregnated by a "transgender inmate." By "transgender inmate," of course, they mean a man. At the time, New Jersey housed twenty-seven men in the women's prison on the basis of their woman identities. The man who impregnated the women was later transferred back to the men's prison.

As previously mentioned, the situation in New Jersey is entirely the result of a legal settlement between the state corrections department and the ACLU to allow men to be housed in the women's prison on the basis of their "female gender identities," which was entered into under the administration of Democratic governor Phil Murphy. The lawsuit that resulted in the settlement was brought by the ACLU of New Jersey in 2019 on behalf of a man named Daniel Smith, also known as Danielle Demers (although he is referred to in the lawsuit only as Sonia Doe). He had been convicted of possession of a destructive device, possession of an explosive substance for an unlawful purpose, unlawful sale of a firearm, unlawfully teaching another to use an explosive, and conspiracy. He was sentenced to five years in April 2018 and sued for the right to be housed in the state women's prison, which he eventually was.

Since his release from the women's prison, he has been active in the online forum Quora, where he frequently posts about topics related to "trans" and prison policies as well as his ADBL ("adult diaper baby love") fetish. He once posted about a sexual encounter that he had with a seventeen-year-old girl and claims to menstruate. He says on Quora, "There is nothing shameful about menstruation. I prefer pads, and when I'm on my period, I keep one in my back pocket. I've always got a pad or two in my purse." This is an adult man who, with the help of the ACLU, sued the state of New Jersey for housing him in the men's prison and now talks openly online about his diaper fetish, his sexual encounters with minor girls, and his supposed "period." No one in a position of power, including the Democratic governor of New Jersey, seems to give any of this a second thought.

A woman named Shakira Reed, incarcerated in the same New Jersey prison, has reported that a man named Cyntara (Jermaine) Gibson gave her a broken nose and two black eyes after she repeatedly refused his sexual advances. Witnesses saw him punching her in the head and reported that there was blood "everywhere." When she would walk by his cell on her way to work, he would expose himself to her. She says that he attacked her because she didn't want to have sex with him. She repeatedly reported this to prison officials, who did nothing. This is a man sexually abusing and then beating an incarcerated woman and the only reason he is allowed to be housed in the women's prison is that he claims to have a woman identity. This woman identity entitles him to be housed in the women's prison because of a settlement agreement between the ACLU and the state of New Jersey, entered into by a Democratic governor. Phil Murphy is still the governor of New Jersey, and he continues to do nothing to remedy the situation.

A man named Mark Campbell is being housed in the Taycheedah Correctional Institution, a women's prison in Fond du Lac, Wisconsin, on the basis of his woman identity. The prison lists him as female. He requested taxpayer-funded "gender-affirming" surgery in 2013 and the Department said no, but a federal court eventually ruled in 2022 that the Department's refusal to provide it violated his rights. The judge stated, "I decline to impose any further prerequisites on Campbell's sex reassignment surgery. She has waited long enough." Campbell's crime of conviction was raping his ten-year-old daughter.

In 2022, a man named Diamond (Ramel) Blount was being held in the women's section of the infamous Rikers jail in New York City. He approached a female inmate in the bathroom after she had finished showering, held her down by the neck, and raped her. A rape kit was administered and his DNA was detected. He eventually pled guilty and was sentenced to serve seven years in state prison. Thankfully, he is being held in a state prison for males.

In 2021 and 2022, a man named Makyyla Holland was being held in the men's section of the Broome County Jail in the state of New York on the basis of his male sex. With the help of the New York Civil Liberties Union, he sued the jail. According to the terms of an August 2023 settlement, the county will pay him $160 thousand dollars in damages and the jail now agrees to house inmates and conduct intimate searches on the basis of the inmates' "gender identities."

There is a YouTuber popularly known as Chris Chan. He was born Christian Weston Chandler and now goes by the name Christine Weston Chandler. In 2021, he was arrested and charged with incest after allegedly having sexual intercourse with his then seventy-nine-year-old mentally disabled mother. He was initially booked by the Henrico Virginia County Sheriff's office, which listed him as female, and later transferred to the Central Virginia Regional Jail, which marked him as male. He was held between August 2021 and March 2023, when he was released pending trial.

In August 2023, the ACLU of Indiana filed a lawsuit against the state's Department of Corrections on behalf of a man named Jonathan Richardson, who calls himself Autumn Cordellioné. Richardson had been convicted in 2002 of murdering his eleven-month-old daughter by strangling her to death. He eventually told a prison official, "all I know is I killed the little fucking bitch." In its complaint, the ACLU argues that by refusing to provide him with taxpayer-funded "gender-affirming surgeries," the

Department is violating Richardson's rights under the Equal Protection Clause of the Fourteenth Amendment.

* * * * *

Proponents of "gender identity" often accuse TERFs of cherry-picking some of the worst examples of this phenomenon to "paint all transwomen as predators." First, that's just not true; there are many more similar examples. Second, though, one has to ask: How many male murderers and sex offenders being housed in women's prisons is too many? How many women have to be raped and/or impregnated in their cells by men who claim to have a woman identity before we stand up and say no? How much more abuse will the Democrats heap upon these women?

Female Inmates Around the World

None of this is limited to the United States. Left-of-center parties are supporting the housing of convicted male rapists and sex offenders in women's prisons all over the world. Adam Graham is a Scottish man who claims to be a woman named Isla Bryson. In January 2023, he was convicted of raping two women. He announced his "gender transition" during his trial and was sent to the women's prison to await sentencing. He was eventually sentenced to eight years in prison and after several protests, he was moved to a men's jail. The Scottish news reported the conviction as "a transgender woman has been found guilty of raping two women when she was a man" and referred to him as "she" and "her" throughout the reporting. Of course, there is no such thing as a woman who "was a man." He would go on to file "hate crime" charges from the prison against a man whom he accused of engaging in "transphobia."

Also in Scotland, a man named Katie (Lennon) Dolatowski is a convicted pedophile who claims to be a woman. He once pled guilty in connection with accusations that he sexually assaulted a ten-year-old girl in a supermarket by grabbing her by the face, forcing her into a bathroom, and pulling down her pants. In a separate incident, he covertly filmed a twelve-year-old girl in a different supermarket bathroom. In 2022, he was sent to the women's prison. After his release, he skipped bail numerous times and was eventually locked up in a men's jail. In April 2023, his father went on record as saying "My son is dangerous trans paedo Katie Dolatowski—lock him up NOW before he attacks another child."

The problem is not going away in Scotland. In May 2023, a man named Amy George (Andrew Miller) confessed to having abducted and sexually assaulted a young girl while wearing a dress and appearing to the girl to resemble a "lady." The girl had missed a bus and was walking home when he offered her a ride, which she accepted. Instead of taking her home, he took her to his own house, where he sexually assaulted her over a period of twenty-seven hours and forced her to watch pornography. She was finally able to call the police after he fell asleep, and officers found him sleeping and wearing a bra, silicone breasts, women's underwear, and tights. Miller told the police that picking up the child was "a motherly thing" and that he had "put her in bed with [him] to warm up." He pled guilty to abduction, sexual assault, possession of 242 indecent images of children and intentionally causing a child under the age of thirteen to look at a sexual image. First Minister Humza Yousaf refused to say whether he would ultimately be held in a women's prison or a men's. All of this has been allowed to occur under the administration of the Scottish National Party.

In May 2022, an Irish man named Barbie Kardashian, who is legally considered female, was convicted of threatening to torture, rape, and murder his mother. In March 2023, he was sentenced to five and a half years with the final twelve months suspended. He has fifteen previous convictions including for threats to kill, sexual assault, assault causing harm, and causing criminal damage to property. This is what he said to a social worker who interviewed him before his trial: "If I got into [my mother's] house I would run towards her and put the knife into her body and into her genitalia; the thing is, I would want to prolong my mum's suffering for as long as possible. I would stab her, but not in her heart or neck, I'd want to put her through lots of torture, fear, and humiliation. I would bring a screwdriver to insert inside her genitalia because I am a woman and women rape using objects; it would definitely be a long, protracted incident, I would want her to bleed out after death after a number of hours, by putting objects into her vagina, pouring boiling water into that area. I know that my mum is smaller than me, she is physically weak and she is frail. When I was living with her since I was nine or 10, I was stronger than her then, and I know she would be overpowered by me. I would only walk away when she was dead." He was housed in the women's prison, in accordance with his self-identification as a woman, thanks to a law that was passed under the direction of an Irish Labour leader with almost no public consultation, but eventually transferred to the men's. I have read similar accounts from Mexico, Brazil, and India. I'm sure there are others.

People often ask questions like "How many examples of this are there?" or "How many convicted male rapists and murderers are being housed in women's prisons, in the U.S. or elsewhere?" The most straightforward answer to that question is I don't know. I don't think that anyone knows. Feminist groups and publications like WDI, Keep Prisons Single Sex, and *Reduxx* do their best to stay on top of the situation, but at this point, I'm not sure that anyone can possibly have answers to those questions because our lawmakers and mainstream media outlets are intent on keeping us all in the dark about the situation. I'm also not sure it matters; even one example of a convicted male murderer or sex offender (or any man at all) being housed in a women's prison is too many, as far as I'm concerned, and it is clear that the actual number is far greater than one. What I can say for certain is that episodes like this are the inevitable result of pretending that sex isn't real or that it doesn't matter. Some men who have been convicted of some of the vilest crimes imaginable are being housed with vulnerable female inmates, all at the hands of the left-of-center parties in power, including the Democrats in the U.S.

Women in Bathrooms, Locker Rooms, and Spas

In July 2021, a spa called Wi Spa in Los Angeles made headlines when a woman named Angel reported to staff that a man was wandering around in the women's section of the spa, where girls were present and naked, and with an erect penis. The woman made a video of the incident, which went viral. The staff can be seen in the video dismissing her concerns and mumbling something about "sexual orientation," to which Angel responded, "I don't care about sexual orientation, I see a penis!" The spa has a clear policy: Nudity is expected in the women's section and in the men's section, and clothing is expected in the mixed-sex sections. However, California defines the word "sex" as follows: "'Sex' includes…, but is not limited to, a person's gender. 'Gender' means sex, and includes a person's gender identity and gender expression. 'Gender expression' means a person's gender-related appearance and behavior whether or not stereotypically associated with the person's assigned sex at birth." In my view, businesses like Wi Spa can be forgiven for being confused about what any of this means, and whether they can legally maintain female-only (or male-only), spaces. I don't know what any of it means either. It is all nonsense.

The man in question turned out to be a guy called Darren Merager, and he has since been charged with indecent exposure (the L.A. jail has him classified as male). This sets up an interesting legal conundrum: Can Merager fairly be charged with or convicted of indecent exposure if California law allows him to be naked and with an erect penis in the women's section of a public spa on the basis of his "female gender identity"? This is how Merager described himself during a 2022 conversation with *L.A. Magazine*: "I'm very neutral, like non-binary, although I don't like that word. I'm legally female. But I have facial hair. I have a penis. I have no breasts. I don't have a feminine voice. I don't wear makeup or dress up like a female. So imagine you're a grocery store [clerk] and you're bagging my groceries and you say, 'Excuse me, sir…' I mean, am I supposed to be offended? That'd be ridiculous. How would this person know? But technically, for legal terms, I am she/her. I put 'female' on my driver's license. But I've had to struggle my whole life fitting into traditional society."

He described changing his sex on his driver's license in January 2019, when the California Gender Recognition Act took effect, saying, "Anybody could walk in and get one." He was right. The California Gender Recognition Act of 2017 allows anyone to simply mark female,

male, or non-binary on a driver's license. The only requirement is that such a person has to submit an affidavit saying that the request "is to conform the person's legal gender to the person's gender identity and not for any fraudulent purpose." But *any* lie about sex is fraudulent. The law was authored by state Senate Democrats Toni Atkins and Scott Wiener, signed by Democratic governor Gavin Newsom, and went into effect in January 2019, just as Merager said.

A similar situation occurred in the Seattle area in 2023, when the Washington State Human Rights Commission (WSHRC) ruled that a Korean women's spa must be forced to admit men who claim to have woman identities. Since its inception, the spa had maintained a strict female-only policy. This is consistent with the Korean tradition of *jjimjilbang*—a system of maintaining sex-segregated spaces in bathhouses where nudity is expected and encouraged. A man named Haven Wilvich (born Caleb Richmond) sought membership at the spa in 2020. They denied his application because he had not undergone "gender reassignment" surgery and still had a penis. So he sued them and won. The WSHRC offered the spa a settlement agreement to avoid prosecution, which would have required the spa to remove all references to "biological women" on its website and provide staff with "inclusivity" training. The spa refused to back down and instead sued the WSHRC in federal court.

That court, however, dismissed the complaint. Wilvich bragged about his victory on social media, exclaiming, "I did it! I worked with the Washington Human Rights Commission [sic] and got Olympus Spa (the main naked lady spa in the area) to change their policies and allow all self-identified women access regardless of surgery and genitals." This is probably perfectly legal because Washington state law prohibits discrimination in public accommodations on the basis of "gender identity." Thanks to the Democrats in charge in Olympia, women and girls who want to visit a female-only spa have to endure the site of penises and testicles throughout it.

In 2021, a male student who claims to have a female "gender identity" allegedly raped a twelve-year-old girl in a girls' bathroom at ASK Academy, a STEM school in Rio Rancho, New Mexico. She was in sixth grade at the time. The girl did not report the incident to her parents or to school administrators, and later descended into mental decline, struggling with depression and anxiety. Her mother got her into therapy, where the girl reported being "bullied" at school but did not mention the rape. Several months later, her mother found her journal, opened it, and read these words, written by her twelve-year-old daughter: "I was raped. I was raped. I was raped. Fucking kill me."

When the mother asked her daughter to explain, her daughter stated that she was washing her hands in the bathroom and didn't take notice of the only other person in the bathroom at the time, but that before she knew it, he had walked over to her, pinned her against the counter, and wrestled her to the floor. He then held her down, ripped her pants, and raped her. All of this was allowed to happen because the school had a policy in place that allowed students to use bathrooms in accordance with their "gender identities." The mother reported the matter to the school and the police and took her daughter to have a medical exam (which confirmed that her hymen had been ripped). The girl's stated reason for not initially reporting the rape was that she was afraid that she would be called a "bigot" because the school had regularly been teaching students about "gender identity" and the importance of "inclusion." It was later revealed that numerous other girls had shared concerns among themselves about the same male student but the school didn't do anything about it. When asked to comment, all the school's Chief Executive Officer could manage to say was that the school is an "inclusive learning environment for all students" and that it does not "discriminate against any student." As of writing, there is an ongoing police investigation and the parents are suing the school for damages.

Just south of L.A., in a town called Santee (near San Diego), in January 2023, seventeen-year-old Rebecca Phillips was at the local YMCA swimming laps. She later testified before the Santee City Council, breaking down a little bit, that:

As I was showering after my workout, I saw a naked male in the women's locker room. I immediately went back into the shower, terrified, and hid behind their flimsy excuse for a curtain until he was gone. I ran into a bathroom stall to change as quickly as I could, organizing my thoughts to share with the people at the front desk. As I did so, I could only think of my five-year-old sister, who I bring to this gym during the summer, ...to enjoy their water slides. This is the YMCA, where hundreds of children spend their summer afternoons in childcare camps. This is the YMCA where my little sister took gymnastics lessons. The locker room was supposed to be her safe haven to go to gossip with her friends, and shower and change.

When I asked the YMCA management what the policy was regarding transgenders, they confirmed that the man that I saw was indeed allowed to shower wherever he pleased. As long as you are not a red flag on Megan's Law [the California sex offender registry], a grown male can shower alongside a teenage girl at your YMCA location here in Santee.

I was made to feel as though I had done something wrong when I talked to people at the YMCA. Somehow, the indecent exposure of a male to a female minor was an inconvenience to them. When my dad spoke to the sheriff's office, they told him that he should never allow me to shower there ever again. The YMCA wouldn't let my father speak to the manager of the Santee branch. After waiting several days, he finally received a call from Terry Moss, who is the Director of Membership for San Diego County. She informed my dad that I was not in any danger at the time of the incident. That I was safe. But I ask

> you this: I'm assuming all of you either have a wife, sisters, daughters, or granddaughters, or you are a woman yourself. Could you knowingly send an underage girl into a room where there was a naked male and say that she was not in danger?

I would never refer to people as "transgenders," but readers can see her point. The YMCA later issued an apology to Phillips.

The man in question, a Navy veteran, turned out to be named Christynne Lili Wrene Wood. He claims to be a "transgender woman" because he has a "female gender identity." Later that month, the feminist magazine *Reduxx* did a deep dive into Wood's social media history and uncovered multiple photos that Wood had uploaded of little girls, often wearing adult dress. *Reduxx* reported that the pictures "were usually superimposed with bizarre captions in which Wood compared himself to children." *Reduxx* states further that some posts have a "more overtly sexual theme" and that in one photo from an online quiz on the topic "How perverted are you?" Wood's score reads "637% perverted" and states "even the most innocent of moments can turn into something raunchy for you." This is "gender identity" and it has the full support of California Democrats.

Riley Gaines is a former swimmer on the University of Kentucky's women's swim team who competed against Lia (Will) Thomas in the 2022 NCAA championships in Atlanta, Georgia. In February 2023, she testified before the Virginia state legislature about a group of bills concerning the topic of single-sex sports. She said, "In addition to being forced to give up our awards, our titles, and our opportunities, the NCAA forced female swimmers to share a locker room with Thomas, a six-foot-four twenty-two-year-old male who was fully intact with male genitalia. Let me be clear. We were not forewarned. We were not asked for our consent and we did not give our consent. If nothing else, I hope you can see how this is a violation of our privacy and how some of us have felt uncomfortable, awkward, embarrassed, and even traumatized by this experience."

It's worth pausing for a moment to emphasize what Gaines is saying here. She is using words like "force," "consent," and "trauma." This highlights exactly what we are talking about—allowing men like Thomas to access women's locker rooms is nothing short of rape culture. In 2017, we had the #MeToo movement, where women were supposed to be permitted to say no to men. Women have fought for the right to say no to men for thousands of years. Women *still* have to fight for the right to say no to men, and that doesn't change if the man in question calls himself Lia. Gaines later testified before Congress to say that she and the other female athletes had to cram into a janitor's closet to change outside of Thomas's presence. Kylee Alons was a female swimmer at North Carolina State University at the time and also competed in the NCAA 2022 Championships. She echoed Gaines's sentiments, stating in 2023 that NCAA organizers "put women in an uncomfortable situation by allowing Thomas to enter the female changing rooms." She continued, "Not only was he advantaged against us, he was stronger, bigger, and stole titles from some of these women, but he was also creating a very uncomfortable environment in the locker room. I tried to keep myself mostly covered just in case he walked in. I ended up changing in a storage closet that was behind our team's bleachers." Women and girls should not have to go to lengths like these to avoid being naked in the presence of men and boys.

Proponents of "gender identity" often say that TERFs are "obsessed with genitals." For example, a man called James Stephanie Sterling (who claims to be "non-binary"), once posted: "Terfs should be kept out of women's spaces in the name of safety. They harass people in toilets, are obsessed with looking at genitalia, a lot of them are men, and they're violent. They're a societal menace and their lifestyle choice should be condemned." But here's the thing: women like Gaines and Alons would not have had to mention Thomas's genitalia in their testimony were it not for the fact that Thomas had flaunted it in the women's locker room, right in front of them.

It came out in February 2023 that the situation with Thomas is even worse than anyone knew. Crain & Company is a sports podcast that runs on the conservative network *The Daily Wire*. Its host, Jake Crain, interviewed Gaines to talk about her experiences competing against Thomas and then decided to do some digging. Crain discovered that Thomas has two accounts on Instagram: "LiaKThomas" and "LiaThimas." The former appears to be fairly benign and posts things like "let trans kids play" (a reference to wanting to allow boys to compete in girls' sports). The other account is a bit more sinister. That account "likes" numerous posts promoting autogynephila. Thomas appears to be in a relationship with Gwen Weiskopf (also a man who claims to have a woman identity) who ran a Crowdfunder in early 2023 to fund his breast augmentation surgery. Weiskopf posts images of himself posing in front of bondage gear and wearing bikinis (where you can see, well, everything), as well as satanic artwork. Some of these feature Thomas—one brags that Thomas is going to "bring about the collapse of Western Civilization" and another characterizes Thomas as a demonic dominatrix. Thomas also appears in numerous photographs with someone who goes by the online name "crybaby_hellbitch." This person also appears to be a man who claims to have a woman identity.

Throughout all of 2022, the national media championed Thomas as a trailblazer. *Sports Illustrated* ran a gushing story called "'I am Lia': the Trans Swimmer Dividing America Tells Her Story." *People Magazine* explained that in the story, "Lia Thomas is opening up her resolve to keep swimming, even after she faced resistance from other athletes.... Before she came out, Thomas said she began to reflect on her gender identity toward the end of high school. And though she had come out to family, her struggle with gender dysphoria became so persistent during her sophomore year at Penn that it began to impact her day-to-day life." It reported Thomas as saying "I was very depressed. I got to the point where I couldn't go to school. I was missing classes. My sleep schedule was super messed up. Some days I couldn't get out of bed." Except it isn't true. Thomas is nothing other than a creepy autogynephile who persuaded the University of Pennsylvania to let him access the women's swim team and the locker room, won medals, crushed records, and intimidated young women by exposing his penis to them. And the entire world went along with it because, supposedly, he is a "she." This is what "trans" does. It is gaslighting, manipulative abuse.

In 2021, a boy forcibly sodomized a ninth-grade girl in a school bathroom while wearing a skirt in a Loudoun County, Virginia school. That school had in place a policy allowing students to use the bathroom that corresponded with their "gender identity," regardless of sex. Knowing that this had happened, the school simply transferred the boy to another school within the district, where he assaulted yet another girl. When the first girl's father attempted to complain at a school board meeting, he was arrested for disorderly conduct. It only came out later, in 2022, that all of this had happened with the knowledge of the school district, and the superintendent was fired.

In 2021 and again in 2022, several women complained about the presence of a man in the women's locker room at the YMCA in Xenia, Ohio (a suburb of Dayton). When they complained, they were told that the man was in fact a woman. He wasn't. One of the women who complained was named Sue Atherton, who is married to a pastor named Mark. Mark has blogged publicly about how he reached out to the president and two vice presidents of the YMCA to inquire about its policies and was told that "It is the policy of the Xenia YMCA to be 'compliant with the Ohio Civil Rights Commission and Ohio law, which requires the Xenia YMCA to allow all members access to its facilities and programs, regardless of religion, national origin, race, color, sex, age, disability, gender identity, or sexual orientation.'" This is not true. According to the website of the Ohio Civil Rights Commission, the bases protected against discrimination in Ohio are "race, color, sex, disability, age, religion, national origin, ancestry, familial status in housing, military status, marital status (for credit only) and retaliation." There is no mention of "gender identity" or sexual orientation. Whether the leadership of the YMCA simply lied to Mr. Atherton or were themselves confused is unclear.

The Greater Dayton YMCA later put out an official statement to the effect that it adheres to state and federal antidiscrimination laws which "allow all members access to its facilities and programs, regardless of religion, national origin, race, color, sex, age, disability, gender identity, or sexual orientation." But again, this just isn't true. Neither state nor federal law mention "gender identity" in their nondiscrimination laws (yet). However, the city of Dayton does. A local city ordinance prohibits discrimination in the areas of employment, housing, public accommodations, and credit transactions on the basis of an individual's race, color, religion, sex, ancestry, national origin, place of birth, age, marital status, familial status, sexual orientation, gender identity, or disability. The same ordinance defines "gender identity" to mean "the gender-related identity, appearance, or mannerisms or other gender-related characteristics of an individual, regardless of the individual's designated sex at birth." The Greater Dayton YMCA, including the Xenia branch, are evidently referring to this city ordinance when they say that they cannot exclude a man from the women's locker room on the basis of his "female gender identity."

The man in question is named Darren Glines (he calls himself Rachel). Although he was initially charged with three counts of indecent exposure, he was eventually acquitted after a local municipal judge decided that as a factual matter, Glines was too obese for his genitalia to be visible and if his genitalia was not visible, indecent exposure could not be proven. During the 2023 trial, a woman testified that Glines had previously approached her at her place of work (a different nearby YMCA) and befriended her. This woman, Kateisha Young, states that at the time, she was very sympathetic to people who claim to "be transgender." She agreed to meet with him for coffee, listened to his story about allegedly being discriminated against at the Xenia YMCA, and gave him a sympathetic hug. That's when he grabbed her genitals and buttocks. She was stunned. She reported the incident to law enforcement and eventually got a restraining order against him. Let this be the takeaway here: All of us on the political left who think that we are sympathetic to people who identify as "transgender" eventually learn the truth that it is mostly a ruse to abuse women and girls. All American liberal and progressive women who think they support "trans" will eventually come face-to-face with this truth.

In this scenario, everyone agrees that Glines has a penis and testicles (male genitalia). Everyone agrees that he was present in the women's locker room at the Xenia YMCA on numerous occasions. Everyone agrees that he eventually started going to a different local YMCA where he befriended and eventually sexually assaulted a female employee. There are no factual disputes here. And yet, a judge found that he could not be guilty of indecent exposure because he was too obese for his penis and testicles to be visible to the women and girls who were in the locker room with him. It doesn't seem to matter to anyone that this man, whether his genitals were visible or not, was permitted to gawk at women and girls in a state of undress. Men are just being permitted to be physically present in women's locker rooms on the basis of their "gender identity" because of laws that Democrats have enacted, and very few people seem to be concerned enough to do anything about it.

In December 2022, a male employee of Denver's Regional Transportation District (RTD) named Willow (William) Senseman started using the women's bathrooms, showers, and locker rooms at RTD facilities, with RTD's permission. Female employees complained and were told that they could either accept it or be fired. According to an employee who wished to remain anonymous, "RTD announced that nobody can discuss the situation, either with other employees or the media and all employees MUST refer to the male employee as a woman and call him by his chosen name or risk being fired from their jobs." The state of Colorado does not protect "gender identity" in its public accommodations law. That law states: "It is a discriminatory practice and unlawful for a person, directly or indirectly, to refuse, withhold from, or deny to an individual or a group, because of disability, race, creed, color, sex, sexual orientation, marital status, national origin, or ancestry, the full and equal enjoyment of the goods, services, facilities, privileges, advantages, or accommodations of a place of public accommodation." But Denver does. Like Dayton, Ohio, Denver has an ordinance in place that protects race, color, religion, national origin, ethnicity, citizenship, immigration status, gender, age, sexual orientation, gender identity, gender expression, marital status, military status, disability, source of income and "protected hairstyles" in public accommodations (I don't know exactly what "protected hairstyles" refers to, but I assume it protects hairstyles worn by black people, who are often discriminated against because their chosen hairstyle defies norms of "acceptability," which, if true, is a good thing in my view). So presumably, RTD complies with Denver law by allowing this man who goes by Willow unfettered access to what should be female-only spaces. The women lose while their concerns go ignored.

In 2023, at a Wisconsin high school, an eighteen-year-old male student exposed his penis to four freshman girls. It was after a swim class and the girls were showering in the locker room. The student just entered, stripped naked, and announced, "I'm trans, by the way," before exposing his penis to them. A legal group representing the girls and their families has submitted a letter to school administrators, demanding answers. The only answer, of course, is that men and boys are allowed to get away with whatever they want to simply by saying things like, "I'm trans, by the way." The district tried to implement a policy banning male students from using the girls' facilities, but that policy was blocked by a federal court.

Something similar happened at a high school in Riverside, California, where a girl is on record referring to a "transgender" (i.e., male) student in saying "He's in the girls' locker room, using girls' restrooms. He spit on my friends that are girls. He shows his genitals in the locker room." The student's behavior was apparently so brazen that it led to an altercation between him and a different female student. A very brave young woman named Megan Simpkins would later slam her own school board for allowing this male student to access what are supposed to be female-only spaces. She said: "There was an incident within our school district that occurred recently regarding a transgender woman, who really is a biological man, having an altercation with a young woman at [the school]. It was infuriating when I had seen the video on social media, but what was detrimental to this is the fact that this man is and has been using the women's restroom and locker room." She warned school officials about the issue of "biological men claiming they are women and, in turn, truly believing that they are entitled to use women's spaces." She said, "Firstly, the question we must address is why are we affirming the mental confusion of this boy and putting the safety of women in jeopardy by allowing mentally confused men to use women's spaces? Of course, any male who claims he is a woman will accept it, but what about the women? What about the true girls like myself who are females down to our DNA? Why don't we ever get a say in whether or not we are comfortable with this? The truth is we aren't, the majority of us aren't, and yet nothing has been done to protect the safety of these women. I will conclude with this—it all starts with you. You are in charge of the safety of us women. Please do something about it." As far as I know, they haven't.

In 2023, Jodi (Gregory) Jeloudov visited the women's clinic in the VA Medical Center in West Palm Beach. He complained that someone or multiple people at the clinic had "misgendered" him and not respected his preferred name. He later said that as he was leaving, he decided to make a stop in the women's bathroom. A woman in the bathroom said, "You don't belong here" to him and his response was "I have long hair; I have on a female dress; I have high-cut boots, and I have on some makeup." After he left the bathroom, two staff members blocked him from going back in. During the incident, a manager asked him why he didn't just use the unisex bathroom. What this means is that he had the option of using a unisex bathroom and he chose to go out of his way to use the women's instead.

He complained to the VA, which responded, "This is unacceptable, and we are immediately reaching out to this Veteran to apologize. We have also launched an investigation to ensure that this does not happen again. VA's policy ... is that Veterans are welcome to use any and all facilities that correspond to their self-identified gender identity. Moreover, it's our job at the VA to make sure that Veterans of all gender identities know that whenever they walk into a VA facility, they will be treated with the care, compassion, and respect that they deserve. That is the standard to which we hold all VA employees. This incident was a failure of that mission, and we will not rest until it is fixed—for this Veteran and for all Veterans who entrust us with their care." This is the U.S. Veteran's Administration falling over itself to pander to a man who got upset that he wasn't allowed to use a women's bathroom. A national patient advocate program representative even reached out to him, but none of this was good enough. Instead, he vowed not to use VA facilities because he didn't "feel safe." Never mind the safety of actual women.

A male tennis coach in Gettysburg, Pennsylvania, named Sasha (David) Yates has been using the girls' locker room while girls are inside changing. He was initially hired as David, but in 2022 decided that he is a woman named Sasha. After a few incidents in 2022, the school board decided not to rehire him, but they later changed their mind because they were worried that if they didn't, he would sue them for discriminating against him on the basis of his woman identity. This is how reports describe one of the 2022 incidents: "Mr. Yates changed his clothing too, stripping down to bra and panties. Students reported that it was clear from what they saw that Mr. Yates was still fully a man." In April 2023, he followed a female softball player into the girls' locker room and tried to strike up a conversation with her. She immediately left. During a September 2023 board meeting, the board voted to renew his contract over the objections of numerous students and parents.

There is an ongoing legal case called *Doe, et al. v. Kappa Kappa Gamma, et al.*, which concerns a group of women who are suing their sorority, the sorority president, and a man listed as "Terry Smith" (a pseudonym for a man named Dallin Langford who claims to have a woman identity and goes by the name Artemis Langford). The sorority forced its members to admit Langford into it, over the objections of several women, and Langford proceeded to behave inappropriately in common areas of the sorority house. Among the allegations in the complaint are that he frequently sits in the second-floor common area watching women; voyeuristically peeps on women while they are in intimate situations while having a visible erection; once watched a woman walking down the hall to take a shower, wearing only a towel; took photos of women during a slumber party without consent; repeatedly questioned women about what vaginas look like and breast cup size; and watched women changing their clothes, in various states of undress. When women complained, the sorority and the university did nothing. Young women are simply expected to put up with this type of behavior because the man in question claims to have a woman identity. The plaintiffs initially sought permission to proceed anonymously and the court denied their request, so they bravely stepped up and revealed their names. In a court filing, the sorority said, "The term [woman] is unquestionably open to many interpretations," called the plaintiffs' action "frivolous," and said that the plaintiffs were only trying to further "their own political purposes." But what is "political" about women not wanting to be naked around men with visible erections? The sorority won at the federal district court level and at the time of writing, the matter is on appeal.

The Biden administration has a policy in place that permits men to be housed in military barracks with women on the basis of their woman identities. In July 2023, it was reported that one young woman complained privately. Just eighteen years old, this military recruit said that she was forced to sleep in between "two individuals who were supposedly changing from male to female" and to shower with others. She was extremely distressed and worried that filing a formal complaint would put her career at risk. She said that she was thinking of resigning from the military rather than be forced to endure the situation. I'm no military expert, but I think an argument can be made that by housing men with female members of the military, the president is putting our nation's security at risk by alienating good, strong, female recruits.

In May 2023, a man named Ali (Dylan) Miles sued a yoga studio in New York City because the yoga studio would not allow him to use the women's bathroom or locker room on the basis of his claimed woman identity. According to his complaint, he told the manager that he "most closely aligned with female gender identity" and that he planned to use the women's bathroom and locker room. He was told that he would not be permitted to do that, but he did it anyway. According to the complaint, "female patrons complained and yelled at [him] about [his] presence and use of the single-sex locker room and bathroom labelled *Women*, and they demanded [he] leave and cease using the facilities." He further alleges that while "feeling shame, humiliation, and frustration, he was escorted to the facilities designated for men," and was "forced to use a locker room and bathroom that was not most closely aligned with [his] gender." But why shouldn't men who intentionally invade women's spaces experience shame and humiliation?

Oklahoma has a law in place that requires public school students to use restrooms that match the sex listed on their birth certificates. Under the law, students who "identify as transgender" who are not comfortable using the restroom that is reserved for members of their sex can use a "single occupancy restroom." But a school in Edmond, Oklahoma knowingly allowed a boy to use the girls' bathroom on the basis of his "female gender identity." In October 2022, it is alleged that he "attacked and severely beat" a female student in the girls' bathroom. The female student's mother, Theresa Gooden, has sued the school for damages and the case is ongoing at the time of writing.

Sonia Rivera is a longtime employee of the New York City Metropolitan Transit Authority (MTA) and a bus driver. One day she entered the women's locker room at the MTA Eastchester Bus Depot when a fellow bus driver, Nana Mangual (a man who claims to have a woman identity) was inside. She told him to use the men's, and he began filming her. When Rivera complained, *she* was arrested and charged with harassment, harassment as a hate crime, and assault. Mangual faced no consequences for being in the women's room in the first place.

I have had my own personal experience encountering a man with a "female gender identity" in a women's bathroom. One day in 2019, I was at a local restaurant, where I happened to know the owner. It is a family-friendly establishment, and the owner had his three young daughters with him that day. I was sitting at the bar with a friend, having a normal conversation, when all of a sudden, I felt a very strange and strong male presence to the right of me, in a way that felt very much like a violation of my personal space. I don't mean that in some sort of weird new-age way; I literally mean that he was right up against me. That kind of thing is sometimes appropriate, say, in a crowded bar where everyone is standing shoulder-to-shoulder. This wasn't that. There was plenty of room everywhere along the bar, and the only reason that I could come up with as to why he would be standing so close to me is that he thought he could make me uncomfortable. He was right. I didn't want to look directly at him, though, so I basically avoided the situation until he had bought a drink and walked toward a table, which happened to be directly behind me and my friend. I quickly glanced behind me and saw a very tall man with long blond hair. He was wearing a long flowy skirt and sandals. His toenails were painted pink. He also had with him numerous tote bags. I returned my attention to my conversation with my friend and we both did our best to ignore him (which was difficult because he kept making a complete nuisance of himself by shifting seats and moving his tote bags around in an obvious attempt to get attention from other restaurant guests, which he did because his conduct was so irritating).

A while later I wanted to use the restroom, and as I turned to get off my barstool, I saw that he was gone from the table where he had been. His beer glass was empty, and his tote bags were gone. I assumed he had left. I went into the women's room, which contains three private stalls, and the first thing I noticed was that in one of the stalls was a pair of feet with pink toenail polish and the same slew of tote bags on the floor. I immediately left to tell the owner. He didn't like the situation any more than I did (especially given that his daughters were present), but he knew there was little he could do, legally, because Washington D.C. (where I live and which is run primarily by Democrats) protects the category of "gender identity" in places of public accommodation. Happily, the man with the skirt, pink toenail polish, and numerous tote bags left shortly thereafter. But still, it bothered me, as it would just about any woman. He had previously gone out of his way to make me uncomfortable by violating my personal space at the bar, and there he was, in the women's room, presumably on the basis of his woman identity. Needless to say, women should not have to put up with this.

Supporters of "gender identity" often dismiss these types of concerns by saying, "Well, male perverts are always going to lurk in women's bathrooms, but that's no reason to exclude transgender women from them." This misses the point for so many reasons. First, it is completely true that male perverts are always going to lurk in women's bathrooms, *but under a legal regime that prohibits men from going into women's bathrooms, at least we have the ability to kick them out when we catch them doing it.* Under a legal regime that permits men to be in women's bathrooms based on their woman identity, in contrast, we lose that ability. Second, how are women supposed to know which men are the perverts and which are the nice ones who just happen to have woman identities? Women can't just look at a man and know for certain whether he is going to attack her or not. This is why we have female-only spaces to protect women and girls in the first place! Third, and perhaps most importantly, *decent men who are not perverts do not wish to access female-only spaces.*

I cannot emphasize this enough. On a different occasion several years later, I was in a women's restroom at a restaurant and while I was washing my hands, a man walked in. Not because he was a creepy pervert, but because he had made an honest mistake. When he saw me, he seemed mortified, blushed, and walked out. I am not mad at men who make innocent mistakes about which restroom is the women's and which is the men's. If a man accidentally walks into the women's thinking it is the men's and instantly realizes his mistake and leaves, no problem. That is what any decent person of either sex would do. It is the men who *want* access to female-only spaces that I don't trust. That is just as true of the male perverts who do not pretend to be women as it is true of the male perverts who do pretend to be women.

All these incidents reveal the dangers to women and girls of enshrining "gender identity" in the law because doing so allows men to access women-only spaces on the basis of their "female gender identity." This is all the result of policies enacted by Democrats in positions of power who simply do not care about the safety or dignity of women and girls.

Female Athletes

Polls consistently show that Americans overwhelmingly support single-sex sports. Title IX, enacted in 1972 to prohibit sex discrimination in education, expressly permits single-sex sports and spaces in its regulations. In 2023, the *Washington Examiner* ran an opinion piece titled "Even Democrats aren't buying transgenderism in sports," citing polling showing that Democrats' support for men competing in women's sports has dropped from 55 percent to 41 percent in two years. Yet time and again, we have seen male athletes be permitted to compete on women's teams under Democrat-enacted laws and policies that allow for participation on the basis of "gender identity." Time and again, women and girls lose.

It is no mystery that men and boys have athletic advantages over women and girls, especially after the onset of puberty. Dr. Emma Hilton, a U.K. feminist and biologist, has proven this time and again. For some reason, in 2023, a group of former players with the U.S. national women's soccer team (the reigning World Cup champions), decided to play in a soccer tournament with a Welsh male soccer team. Within forty minutes of play time, the men had scored sixteen goals and the women scored zero, and officials ended the match. One can only wonder what the score would have been had the match been permitted to continue until ninety minutes plus extra time.

All the way back in 2013, Fallon Fox (a man) was beating up women in the mixed martial arts (MMA) ring. In 2014, he competed against Tamikka Brents, beating her so hard he gave her a concussion and an orbital bone fracture, essentially ending her career. Alana McLaughlin is a former member of the U.S. Army Special Forces and current MMA fighter. In 2021, he competed in the women's MMA, beating up Celine Provost. He calls himself "Lady Feral" and his X bio reads: "The lady feral, hard femme, trantifa supersoldier, eater of fish, titles, she/her" with a trans flag, and his cover photo features a neon pink assault rifle. Men like Fox and McLaughlin get away with beating up women in the ring by saying they "are transgender."

Lia (Will) Thomas is probably the most well-known male athlete who has competed in women's sports in the U.S. In 2022, he smashed NCAA records and stole awards from female competitors. He towers over his female competitors and Americans rightly got angry when he was permitted to receive awards and medals, taking spots from the female athletes who deserved them. In 2022, the body that oversees competitive swimming globally announced that it would not allow "transgender women" to compete in women's events if they "transitioned" after the age of twelve, in part because of Thomas's participation in the NCAA championships. I have had more than one person (all Democrats) tell me that Thomas is personally responsible for making them investigate what on earth is going on in America with respect to "gender identity." In March 2023, *ESPN* released a segment honoring the achievements of female athletes in observance of Women's History Month, *including Thomas*. Throughout the segment, *ESPN* referred to Thomas as "she" and "her." Riley Gaines has become an outspoken advocate for keeping female athletics female and the entire U.S. National Women's Swimming Team later announced that they would quit if Thomas was permitted to try out for the team. But Thomas is hardly alone.

In 2018, four female high school students (Selina Soule, Chelsea Mitchell, Alanna Smith, and Ashley Nicoletti) in Connecticut sued their state athletic association over its policy of allowing male athletes to compete in women's track. The way that the athletic association allows male athletes to compete on women's teams is via its "Transgender Policy." Each of the plaintiffs had had to compete against a male athlete. The case is called *Soule v. CIAC* and it is still ongoing, after five years of the federal judiciary essentially ignoring these young women's concerns. At one point during the course of the litigation, the plaintiffs' lawyer was ordered not to refer to the male athletes as male, even though they clearly are.

In 2017, a young man named Jonathan Eastwood was running on the men's cross-country team at the University of Montana. By 2019, he was calling himself June (sometimes Juniper) and running on the women's team as a senior. That year he was named Woman of the Week during the Big Sky Conference Tournament. In 2020, he took first place in the women's mile event during the Big Sky. In 2020, the state of Idaho enacted a law mandating that schools throughout the state maintain single-sex sports. That law was challenged by a man named Lindsay Hecox who thinks that he should be able to compete in women's sports based on his woman identity. That case is still ongoing too. Around twenty other states have passed similar laws, many of which are the subject of litigation in cases brought by men who claim to have woman identities (who are often represented by the ACLU).

The stakes for female athletes could not be more dire. In October 2022, a female high school volleyball player in North Carolina named Payton McNabb suffered severe injuries to her head and neck after a male player on the opposing team hard-spiked a ball at seventy miles per hour into her face. The male player was, of course, permitted to play in a girls' volleyball game on the basis of his claimed woman identity. Rather than deal with the situation directly, the entire Cherokee County school board voted to forfeit all matches for its schools' women's volleyball teams against Highlands School (the school that had permitted the male athlete to play on its women's team). In other words, the adults on the school board just forfeited games against the team rather than stand up to a boy who claims to have a "female gender identity," as though that were perfectly normal.

In March 2023, a forty-six-year-old male cyclist named Tiffany (Trent) Thomas won a women's cycling competition in New York City called Randall's Island Crit cycling race. According to *The Daily Mail*, he did so after "blowing the competition out of the water to snatch first place." Thomas had taken up cycling in 2018 and quickly went on to dominate women's races. He won a spot on the women's cycling team LA Sweat, whose website states: "We're on a mission to empower other women to cut the crap and be unafraid to get out there and ride." But by allowing men to compete on its team, it is clear that LA Sweat is not "cutting the crap."

Tara (Todd) Seplavy is a deputy editor at Hearst Magazines, which includes both *Bicycling* and *Women's Health*. He has been competing in women's cycling races at least since 2017. According to his website, he is "passionate about the sport of cycling and about getting more people onto bikes!" His website doesn't bother to mention that he's male. He once bragged that the women's cycling community had given him unconditional acceptance. He continued: "What I have experienced in the women's cycling community are people who are passionate and dedicated to growing cycling for all riders. There is a true want from the community to grow participation beyond its current boundaries. Seeing this desire to grow in a meaningful and intersectional way makes me want to give back more of myself, to reinvest into my love of bikes and into the sport." During that interview, he did not mention that he has posted pictures of himself holding a baseball bat painted in the pink and blue colors of the "trans" flag on Instagram, which is extremely threatening; it is hard to imagine women opposing his inclusion under those circumstances. By May of 2023, he had competed in four women's cycling races that year, beating out countless actual female cyclists.

Another male cyclist, Austin Killips, won the women's category in the Tour of the Gila in New Mexico in 2023. This brought widespread condemnation from female athletes, with three-time Olympian Inga Thompson accusing the world's cycling governing body of "killing off women's cycling" and tennis champion Martina Navratilova saying that "trans identified male athletes" have no place in women's sports. Previously, former cyclocross champion Hannah Arensman had lost to Killips in the national championship finals and stated that she had decided to end her cycling career as a result. She said: "I have decided to end my cycling career. My sister and family sobbed as they watched a man finish in front of me, having witnessed several physical interactions with him during the race. I feel for young girls learning to compete, who no longer have a fair chance at being the new record holders and champions in cycling because men want to compete in our division." Killips went on to win the women's competition in the Belgian Waffle Ride in North Carolina that year (that ride eventually implemented a policy prohibiting men from participation).

Killips also raced in the women's division in the 2022 U.S. Cyclocross National Championships, along with another male cyclist who claims to be a woman named Jenna (Jimmy) Lingwood. Lingwood had competed in the men's competition until 2018, when he decided that he was a woman. In the 2022 nationals, he won a women's masters title, beating out female athlete Erin Feldhausen. Killips ended up coming in third in the finals that year, stealing a bronze medal from yet another actual female athlete. The following year, Lingwood won Day 9 of the elite women's race (along with a $950 prize) at the Tour of America's Dairyland competition in Wisconsin. Jordan Johnson is yet another male cyclist who participates in women's races. Johnson is a category 3 cyclist, which means that USA Cycling does not require him to suppress testosterone at all. In April 2023, he won the women's Oval Criterium at Colorado State University. That June, he advanced to the finals in USA Cycling's women's Track Talent ID program.

Chelsea (Connor) Wolfe is a BMX competitor. In 2020, he said that "[his] goal is to win the Olympics so [he] can burn a US flag on the podium." He did go on to compete in the Tokyo Olympics in 2021 as an alternate in the women's category. On his way there, he placed fifth in the 2021 BMX Freestyle Park finals, placing him third overall in the U.S. women's team rankings. He later went on to place first in the UCI Elite Women's division of round 3 of the 2022 USA BMX Freestyle Series. As of writing, Wolfe was on track to qualify for the women's U.S. Olympic team for Paris 2024.

There are countless examples of male athletes competing in women's cycling. One who deserves special mention is Veronica Ivy (a.k.a., Rachel McKinnon, a.k.a., Rhys McKinnon), who I'll talk about at more length in Chapter 5 regarding his appearance on *The Daily Show* with Trevor Noah. Ivy is a male cyclist who decided that he's a woman in 2012. He started competing in women's cycling in 2018 and won the UCI (global cycling governing body) Masters World Track Cycling Championship in the women's sprint 35-44 age bracket that year. He has been disgusting feminists and female athletes ever since. He once posted in 2019, in a reference to TERFs, "I mean, I'm more specific and want them to die in a grease fire." That same year, he posted, "It's okay to be happy, even celebrate, when bad people die." A feminist asked him if that was a reference to Magdalen Berns, a U.K.-based feminist who died tragically in September 2019 of a brain tumor. He responded, "If they're a trash human actively trying to harm marginalized people because of who they are? I think it's justified."

In 2023, after the UCI took steps to limit the participation of male athletes in women's cycle, he posted on social media, "F*CK THE UCI" and "Buckle up, b*tches." The UCI finally moved to have him suspended and his response is worth quoting in full:

> The UCI is currently moving to have me suspended and fined for calling out their nakedly TRANSPHOBIC ban of trans women from ALL elite competitions.
>
> The reporting on this has been poor: trans women are banned from ALL elite competition, which includes NATIONAL championships, by the way! Nats are run under UCI rules and are on the UCI calendar, so we're banned from our own national championships even if our national federation allows us in non-UCI events. Way to go @cyclingcanadaofficial by the way <3
>
> What's got the UCI's panties in a bunch?
>
> I posted 'F*ck the UCI' and referenced a joke by Iliza Schlesinger in her comedy special 'War Paint,' adding the word 'motherf*ckers.'
>
> So the UCI is uppity about 'f*ck the UCI' and 'mother-f*ckers' when directed at an ORGANIZATION and no individual person (although I do call out Xavier Bigard for being a fool and a bigot--I stand by that, profesionally).
>
> They think such language is 'threatening,' 'abusive,' and 'insulting.'

> But their unscientific, unethical, and ILLEGAL ban of trans women from women's competition ISN'T threatening, abusive, and insulting?
>
> How do I put this politely: anyone who thinks this way can EAT SH*T.
>
> Banning trans women from women's sport is the threat, the abuse, the INSULT.
>
> I'm not sorry I hurt their fee fees. Grow up you snowflakes.
>
> OH! The kicker on all this is that they want ME to PAY for their proceedings against me.
>
> HAHAHAHAHA. NOPE. Good luck with that you fools.
>
> Thanks for making my lawsuits against you even easier! You keep digging. I love it.
>
> Keep it up.
>
> How convenient that they didn't include the HATEFUL, TRANSPHOBIC, and BIGOTED comments on my Instagram posts in their exhibits!!
>
> Their policy decision caused untold ABUSE, DEATH THREATS, and other INSULTS to come my way.
>
> But 'F*ck the UCI' and 'motherf*ckers' was just TOO MUCH for them! Oh woe is me!
>
> Someone get them a fainting couch!

Then he posted a bunch of random hashtags. Welcome to "trans."

In April 2023, a man named Kae Ravichandran won the newly created "non-binary" category in the Boston marathon. It is worth pausing for a moment to understand what happens when sporting events create "non-binary" categories—the male athletes who claim to be "non-binary" will almost always beat out the female athletes who claim to be "non-binary." These events should just acknowledge that they are mixed-sex and be done with it, rather than kowtow to the nonsensical idea that there is some coherent category of people who are neither male nor female. He went on to place in the top three of the women's Finger Lakes 50K trail race in June of that year. One wonders why, if this man claims to be "non-binary," he was permitted to compete as a woman. He describes himself on X as a "she/they/just a trans runner girl." On June 22, the same day he placed in the top three of the women's category, he posted: "cis cis cis cis cis cissy," in what may be an oblique reference to "sissy porn."

In 2023, at least two male athletes beat out female athletes to make their way to the California Interscholastic Federation's high school state track and field championships. Athena Ryan took second place in the high school women's 1600-meter race at the North Coast Meet of Champions. The fourth-place finisher, Adeline Johnson (an actual girl), missed her chance to compete in the state by just one spot. Ryan had previously competed in the men's competition (where he belongs) but began competing in the women's competition in 2022. In 2023, he ran the 1600 in 4:55:91. The slowest time in the male category was 4:46:54; had Ryan competed in the male category he would have finished at the bottom of the pile. Instead, he took second place in the female category, securing his spot in the state championships.

Also scheduled to compete in the 2023 California state championships in the female category was Lorelei Barrett, who took third place in the girls' qualifier for the 1600. Like Ryan, Barrett is male. During the race, a group of women affiliated with the group Women Are Real protested his participation, holding signs that read "Protect Female Sports." They reported that numerous people approached them to ask them what their protest was about and when they explained, people were shocked to learn that a male athlete had taken second place. A male athlete named Diamond Solorzano competed in and helped the girls' team from North Valleys High School win the 2023 Nevada state championship in the 4x200 meter and 4x400 meter relay races. This means that the girls on the other teams lost out on a chance to win because a young man (he was a senior) competed on the North Valleys women's team.

Emma (Emmet) Farnan is a man who has played on the Southern Headliners Rugby Club women's team in the Premier Rugby Sevens League while attending school at Notre Dame. He is listed on the 2023 women's roster playing the "prop" position, which is typically assigned to the biggest two players on the team. In August 2023, while competing in the women's division of the Premier Rugby Sevens semi-final, he was seen on camera (possibly deliberately) spreading his legs, grabbing his groin, and adjusting himself. Previously, as a senior at Notre Dame, he completed a half marathon in under two hours while chugging a can of Coors Light at every mile. He once provided images of himself to the *Daily Mail* which show him to be quite obviously male. The *Mail* reported the story as "Transgender women's rugby player insists she has NO advantage over her competitors—and says she is 'a shell of the athlete' she was before transitioning." Even if it weren't obvious from the images that he is clearly male, the reason we know that he is male is this reporting. The *Mail* is referring to him as a "transgender" athlete and using "she" and "her" to describe him.

World Rugby is an international federation that has concluded that "safety and fairness cannot presently be assured for women competing against trans women in contact rugby," so Farnan is not able to advance beyond his current level of competition and he is frustrated about that. He has said, "And it's really tough to be in a position where my career isn't limited because I go and tryout and I'm told I'm not good enough, my career is limited because of my medical history." And with that, he characterized the fact of his maleness as his "medical history."

Brooklyn Ross is a man who was permitted to compete in women's tennis in college and in 2023 was scheduled to compete in the women's category of the Wyoming Governor's Cup, prompting the (female) president of the state's tennis association to resign in protest over the unfairness. He eventually dropped out, citing concerns for his own safety (without providing any evidence of any threats to his safety).

Alicia Rowley is another male tennis player who, in 2023, won a Women's National Tennis Championship. In response, tennis great Martina Navratilova said, "Come on @USTA—women's tennis is not for failed male athletes—whatever age. This is not right and it is not fair. Would this be allowed at the US Open this month? Just with self-ID? I don't think so." Navratilova's reference to "self-ID" was to the fact that U.S. Tennis allows any man to compete in the women's category. For professional competitions, the only requirement for a male athlete to compete in the women's category is that "the athlete has declared that her gender identity is female" and that "the declaration cannot be changed, for sporting purposes, for a minimum of four years." It requires that "hormonal therapy appropriate for the assigned sex" to have been "administered in a verifiable manner and for a sufficient length of time to minimize gender-related advantages," but it doesn't impose any specific requirements about what that might entail.

Men are competing in women's disc golf, snowboarding, and other sports all over the U.S. It's happening in jiu-jitsu. It's happening in fencing. Women who complain are punished. In Illinois, a sixteen-year-old female swimmer was banned from the YMCA and kicked off her team when she complained about the presence of grown men in the women's locker room. She was told that her complaint constituted "hate speech." One woman who is not doing female athletes any favors is Megan Rapinoe, a major U.S. soccer star who retired in 2023 after missing a penalty kick in the 2023 FIFA World Cup. Rapinoe says that she "sees trans women as real women" and that any disagreement necessarily leads to violence against men who have woman identities.

Again, though, this phenomenon is not limited to the U.S.

A man (who claims to be a lesbian) named Riley J. Dennis describes himself on his website as "an American-Australian video creator and writer" who "used to make YouTube videos covering a wide range of topics, including exploring the themes in some of her favourite TV shows." It is true that Dennis talked about TV shows on his YouTube channel. But what he isn't saying is that his favorite pastime used to be telling lesbians that they are "transphobic" if they don't want to have romantic or sexual relationships with men. He often said that "genital preferences" (i.e., having a sexual orientation) are "transphobic" and specifically, that lesbians are a problem if they don't want to be around penises. He appears to have deleted all his anti-lesbian videos from his channel since then, but you can see them all very clearly by visiting the channel of the late Magdalen Berns (a British radical feminist lesbian content creator who tragically died of a brain tumor in 2019 at the age of thirty-six). In April 2023, it was revealed that Dennis is now one of many men competing in women's football (soccer, to us Americans) in New South Wales, Australia, and that he had injured several women on an opposing team.

In Canada, a man named Ash Davis was awarded "Men's Hardest Hitter" in Canadian rugby at a banquet event in 2022. By 2023, he was competing in women's rugby. In June of that year, he had to be removed from a women's rugby match after injuring three women who had to stop playing and receive medical treatment. Canadian policy allows rugby players to participate "as the gender with which they identify." There is no requirement for a player to demonstrate any attempt to medically or surgically alter their bodies before playing on the team of their choice.

Valentina Petrillo was born Fabrizio and has been competing in Italian women's track events since 2020, when he changed his name and started his "gender transition." He has set several women's track records and ranked fifth at the 2021 World Para Athletics European Championships. In 2023, he won a women's world championship race.

Hannah (Callum) Mouncey is a man who plays women's handball in Australia. He made his start after moving to Canberra in 2009. He played twenty-two games with the Australian men's national handball team before announcing in 2016 that he's a woman. In 2018, he began training with the Australia women's national handball team and played that year in the

Asian Women's Handball Championship. The Australian women's team qualified for the 2019 World Women's Handball Championship but he was not permitted to compete because some women did not wish to share the showers or changing room with him. Nonetheless, he has been permitted to compete on the women's team ever since. Although his announcement that he is a woman came in 2016, in 2017 he bragged on X that he is "hung like a horse." In 2023, he celebrated new guidelines regarding the ability of men to compete in women's sports, calling them "awesome." Handball, incidentally, is a contact sport. Players are permitted to tackle using their hands or their whole bodies.

Laurel Hubbard famously competed in the Tokyo 2020 Olympics in the women's weightlifting competition after competing in women's weightlifting in New Zealand for several years. He had previously set national records in men's weightlifting, but those records were later broken by another male weightlifter. His solution? Simple—become a woman. Hubbard, of course, is not a woman, a point American weightlifter and bronze medalist Sarah Robles made abundantly clear when a reporter asked her what she thought about Hubbard competing in the women's competition and she replied, simply, "No thank you."

In April 2023, a man named Glenique (Glenn) Frank was permitted to compete in the women's category during the London Marathon, beating out 14,000 female runners. He had run in the men's category in the New York Marathon several months prior to London. Shortly after the event, he bragged about all the marathons he had competed in before shouting "GIRL POWER!" and telling everyone that he is "going to be a granny." Marathon organizers defended the decision to allow him to compete in the women's category because the marathon is an "event that champions inclusivity." Never mind the inclusion of the actual female athletes.

There is a man in the U.K. named Julie-Anne Curtiss. He describes himself on X as an "unapologetic anarcho-socialist" and as "a woman who deeply loves the world and wishes it was a better place." He plays rugby and wants very much to play on his local amateur women's team. Sadly for him, England's Rugby Football Union (RFU) found in 2022, based on all available evidence, that "there are physical differences between those people whose sex originally recorded as male and those as female at birth, and advantages in strength, stamina and physique brought about by testosterone and male puberty are significant and retained even after testosterone suppression." It therefore decided that "this science provides the basis of the new gender participation policy that concludes the inclusion of trans people originally recorded male at birth in female contact rugby cannot be balanced against considerations of safety and fairness."

In May 2023, Curtiss launched a crowdfunder to raise money to cover the legal costs of suing the RFU. He stated, "First and foremost, I am a human being. I happen to love playing rugby." I have no doubt that both of those claims are true. He stated further, "I also happen to be trans." By this, he means that he is a man who claims to have a woman identity and thinks he should be allowed to play women's *contact* rugby based on that claimed identity. I don't know much about rugby and have never played the game. I do know however, that contact sports (including rugby) permit players to inflict significant physical impact force on other players. If I hadn't been paying attention to matters like this for so many years, I would find his demand to be able to inflict significant physical impact force on female athletes to be astonishing. However, I am no longer astonished by the entitlement of these men who claim to have woman identities. They will stop at nothing.

Curtiss has publicly complained on his blog that there is a "genocide of transgender people in the United Kingdom" because "many still do not accept the premise that trans-women ARE women." I don't know what polling in the U.K. looks like, but I previously noted that polling in the U.S. demonstrates that the vast majority of Americans understand that the following phrase is false: "Transgender women are biological women." Even 65 percent of Americans who call themselves "very liberal" and 80 percent of Americans who call themselves "liberal" know that phrase is false. The idea that knowing that sex is real and that men are male constitutes "genocide" is disgusting.

This is just a smattering of the horror stories about the men who are stealing women's titles and trophies all over the world. They are allowed to get away with it because they claim to have woman identities. The left-leaning parties in power, including the Democrats in the U.S., encourage this. Meanwhile, women and girls lose.

It's looking like more and more women and girls have had enough. Tennis great Martina Navratilova is probably the most high-profile female athlete who has been speaking out courageously. Bethany Hamilton is a surfer who lost her arm in a shark attack at thirteen and kept on competing through her adversity. In early 2023, she announced that she would boycott the World Surf League over its policy of allowing men to compete in women's surfing based on their woman identities. An Australian female boxer named Ebanie Bridges has refused to compete against male boxers, stating, "No, never. I think it's wrong, especially in boxing. I think in all sports." She continued, "It's like saying all of a sudden Mike Tyson wants to be a girl now and he goes on fights you—no way!" Kim Russell was the head coach of the Oberlin College women's lacrosse team, until she wasn't. After years of leading the team to victory, Russell posted on social media a congratulatory message to Emma Weyant, now an Olympian swimmer, who had her first-place podium spot at the 2022 NCAA swimming championships taken from her by Lia (Will) Thomas. Oberlin then subjected Russell to a series of disciplinary meetings. She says about those meetings, "I was burned at the stake. I was stoned. I was basically told I was a horrible person, and it was heartbreaking, really." They removed her as coach, and the college's webpage about the matter reads, simply, "After five seasons as the head women's lacrosse coach, Kim Russell transitioned into the role of employee wellness project manager in September of 2023."

In February 2023, the Mid Vermont Christian School girls' basketball team withdrew from the Vermont Division IV state tournament because an opposing team included a male player. Also in Vermont in October 2022, a family sued a school district after a coach and his daughter were punished for complaining about the presence of a male athlete in the girls' locker room. Travis Allen (the girls' soccer coach) and his daughter Blake (who played on the girls' volleyball team) were both punished when they complained. Allen was suspended without pay and Blake (and several other girls) were banned from the girls' locker room. In a victory for free speech (and for sanity), the school eventually agreed to reinstate Allen as the coach, lift Blake's ban from the girls' locker room, and pay the family $125,000. It is not clear whether the school will continue with its policy of allowing boys to use the girls' locker room based on their claims to be girls.

In April 2023, Payton McNabb (the North Carolina high school student who had been injured after a male volleyball player spiked a ball at her head) joined Riley Gaines to testify in support of a North Carolina bill to protect women's sports. McNabb stated that she still struggles with the effects of her injuries, including impaired vision, partial paralysis on the right side of her body, unremitting headaches, anxiety, and depression since she suffered a concussion at the hands of a male athlete. A woman named Evie Edwards published an op-ed in *The Carolina Journal* in support of the bill titled "I'm a female athlete, mother, and Democrat calling on NC to save women's sports." In her piece, she lamented, "I am a liberal woman. I am a wife, mother, and a registered Democrat. Most of the people I associate with are open minded. But we tend to agree, from a practical standpoint, that the inclusion of male bodies in female sport is unfair. Policies that force this ideology on girls and women are wrong and need urgent discussion. This should not be a partisan issue. I'm encouraged by the support of Republicans and baffled and disappointed by the lack of support from my Democratic Party." The bill eventually passed and was vetoed by the state's Democratic governor. But in an astonishing move, the legislature overrode the veto, *with two Democrats supporting the override.*

April Hutchinson is a powerlifter from Canada and she's speaking out after a county judge ruled that USA Powerlifting was in violation of state law by refusing to allow men to compete in the women's category. In 2018, a man named JayCee Cooper applied to compete in women's powerlifting. After USA Powerlifting denied his request, he sued them. Hutchinson is speaking out and fighting back, calling the forced inclusion of male powerlifting in the women's category discrimination against women and says that it needs to stop TODAY. USA Powerlifting has appealed the ruling and that appeal is pending as of writing.

The whole world is waking up to this charade. In March 2023, the organization World Athletics (the global governing body for track and field) announced that it would not permit men (who it referred to as "male-to-female transgender athletes who have been through male puberty") to compete in women's competitions. This is a positive step and a great win for female track and field athletes. In my view, however, it does not go far enough. There is simply no such thing as a "male-to-female transgender athlete." Pretending that someone can change sex is a complete denial of material reality and women and girls, including female athletes, pay the highest price.

British Cycling, which governs cycling competitions in the U.K., has announced that men (who it refers to as "transwomen") will not be permitted to compete in women's competitive cycling events under any circumstances (the policy does not extend to non-competitive events). It will allow women who claim to be men (i.e., "transmen") to compete in the women's category if they are not on testosterone and to compete in the men's category if they are on testosterone and if they wish to compete as men. However, following these matters can be very tricky. The new policy *still* recommended that athletes be permitted to use the locker rooms that aligned with their "gender identity," rather than their sex.

In response to this new policy, a male cyclist named Emily Bridges complained that the new policy was a "violent act" and accused the organization of "furthering a genocide." Literally all that happened is that British Cycling said that sex is real and that men will no longer be permitted compete in women's cycling simply because they claim to have a woman identity, and Bridges calls this "furthering a genocide." It is a grossly offensive description. As U.K. feminist Joan Smith said, "Using words like 'genocide' is profoundly offensive to the descendants of Jews who died in concentration camps during the Second World War, the Tutsi minority murdered in Rwanda in 1994, or the Muslim men bundled into mass graves at Srebrenica in eastern Bosnia a year later." But, as

Smith also says, "claiming victim status is a core tactic of the gender cult, which depends on hyperbole to disguise the fact that its aim is to allow a group of entitled men to do whatever they like, including destroying women's sport."

On April 20, 2023, the U.S. House of Representatives passed the Protection of Women and Girls in Sports Act, which is supported by the U.S. chapter of Women's Declaration International. It was sponsored by a Republican, and not a single House Democrat voted yes. They should have. It is a powerful piece of legislation that would bolster Title IX by explicitly protecting women and girls in athletics—a goal that liberals and progressives should have no trouble getting behind. If women are fully human, after all, then we have human rights, including the right to fair athletic competitions.

Black Women

The imposition of "gender identity," disproportionately and in many ways, uniquely, affects black women more than women in other racial categories. I am not a black woman and cannot speak for black women. However, several women who actively work with WDI USA have formed a Black Women's Caucus to address this problem and in early 2023, they put out a statement to explain their position. The statement has proven to be immensely popular. J.K. Rowling posted it on X, and as of writing, the statement has received over two million views on the WDI USA website from all over the world. It reads:

> We, the members of the Black Women's Caucus of Women's Declaration International USA, believe that it is crucial for Black Women to denounce gender identity ideology. This ideology promotes the idea that sex is nothing more than a social construct and that an individual can choose to *be* a man or a woman regardless of her or his sex. Gender ideologues employ the "forced-teaming" tactic against Black women in order to shame us

into being work mules for their campaign of male sexual privileges that they call "transgender rights." While these efforts are masked as progressive and inclusive concepts, gender identity ideology is actually intrusive and harmful to women, and uniquely so to Black women.

Gender identity ideology erases the unique experiences of women and reinforces the harmful stereotypes of femininity and masculinity. It is also incompatible with the fight for women's rights because it allows men access to spaces and activities designated for women such as bathrooms, sports teams, and housing. It has been reported that 1 in 4 Black girls are sexually assaulted before the age of 18 and 35% of Black women report experiencing physical sexual violence. Policies that allow men unfettered access to female-designated facilities put Black women and girls, a demographic disproportionately impacted by male violence, at an even higher risk.

Black women are 2.5 times more likely to be murdered by men than White women and this is why the fight against gender ideology is pertinent for Black women; we are the demographic most in need of protection from male violence. There have already been deadly consequences where an employer ignored a Black woman's whistleblowing regarding a male who demanded to be recognized as a woman. Monica Archer, a caseworker in a women's shelter, warned her employers about a client, Harvey Marcelin living as Marceline Harvey, who'd made threats against her and other shelter employees. Archer was fired for speaking out. Marcelin had already served 50 years for murdering and dismembering two women and after Archer's whistleblowing was ignored, Marcelin was found to have murdered and dismembered a 68-year-old "gal-pal" he had met while living in the women's shelter.

Marcelin has since been reimprisoned, but locking away criminally-violent men who claim to be women doesn't end the horror for all women. As of 2021, California has imprisoned men who claim to be women in women's prisons. Since then, there have been women who have come forward claiming to have been harassed and sexually assaulted by some of these men. Studies have shown that even when men claim to be women, they display a typically male pattern of criminality with respect to violent crimes. Additionally, 49.7% have been convicted of sex crimes. Therefore, incarcerated women are forced to be housed with male criminals of whom half have a history of sexual violence. Since Black women are seven times more likely than White women—and more than twice as likely as Hispanic women—to be incarcerated during their lives, these inhumane conditions of incarceration disproportionately and unfairly affect a maligned and especially vulnerable group of Black women. Being raped while incarcerated amounts to torture at the hands of the state.

Black girls are another vulnerable subset of the Black female population who have already borne the brunt of gender identity ideology. In 1993, Luis Morales, a man pretending to be a woman, along with his boyfriend and fellow member of the Almighty Latin King and Queen Nation gang, kidnapped a 13-year-old Black girl named Ebony Nicole Williams. Ebony was brutally and repeatedly raped and tortured by Morales, who was motivated by sexism and racism. Morales's boyfriend, Carlos Franco, then mercilessly stomped on Ebony's neck until it was broken before both men packed her petite body into a box, dumped the box near an expressway, and set the box on fire. The violence Morales and Franco inflicted upon Ebony was so extensive that she could only be identified through dental records. In 1996, Morales was sentenced to 25 years in prison for Ebony's murder. He suggested that he had avoided the rape conviction due to his "gender identity."

Unlike Ebony, Morales has been able to grow older and pursue happiness. While detained, Morales became a media sensation and noted advocate for the "rights" of incarcerated men claiming to be women and, after a lawsuit in 2003, was granted wrong-sex hormones paid for by the state of New York. Since being paroled in 2018, Morales has appeared as a member of the Sylvia Rivera Law Project's advisory committee. To honor Ebony's memory and to protect other Black girls, we stand unapologetically against gender ideology.

The impact of gender ideology is not only being felt in the area of male violence against women. It is also a socio-economic issue. Men overall receive a disproportionate amount of sports scholarship funding compared to women, and Black women and girls make up only 9% of student athletes. Making men who pretend to be women eligible for sports scholarships designated for women and girls further disenfranchises Black women and girls from opportunities to fund their education.

Also, Black women are especially likely to be homeless due to inability to find affordable housing. Classifying men as women further aggravates the disparity. When we include men in female-designated housing programs, we do so at the expense of Black women.

We urge all Black women to denounce gender identity ideology and instead advocate for policies that protect the rights of Black women and girls. This fight is especially crucial for Black women, as we are the demographic most in need of protection from male violence but with the least access to that protection. We must stand up against any movement or idea that seeks to erase our experiences or undermine our fight for equal justice, safety, and dignity.

Black women have spent decades undoing the trauma of colorism, hair texturism, and featurism. We can't then turn around and embrace a movement that encourages self-hate and perpetuates the same standards of femininity that were often used against Black women and girls. We can't teach our daughters the lie that we can be born in the wrong body and expect them to feel comfortable with their skin color, hair texture, or other bodily features. It is against our best interest as Black women to support gender ideology and we urge other Black women to support women's rights, instead.

—Women's Declaration International USA – Black Women's Caucus Lorraine Nowlin, Coordinator

I asked Dr. Suzanne Forbes-Vierling, a black woman and former Democrat, what she thinks about all of this and this is what she told me:

I used to be a faithful Democrat. Like many Black women across the nation, I felt safe inside this party and never questioned the sincerity of the candidates and leftist media. I started taking note of the betrayal when I saw how the privatization of foster care turned into a lucrative business, essentially turning the children in custody into a commodity. The Democrats have been successful in communicating to Black women under the bigotry of low expectations—that harmful, violent legislation is "empowering," "inclusive" and "social justice" in an effort to secure the faithful Black vote that typically rewards the Democrats with the White House.

There is a tried-and-true technique that has been successful with child welfare policies, for example. Black people are tossed between the liberals and the conservatives. Liberals push an agenda of interest and use something from Black culture to put in front of the agenda like a shield or Trojan Horse. Then they toss something "racialized" in front of the agenda over the net to conservatives. Then they quietly step back. For example, putting it out to the world that a Black woman was going to be selected for Vice President and Supreme Court Justice. The next step is for them to wait for conservatives to respond, sometimes directly attacking said issue and unfortunately sometimes directly attacking Black folk—such as the belief that Black culture is not competent in response to liberal chess moves. Next, Black folk—bonded and faithful to the Democrats—miss the first strike from the Democrats and respond to the often vitriolic reaction from the Republicans. Liberals then console Black folk by pointing a finger at conservatives, "Look at those mean racists! How could they do that to you?!" while presenting themselves as saviors of Black people.

Black folk respond in kind with rewarding Democrats with the vote. Rinse and Repeat.

Most recently, we watched this tennis game where Black women were tossed between Democrats and Republicans with the Democrats on the offense—serving first. This tennis game was used with Kamala Harris and Ketanji Brown Jackson with Biden announcements of "I'm going to select a Black Woman" knowing how the Republicans would respond and knowing that Black folk would have an emotional response and strike back towards the Republicans in order to defend what would undoubtedly be considered a response to "racism" against these two women. The Democrats come in to console Black folk and shame the Republicans and present themselves as saviors, securing these two women and the faithfulness of the Black vote, in particular, the Black woman's vote.

Today, the Democrats have moved into unrecognizable territory where with no hesitation have legally placed American women in harm's way. The Democrats essentially legalized sexual assault and rape in American prisons when they decided to place male bodied individuals who declare themselves women inside women's prisons. This was my "straw that broke the camel's back" moment. How could they do this knowing the legacy of chattel slavery?

While the women who are suffering in American women's prisons are all nationalities, and yes, my heart and soul in this fight is for ALL women (yes, I am an "All Lives Matter" kinda woman!) I take note of seeing Black women's faces prominently featured in the lawsuits in

> response to these violent Democrat policies that have resulted in children born inside prisons and destined for a life in orphan status. The irony being that Democrats—as we all know—go to great lengths to hold on to and expect the near exclusive vote from Black women. The Black vote is like cashing a check for $billions once tabulated on election day—delivering absolute power for at least four years with literally no tangible promises made or kept to Black women.

White women who fight back against "gender identity" are often told that we are racist. The assertion is based on the idea that demanding single-sex bathrooms is akin to the white supremacist insistence on racially segregated bathrooms. This is absurd. As I argued in *The Abolition of Sex*, women and men are simply different in ways that women of different racial, ethnic, national, or religious backgrounds are not different. More to the point, women and men are different in ways that matter *for the purpose of using a pubic bathroom* that women of different racial, ethnic, national, or religious backgrounds are not different. Even with our diversity and complexity, all women are women and only women are women. Plenty of black women oppose the imposition of "gender identity" in their lives and are speaking out to say so. I'm proud to stand with them.

Lesbians

On December 29, 2022, Lauren Levey, a member of the WDI USA board of directors, sent the message below to U.S. Senate Majority Leader (also her senator) Charles Schumer. She sent it to both Senator Schumer's public account and one of his top staffers, and also submitted it via his Senate website.

Dear Senator Schumer,

I am a resident of Greene County, New York. I've been a Democrat all my life because I hold the values of the political left, including full equality of opportunity for women and minorities to participate in all aspects of U.S. political life, economic life, education, sports, and culture; and universal access to health care, adequate housing, adequate nutrition, and other social services. Until now. Now there is an irreconcilable conflict between these values that support liberty and justice and democracy and responsive government, and the top-down, authoritarian, corporate-funded, global campaign to roll back women's rights and lesbian's rights by erasing the category of sex in law, thereby preventing women and lesbians from organizing for our rights as a sex class. The rallying cry of diversity and inclusion silences and excludes women and especially lesbians, while including any man who wishes to be included in those sex-based categories.

As a woman, a lesbian, and a Jew, the values of the left have personal application for me, as well as being in line with my views on social justice. Despite the fact that antisemitic attacks appear to be at the highest incidence rate in my lifetime, I am currently experiencing the greatest infringement on my rights as a woman (the sex), and especially as a lesbian. This infringement is directly due to the lie called "gender identity", which has been inserted into law and policy at every level almost entirely without debate. This insertion has been accomplished in the US by the Democratic Party; and it has been accomplished sometimes by stealth and sometimes simply by edict, without public discussion of the impact of "gender identity" on women, homosexuals, children, and men and women who simply do not conform to sex-stereotypical behaviors. The public overwhelmingly doesn't buy it; every American, whether or not he or she claims otherwise, knows that a woman is an adult human female. That the Democratic Party denies this is having grave consequences, some of which will be felt by the Party itself. But my purpose in writing to you today is to discuss how "gender identity" affects lesbians in particular.

Lesbians are females, we are exclusively attracted to other females, and we are frequently not seen as feminine in presentation or behaviors. However we behave or present, lesbians are not ever male. By definition, lesbians are never attracted to a feminine "gender"; we are attracted only to females who may or may not be feminine. Lesbians are not "LGBT" people. We are not even "LGB" people. We are simply lesbians. Force-teaming us, by law, with the TQ+—men who lie about their sex, men who get off on wearing high heels and wigs, men who pursue a lesbian fetish, men who enjoy drag shows and other porn, men who are attracted to children—has been devastating to lesbians. Here's how:

- Lesbians are once again forced by law to be re-closeted as outlaws, to meet in secret to evade the presence of male predators who the law says must be included in all of our public spaces.
- Lesbian university students are being forced to share dormitory rooms with men.
- Incarcerated lesbians are forced to share living space with violent male predators.

- Lesbian bars, which existed even in the 1950s when being lesbian was a crime, no longer exist. They are universally overrun with men who claim to be lesbians, who come into those bars to harass lesbians, and who can no longer be expelled.
- Lesbian online dating sites are filled with men who claim to be lesbians. Lesbians are being thrown off such sites when we object or identify them as men.
- Lesbians are harassed openly and with impunity in the streets as trans-exclusionary "terfs", right-wing bigots, and Nazis who deserve to be tortured and killed for rejecting the notion that men can be women; as people who are really men but won't admit it; and as "ugly" when we fail to comply with men's "beauty" standards.
- Lesbians, along with other women who reject "gender identity", are physically attacked when we try to speak out about our rights in public places; and in recent months police have failed to protect our political rallies.
- Lesbian girls and other nonconforming girls are being told they are probably boys, and are having their bodies mutilated with irreversible hormones and surgeries that will not only sterilize them and harm their hearts and bones, but will also likely preclude sexual gratification, forever. "Gender identity" indoctrination of kids is carried out in public schools, often deliberately without parents' knowledge. State agencies are undermining the parent-child relationship in order to promote gender identity ideology. This is how cults behave.

> Lesbians are being subjected to a global campaign of erasure in public law and policy that results in physical harassment and attacks throughout public life that goes largely unprevented and unpunished. Government representatives, including legislators, judges, and police, stand by, seemingly in approval of the acts of hate perpetrated against us. The current position of lesbians reminds me of the position of Jews in Germany in the years leading to the Holocaust, with gangs of violent "trans youth"—masked, hooded, violent, and dressed in black—attacking lesbians with escalating violence and with impunity.
>
> This campaign is driven in the US by the Democratic Party. There is no legitimate, definable category based on "gender identity." In contrast, the categories of sex and sexual orientation (based on sex) are easily definable based on material evidence.
>
> Lesbians have had it. Increasing numbers of other women have had it. Numerous mutilated children and adults have rejected gender identity ideology and are preparing their lawsuits. Many gay men have had it. We have warned you. I have personally warned you, Senator Schumer. The Democratic Party is poised to fall on the sword of "gender identity." This is on you.
>
> Sincerely,
> Lauren Levey

Similar to the Black Women's Caucus, WDI USA has a Lesbian Caucus. They work hard to ensure that lesbians are recognized as full human beings throughout law and society.

I am neither a lesbian nor a gay man. However, having spoken with many lesbians and gay men, all of whom hail from the political left, about "gender identity," I can say with confidence that many of them are quite unhappy about it. And why shouldn't they be? The fight for the right of same-sex attracted people to have relationships of their choosing was hard-fought, and still is being hard-fought in many corners of the world.

In what might be the height of insult, the Westmount Collegiate Institute, a high school in Ontario, teaches its students that "a lesbian is a non-man who is attracted to another non-man." On June 5, 2023, it announced that "Today, we focus on lesbian people and what they stand for! Like many others in the queer community, lesbians suffer from a lot of discrimination. Today we are celebrating them and their stories!" Johns Hopkins University did the same thing that same year when it posted a set of definitions on its website, including the following definition of lesbian: "A non-man attracted to non-men. While past definitions refer to 'lesbian' as a woman who is emotionally, romantically, and/or sexually attracted to other women, this updated definition includes non-binary people who may also identify with the label" (they later took it down, mostly in response to pushback from feminists, including lesbian radical feminists all over the world). Its definition of "gay man," in contrast, is a "man who is emotionally, romantically, sexually, affectionately, or relationally attracted to other men." Many lesbians were left asking, "Why are we non-men but gay men get to be acknowledged as men?"

This is precisely the problem with acronyms like "LGBT," "LGBTQ," "LGBTQ+" or any other letters or symbols someone might place there and with the word "queer." These acronyms are a lie. They exclude lesbians and gay men—homosexual people whose sexual orientation is based on sex, not on the nonsense called "gender identity." The letters T and Q (and whatever the + symbol is intended to signify) stand for people who want legal protection for lying about who they are. In recent years, numerous groups have sprouted up, calling attention to this very fact. Such groups include the LGB Alliance, of which there is an American chapter, Get the L Out, Lesbians United, The Lesbian Project, and the

Gay Men's Network. All these groups are focused either on the exclusive interests of lesbians or gay men, or collectively on the interests of both. All of them reject the lie of "gender identity." All of them are grounded in the political left and all of them are sick of what the leftist parties in their countries, including the Democrats in the U.S., are doing at the altar of "gender identity."

The Democrats in power need to stop lying. If they support lesbians and gay men, they need to say so explicitly and knock it off with "TQ+" nonsense.

CHAPTER 3

THE SAVAGERY OF "GENDER-AFFIRMING CARE"

Our entire society is harming minors and young adults, sometimes to the point of death, at the altar of "gender identity." This started under President Obama, continued apace with ample funding under Trump, and continues to this day under President Biden. By "harming," I mean sterilizing, amputating, and sometimes killing. We are doing this to young people who are confused about the material reality of their own sexed bodies. The phrase "puberty blockers" refers to drugs that stunt puberty. They are sometimes prescribed for minors who have "precocious puberty"—they have started puberty earlier than their peers. When discussed as a form of "gender-affirming care," they refer to drugs that are given to kids who think they "are trans." This is happening despite there being no evidence that they help confused kids and plenty of evidence that kids who take them end up psychologically and physically worse off than they otherwise would have been.

People will say that there are no surgeries performed on minors, but it isn't true. A study released in the *Journal of the American Medical Association* in August 2023 found that the overall number of "gender-affirming surgeries" had tripled in the past three years, with more than 1,200 surgeries performed on patients eighteen or younger. Sometimes, minors' parents consent because they are bullied and told by medical and mental health providers (who they should be able to trust) that their children will commit suicide if they don't. Other times, the parents resist and end up losing custody of their children. All under color of law; all brought about by Democrats in positions of authority. What's more, the mean age of young people struggling with matters of sex and gender is rapidly decreasing. A lot of people think this will eventually become the biggest medical scandal in American history. Now would be a good time for liberal and progressive women to start speaking out about it.

The U.S. Government's Medical Experiment on Children

On January 19, 2023, the *New England Journal of Medicine* published a study, "Psychosocial Functioning in Transgender Youth after 2 Years of Hormones," funded by the National Institutes of Health (NIH) and conducted by eight "gender medicine" doctors. If you have paid much attention to the movement to abolish sex, you will have heard about "puberty blockers." This phrase refers to hormones that are designed to suppress puberty. They have been approved by the FDA to suppress puberty in children who begin puberty at earlier than normal ages, in order to prevent the mental and emotional harm of having to go through puberty earlier than one's peers. These children are taken off the hormones once they reach an age where puberty onset is more common among their peers. The drugs have also been approved to treat some cancers. They have NOT been approved for teenagers who think they are the opposite sex. Yet, they are routinely prescribed for this purpose anyway.

This NIH study goes beyond puberty blockers (although a subset of the study's participants had previously been on puberty blockers to suppress their correct sex puberty). This is, instead, a study about the impacts of wrong-sex hormones on minors. It looked at the impacts of testosterone on young women and estrogen on young men (some as young as twelve). The study's main conclusion is that "gender-affirming hormones improved appearance congruence and psychosocial functioning." However, *two young people committed suicide during the course of the study and, as far as I can tell, no effort was made to shut down the study or even ask why these suicides happened.*

No one changes sex. Ever. The SRY gene is the gene on the Y chromosome that makes males male. According to Dr. Peter Koopman, who co-discovered the gene in 1990, it "leads to the development of male characteristics in mice, humans, and most other mammals" and "acts to trigger a cascade of gene activity that results in the formation of testes, instead of ovaries, in the embryo. Testes then stimulate the formation of other male characteristics." There is no amount of externally administered testosterone that can make girls male and no amount of externally administered estrogen that can make boys female. At best, these drugs can make young people appear to resemble the opposite sex. At worst, they can cause sterility, disease, and death. Yet the U.S. government is conducting these experiments on young people based on the lie that changing sex is actually possible.

The NIH has been conducting medical experiments on children since at least 2015. As recently reported in *The Star News Network* (and almost nowhere else), in 2019, Dr. Michael Laidlaw (an endocrinologist in California) and Dr. William Malone (the medical director at St. Luke's Endocrinology and Diabetes Clinic in Twin Falls, Idaho) sent a letter to Dr. Jerry Menikoff, who is currently the Director of the Office for Human Research Protections at the Department of Health and Human Services (the NIH is an agency within HHS). From 2007 to 2008, he served as the Director of the Office of Human Subjects Research at the NIH itself. The letter warned that "Given the numerous deleterious side effects of these medications that we will describe, and the lack of FDA approval for cross-sex hormones even in adult populations, the likelihood of serious harms accruing in these young patients is very great." It concluded, "Because this study poses irreversible medical harms (including infertility) to children, we request an immediate moratorium and investigation. Thank you for your prompt attention to this important and urgent matter." The response they received was brief, bureaucratic, and not meaningfully responsive to the concerns raised. Dr. Laidlaw told the *Star News Network*: "They blew us off. Now two kids have died by suicide and the rest have been harmed in other ways by high dose opposite sex hormones, likely permanently. When will this be investigated by authorities?" In short, the NIH was warned about the dangers of this study and proceeded with it anyway, having ignored two prominent endocrinologists who raised the alarm. And now two young people are dead.

The study participants were 315 "transgender and non-binary" young people aged twelve to twenty years old who were "recruited from gender clinics at the Ann and Robert H. Lurie Children's Hospital of Chicago, UCSF Benioff Children's Hospitals, Boston Children's Hospital, and Children's Hospital Los Angeles." The participants were examined at six, sixteen, eighteen, and twenty-four months after initiation of "gender-affirming hormones" (GAH). The study administered various tests, whose purpose was to measure "individual trajectories of appearance congruence [how much a person's physical appearance matches his or her "gender identity"], depression, anxiety, positive affect, and life satisfaction over a period of 2 years." The study also examined "how initial levels of and rates of change in appearance congruence correlated with those of each psychosocial outcome."

All study participants were on GAH—opposite sex hormones that are delivered exogenously (i.e., from outside the body). All women have some naturally-occurring levels of testosterone and all men have some naturally-occurring levels of estrogen. This isn't that. This is the external administration of opposite-sex hormones. The study's main conclusion is that "GAH improved appearance congruence and psychosocial functioning." The authors came to this conclusion despite the fact that two of its participants had committed suicide and eleven contemplated it during the course of the study. The study simply refers to these suicides as "adverse effects." These NIH-funded doctors who published the study are reducing dead teenagers to "adverse effects" in their zeal to push their foregone conclusion that "gender-affirming care" is a good thing.

Conducting medical experiments on minors is ghoulish and disgusting and never should have happened, but this more recent development makes things even worse. The study casually observes: "Two participants died by suicide during the study (one after 6 months of follow-up and the other after 12 months of follow-up), and 6 participants withdrew from the study. For these eight participants, data that had been collected before death or study withdrawal were included in the analyses." If I am reading this accurately (and I have been told by clinicians that I am), this is saying that *the study authors continued with the study not only knowing that it was likely to harm young people but also after two young people actually killed themselves during the course of it.*

These facts, none of which are in dispute, are being documented in the *New England Journal of Medicine*—a prestigious journal that very few people read because it contains medical jargon that few of us understand. Most people who do read it are likely to assume, because it is an authoritative source that uses complex medical language, that it is legitimate. Meanwhile, doctors continue to conduct these scandalous medical experiments on minors with impunity while claiming respectability. They are hiding behind their credentials and the high degree of social trust that doctors carry. They get away with creating confusion while harming young people by confusing everyone into thinking that there is some legitimate reason for the ghastly things they are doing. *And the U.S. government is funding it.*

In March 2023, the *American Journal of Public Health* published an article authored by four doctors affiliated with various agencies within the Department of Defense titled, "Caring for Military-Affiliated Transgender and Gender-Diverse Youths: A Call for Protections." It advocated that children as young as seven have "an inherent ability and right to consent" to puberty blockers and wrong-sex hormones. The authors stated further: "Some well-intentioned military-affiliated clinicians may not be aware that a 'watchful waiting' approach has a different risk profile than a gender-affirmative approach (which allows for gender identity exploration), and that 'conversion therapy' is unethical, harmful, and generally illegal. Patients may face 'gatekeeping' and major delays in care, including protracted and pathologizing psychiatric evaluations that question patient motives." This is arguably the height of insanity. These are military-affiliated doctors arguing that if a seven-year-old child thinks that he or she might be the opposite sex, the appropriate clinical approach is to believe them and go straight to "gender affirmation." It is arguing that helping a child embrace his or her actual sex is "unethical" and "generally illegal."

It's worth taking some time to note how the phrase "conversion therapy" is being used here. That phrase used to mean the use of horrific medical and psychological practices on lesbians and gay men. It used to be thought that same-sex attraction was immoral (and it was often criminalized), so the only way to deal with it was to resort to harmful medical interventions. Today, the phrase "conversion therapy" is used to mean helping human beings embrace the material reality of their sex. It is dangerously manipulative and should be an outright scandal. According to many lesbians and gay men, "gender-affirming care" is *itself* gay conversion therapy. Many view "gender-affirming care" as "transing the gay away."

Dr. David Bell is a former staff governor at the Tavistock and Portman NHS Foundation Trust on its Gender Identity Development Service in the U.K. Tavistock is a clinic that has historically provided so-called "gender-affirming care" to confused young people in the U.K. In July 2022, it was announced that it would close in 2023, after a report by Dr. Hilary Cass said that its model of care was "leaving young people at considerable risk of poor mental health and distress." On January 27, 2023, Dr. Bell published a letter in *The Guardian*, stating "the U.K. should, like Finland, Sweden and France, follow a more cautious path; we should end medication and medical transition for children and adolescents now." The shuttering of the Tavistock was later postponed. Meanwhile, stateside, the poisoning of vulnerable children continues apace, courtesy of the U.S. government.

All these young people (the ones who have died, the ones who have been sterilized, and the ones who have otherwise been permanently harmed) and their parents deserve so much more from a government and a medical profession they should be able to trust. According to recent reports, the NIH study has been fully funded through 2026. What is happening is unconscionable. It is high time that the general public sees what they are doing and that the media holds these actors to account.

"Gender-Affirming Care"

I am old enough to remember the days when people would talk about having a "sex change operation" or, more concisely, "a sex change." Someone might say, "A guy in my town had a sex change." According to Merriam-Webster, the first known use of the phrase "sex change" was in 1949. Today, Merriam-Webster takes great pains to note that the phrase is "usually considered to be offensive because it can be understood to imply that transgender people must undergo a physical change before they can be the gender that they already know themselves to be." I would argue that the phrase "sex change" is not offensive but inaccurate, because there is no such thing as changing sex. Today, as discussed in the NIH study above, the more common term in the medical field is "gender affirming" and it can be used in conjunction with "hormones" and/or "surgery" (i.e., "gender affirming hormones" or "gender affirming surgery"). More generally, it is referred to as "gender-affirming care." These phrases are all euphemisms for practices that permanently harm otherwise physically healthy people.

From a feminist perspective, the entire concept of "affirming gender" is sexist. Feminists seek to abolish gender, by which we mean sex stereotypes. We don't want women and girls (or men and boys) to have to comply with the expectations that society imposes on us on the basis of our sex. From a humanitarian perspective, permanently altering a person's body medically to "affirm" the concept that a person can have a "gender identity" in his or her head is just ghoulish. I discussed "gender-affirming hormones" (i.e., puberty blockers and wrong-sex hormones) above. I'll spend a few minutes explaining "gender-affirming surgery" (GAS) here.

By far, the most common type of GAS performed on "transgender" people is colloquially referred to as "top surgery," also known as a double mastectomy. Although there are some differences between surgeries based on certain factors (e.g., how much skin, breast, and fat tissue to remove, and whether to remove nipples), in essence what we are talking about here is total breast removal. Often, this surgery follows a period of "binding," whereby a young woman will wear a "chest binder." Chest-binding is not unlike foot-binding: both are practices designed to permanently alter a young woman's body. It is very difficult to find data on how many women/girls who claim to be men/boys get this surgery. According to a 2019 study reported in the National Library of Medicine of the NIH called "Demographic and Temporal Trends in Transgender Identities and Gender Confirming Surgery," somewhere between 8 and 25 percent of women and girls who claim to "be transgender" have this surgery.

Genital surgeries available to men ("transgender women") generally include: vaginoplasty, penectomy, and orchiectomy. In case you don't know what those things are, a vaginoplasty, according to the magazine *Very Well Health*, is a surgery in which "the skin from outside of the penis is removed and inverted to create the lining of the vagina. The head of the penis is also reshaped to create a clitoris. Finally, scrotal skin is used to create the labia majora and minora." If all the hair is not removed from the scrotum, then sometimes the hair remains inside. Sometimes parts of the colon are used instead, resulting in fecal matter existing inside, which often smells like exactly what you would expect it to smell like. Men who undergo this procedure have to dilate their fake vaginas, daily at first and then eventually several times a week, for the rest of their lives.

According to the Cleveland Clinic, "A penectomy refers to the surgical removal of the penis. You can have a partial penectomy or a total penectomy. The surgery is the most common way to treat cancer of the penis. You can also have a penectomy as a gender affirmation surgery. There are two main reasons for having a penectomy: treating cancer and gender affirmation." Also according to the Cleveland Clinic, "An orchiectomy is a surgical procedure to remove one or both testicles. Providers use this procedure to treat and prevent testicular cancer as well as treat male breast cancer and prostate cancer. Transgender women may choose to have an orchiectomy when transitioning from male to female." The framing of the Cleveland Clinic's descriptions of penectomy and orchiectomy are cavalier and, I assume, probably insulting to men who have had to have these procedures performed to treat cancer. From my reading of those descriptions, the Cleveland Clinic appears to be framing the treatment of cancer—a life-threatening illness—and "gender affirmation" as roughly equivalent. I would think that men who have survived penile or testicular cancer due to these treatments might not appreciate that.

The most common genital surgery performed on women who claim to be men is called "phalloplasty" and it is absolutely gruesome. According to Johns Hopkins Hospital, it is "surgery for masculinizing gender affirmation" and "a multistaged process that may include a variety of procedures, including: creating the penis, lengthening the urethra so you are able to stand to urinate, creating the tip (glans) of the penis, creating the scrotum, removing the vagina, uterus, and ovaries, placing erectile and testicular implants, and skin grafting from the donor tissue site." By "skin grafting from the donor tissue site," it means: "using skin flaps, which are areas of skin moved from one area of the body to another." I highly recommend that readers do a Google image search of what this looks like in practice. It is bloody, harmful, and permanent. I have watched YouTube videos of women who have had this done to them and now regret it, and they are devastating.

In August 2022, *The Post Millennial* reported on the case of a TikTok user who goes by "Cryspy" in an article called "Phalloplasty Ruined my Life: Biological Female Reveals Horrifying Complications of 'Gender Affirming' Surgery." Cryspy stated: "I started phalloplasty back in March 2020, and we are in March 2022 and we're not even half-way through the process." By that time, she had undergone twelve surgeries in two years due to complications. She continued: "I have a fistula, which is an abnormal connection between my urethra and my rectum. At age 27, I am pooping in a bag." According to *The Post Millennial*, citing the NIH itself, fistulas are "the most common complication of phalloplasty that occur in around 25 percent of patients. A fistula is an abnormal connection between an organ, vessel, or intestine and another organ, vessel or intestine, or the skin." It reported that "Cryspy describes having a recto-urethral fistula, an abnormal connection of the urethra to either the anus or rectum. This results in fecal matter, foul-smelling discharge, blood, gas, and urine emptying from the body through the urethra. Sometimes a fistula is accompanied by infection and inflammation of tissues, and urine leaking into this area makes this condition worse." As many as 51 percent of phalloplasty patients end up with urethral stricture (scarring). The Crane Center for Transgender Surgery reported in 2017 that over 94 percent of them will need a urethroplasty to ever urinate again. Fifty percent of urethroplasty surgeries fail and some women who have this surgery require lifelong catheters to urinate.

On February 9, 2023, a woman who worked for four years as a case manager at The Washington University Transgender Center at St. Louis Children's Hospital published an article in *The Free Press* called "I Thought I Was Saving Trans Kids. Now I'm Blowing the Whistle." Its subtitle was "There are more than 100 pediatric gender clinics across the U.S. I worked at one. What's happening to children is morally and medically appalling." Her name is Jamie Reed. In her article, she stated, "The center's working assumption was that the earlier you treat kids with gender dysphoria, the more anguish you can prevent later on. This premise was shared by the center's doctors and therapists. Given their expertise, I assumed that abundant evidence backed this consensus. During the four years that I worked at the clinic as a case manager—I was responsible for patient intake and oversight—around a thousand distressed young people came through our doors. The majority of them received hormone prescriptions that can have life-altering consequences—including sterility. I left the clinic in November of last year because I could no longer participate in what was happening there. By the time I departed, I was certain that the way the American medical system is treating these patients is the opposite of the promise we make to 'do no harm.' Instead, we are permanently harming the vulnerable patients in our care."

The same day that she came out with these accusations, the Missouri Attorney General's office announced that it had launched a formal investigation two weeks previously. The *New York Post* published an editorial calling on everyone to "End the horrors of the pediatric gender-industrial complex, now." A few days later, it came out that a school had reached out to the clinic in 2021 seeking advice about how to handle what appeared to be a contagion of fifth-grade girls "coming out as transgender" and the advice the clinic gave was to "affirm" the students' "gender identity." Throughout the exchange, at no point did the clinic suggest consulting with the students' parents. Finally, in September 2023, the clinic announced that it would no longer provide puberty blockers or wrong-sex hormones to confused young people.

Meanwhile, a similar situation was brewing in Texas. In January 2023, Texas Children's Hospital and Baylor College of Medicine gave a presentation to a group of medical professionals titled "Medical and Psychological Care of Gender-Diverse Youth." This presentation encouraged doctors to administer puberty blockers and cross-sex hormones during adolescence. It encouraged "gender affirming surgeries" for adolescents on a case-by-case basis. The Texas Attorney General then launched an investigation. By May of that year, an employee of Texas Children's Hospital had come forward to talk with *The City Journal* anonymously about the situation in general and about one doctor—Dr. Richard Roberts—in particular. The whistleblower stated: "If there's a patient who comes in who wants an increase in testosterone, for example, he'll totally do it. He'll up the dose. I have personally seen letters and referrals that he has made for double mastectomies.... It's just really sad. [Kids] are looking for affirmation. They're seeking the validation and approval of the adults that are in their lives." The whistleblower reported that parents go along because they are "scared of being reported to Child Protective Services. They're scared that if they don't affirm their child, that their kid is going to commit suicide and do self-harm—which is a lie. And they're intimidated by these doctors that are on the side of the kid and have a lot of power. They could report [the parents] and then their child could be taken away from them."

The whistleblower then stated: "I'm absolutely sick to my stomach. Absolutely just devastated.... And I'm so 100 percent against this whole ideology and this movement of children just feeling like they were born in the wrong body and then being 'affirmed' by adults who want to take advantage of them and make a buck. Transgender medicine is hugely lucrative. It's like $70,000 to $80,000 dollars per kid if they go through with the whole thing—all the pharmacology drugs, all these companies that are making millions of dollars."

To date, at least nineteen states have put in place some restrictions on the ability of doctors to harm minors with so-called "gender-affirming care." Most have enacted legislative bans; others have restricted access via other methods, including medical board rules and administrative actions through child welfare agencies. Meanwhile, the Democratic Party elite has stayed mostly mum, although Admiral Rachel (Richard) Levine, Assistant Secretary for Health at the U.S. Department of Health and Human Services, has announced that "gender-affirming care for minors has the 'highest support' of the Biden administration."

Two months after Jamie Reed blew the whistle in Missouri, another article appeared in *The Free Press* titled "I Felt Bullied: Mother of Child Treated at Transgender Center Speaks Out." The article stated: "She was told medical intervention would help relieve her 14-year-old's psychological distress. That's not what happened." In that article, a mother named Caroline (a pseudonym) describes her interactions with the center after she took her son there to address his confusion about his sex. Caroline had initially resisted the administration of puberty blockers for her son, but she says that she ultimately felt bullied by the center into agreeing. Clinicians at the center advised Caroline that if she was concerned about her son's future fertility, he could be referred for sperm banking before starting puberty blockers. According to the article, "Caroline was becoming more disturbed by how the therapist seemed to gloss over the enormous implications of the decision in front of them. 'She said that if future fertility was a concern, we could look into banking his sperm before the blocker went in.' She recalls wondering how she found herself in a conversation about banking the sperm of her 14-year-old. 'It was weird, and I didn't like where this was going. It was just so overwhelming.'" They told her that if she didn't agree to puberty blockers, her son was at risk of suicide.

After going on the blocker, Casey's (also a pseudonym) mental health declined precipitously. His grades dropped and he experienced depression and suicide ideation (though he assured his parents that he had no intention of going through with it). Caroline demanded that the blocker be removed but the center refused because of a joint custody agreement with Casey's father, who supported it. Casey was scheduled to have the blocker removed in the summer of 2023 and appears to have resigned himself to experiencing a normal male puberty, but no one really knows what long-term impacts there might be because there have been no longitudinal studies concerning the impacts of puberty blockers on otherwise physically healthy minors.

There is just no other way to say it: under the rubric of "gender-affirming care," our society is permanently destroying the otherwise healthy bodies of teenagers and young adults at the altar of "gender identity," with the support of the highest levels of the U.S. government in general and the Democratic Party elite in particular.

"Detransitioners"

There is a large (and growing) population of people who have "detransitioned." I use quotes there because the term is controversial. These are people who "transitioned," that is, took steps to make their bodies appear to resemble the opposite sex (often under tremendous pressure from mental and medical professionals as well as teachers and school administrators), regretted that decision, and then "detransitioned." The main reason those terms are controversial is that there is no such thing as "transition," in the sense of "changing sex" because no one changes sex. Still, colloquially, the word "detransitioners" refers to the category of people who have undergone some form of "gender-affirming care" and then learned to accept the material reality of their sex.

Reading the stories of "detransitioners" is hard because what is happening to these young people today is horrific. They are being told that if they have a "gender identity" that is different from their actual sex, they must change their bodies to fit their "gender identity" instead of coming to terms with the material reality of sex. Many of these young people suffer from other mental health issues that go unaddressed. They are just beginning to explore their sexuality and discovering that they might be lesbian or gay. Many are somewhere on the autism spectrum and others suffer from depression and/or anxiety. None of these topics are ever addressed. Instead, the psychological and medical establishments simply rush to "affirm gender." They often tell the parents of minors that if they do not consent to "gender-affirming care" for their children, their children will commit suicide and ask, "Would you rather have a live son or a dead daughter?" I think it is important that their stories get out and that we listen to what they have to say if we are going to be able to fully appreciate just how horrific this industry is. Because I cannot speak on their behalf, I will do my best to tell their stories in their own words.

In December 2020, a young woman in the U.K. named Keira Bell made headlines when she won her case against the Tavistock clinic in the U.K. Bell had been given puberty blockers and, later, testosterone, by the clinic and her body underwent some very serious (and totally predictable) changes. She states, "By the time I got to the Tavistock, I was adamant that I needed to transition. It was the kind of brash assertion that's typical of teenagers. What was really going on was that I was a girl insecure in my body who had experienced parental abandonment, felt alienated from my peers, suffered from anxiety and depression, and struggled with my sexual orientation. After a series of superficial conversations with social workers, I was put on puberty blockers at age 16. A year later, I was receiving testosterone shots. When 20, I had a double mastectomy. By then, I appeared to have a more masculine build, as well as a man's voice, a man's beard, and a man's name: Quincy, after Quincy Jones. The consequences of what happened to me have been profound: possible infertility, loss of my breasts and inability to breastfeed, atrophied genitals, a permanently changed voice, facial hair. When I was seen at the Tavistock clinic, I had so many issues that it was comforting to think I really had only one that needed solving: I was a male in a female body. But it was the job of the professionals to consider all my co-morbidities, not just to affirm my naïve hope that everything could be solved with hormones and surgery." Bell made history when she sued the clinic and won, although the ruling was later overturned on appeal.

In February 2023, Luka Hein testified before the Labor, Health, and Social Services committee of the Wyoming state legislature in support of a bill that would prohibit doctors and nurse practitioners from prescribing "transgender-related treatments" (i.e., "gender-affirming care") to minors. This is a word-for-word transcription of her testimony:

> My name is Luka Hein. I'm here today not only as someone who has lived experience and has gone through the gender transition system as a minor, but as someone who has been harmed by it and is a victim of these practices. I was a young teenager with a history of mental health issues, who had been groomed and preyed upon and exploited online. Yet the medical system did not address any of my underlying issues or why I had distress or why I felt the need to escape my body at such a young age. Instead, I was put down a path of permanent medicalization. One that I am trying to reverse, but I am unable to, due to these practices being nonreversible.
>
> At 16, the very first medical intervention I ever had was a double mastectomy in the name of gender affirming care. I only had one consultation with the surgeon, and one with the gender clinic, before I was allowed to do this. I was not able to fully give consent at the time, due to both my age and my mental health issues. A few months later, I was then put on cross-sex hormones and started taking testosterone. At 21, I now live with lifelong complications from that, and I have no idea if they will go away. My joints constantly hurt. I have no idea if I will ever be able to carry a child someday, not to mention the fact that

my breasts are gone. There was nothing wrong with my body. I was just a teenager who was uncomfortable. And instead, I was pushed down a path that taught me that growing up was a disease that needed to be cured with surgery and medicine.

Children deserve the ability to grow up whole. They cannot consent to being a lifelong medical patient. I sure know I could not. At 16, I did not understand what the long-term impacts of this care would be, if you could call it care. But the doctors were eager to push me down this path. To this day, the underlying issues I face were never treated by these professionals. They were pushed to the side, all in the name of gender-affirming care. My parents were baited with the idea that I would kill myself if they didn't go along with it, despite the fact that I had always maintained that I was never suicidal. They were told by the doctors, "Would you rather have a living son or a dead daughter?" These are not the words of a medical professional, but the words of an activist. As more and more people like me are stepping forward as victims of this care system, we need to realize that children cannot consent to this. They deserve to grow up whole, and they deserve to grow up knowing that their body is not something that needs to be altered. Adults are different. They can maybe understand, and they can do what they want. But children deserve to not only be protected but given the ability to grow in a way that will not make them a lifelong patient.

Thank you.

The bill in question was called "Chloe's Law," named for a young woman named Chloe Cole. Cole was eighteen years old when she started speaking out about her experiences with "gender-affirming care." She describes herself as a "former trans kid" who "detransitioned" after being on puberty blockers and having had a double mastectomy at fifteen. By the time she was sixteen, she realized something was wrong and stopped. By eighteen, she was traveling across the country, conducting interviews, and offering testimony about what had happened to her. Her aim was to raise the alarm about "gender-affirming care" on minors, which she refers to as "child abuse" and "medical experimentation."

On September 6, 2022, she testified in California in opposition to Senate Bill 107, which would prohibit healthcare providers and insurance companies from releasing medical information related to a child receiving "gender-affirming healthcare" in response to a legal action based on another state's law that bans "gender-affirming healthcare." In short, SB 107 was intended to turn California into a safe haven for confused kids and to protect doctors and therapists who promote "gender-affirming care" for minors. This is what she said:

> My name is Chloe Cole. I'm 18 and my story is not hyperbole. Starting around the age of 12, I began to believe that I was transgender. This belief was not organic. All the media I consumed as a kid showed me how stupid and vulnerable being a girl was. All the sexualized images of women gave me an unrealistic expectation of womanhood. I spent a lot of time online and quickly saw all the praise coming out as trans got on Instagram and other social media. I was a bit awkward in school and had some trouble making friends. Like many dysphoric children, I also suffer from a variety of mental health conditions, so I easily fell prey to the narrative that if I felt different and did not want to be a highly sexualized girl, that I must be a boy. I obsessed over becoming a boy. I believed that all

of my insecurities and anxiety would magically disappear once I transitioned.

The mental health professionals did not try to dissuade me of this delusional belief. I was fast-tracked into medical transition after I was diagnosed with dysphoria. In California, a child can pick their gender identity and a care provider questioning that would be considered conversion therapy. This wasn't a misdiagnosis, it was mistreatment. My parents were told that the options were transition or suicide. They complied because they were not offered any other treatment solution for my distress. My distraught parents wanted me alive, so they listened to my doctors. I was placed on puberty blockers, testosterone after expressing my gender dysphoria to my therapist and I was approved for a double mastectomy all by the age of 15. No one explored why I did not want to be girl. More and more kids are falling for the false promise of happiness if they transition. Gender clinics in the US are turning a blind eye to European countries, who are pumping the brakes on this experiment on youth.

Who here really believes that, as a 15-year-old, I should have had my healthy breasts removed or that it should've been an option? When the CDPH got less than 300 reports of people getting hospitalized as a result of vaping, San Francisco banned vape products that same year, so I know that you care about the health of children, yet you are allowing doctors all over the state to remove the healthy breasts of children. How many more children's bodies will be destroyed before you actually listen? What is the sweet spot? 100? 200? 1000? SB107 will open the flood gates for confused children like me to get the

> gender interventions that many so regret. I am the canary in the coal mine.

Notwithstanding this moving testimony, the California legislature voted to enact the bill and the Democratic governor signed it later that year. Cole is suing the medical professionals at Kaiser Permanente who performed these procedures on her. Cole would later go on to testify before Congress in August of 2023. She told members of Congress, "My breasts were taken away from me and the tissue was incinerated." "Before I was able to legally drive," she said, "they amputated my breasts." They were "perfectly healthy, but still they were cut off and burned, like trash." "I had a huge part of my future womanhood taken from me." She concluded her testimony, "Let me be your final warning." Every single Democrat in that room on that day heard what she had to say.

Many "detransitioners" were given life-altering hormones and surgeries as minors. As devastating as that is, it is equally important to remember that many "detransitioners" are young adults who have been similarly deluded into thinking they can change sex. Cat Cattinson is a singer with a YouTube channel and a "detransitioned" woman. She talks about how important it is to acknowledge that the situation is not better for young adults than it is for minors. "While banning gender care for under-18s is a step in the right direction, it will not have as dramatic of an effect as some may think, given that these dangerous substances are just a phone call away as soon as a child turns 18. Once that magic birthday occurs, nothing protects him from the gender industry. No mental or physical health history will be explored; no degree of illness will be enough to stop the administration of life-altering drugs and surgeries. Without the protection of parents that younger kids enjoy, those barely-18 'adults' with still-developing brains are possibly the most vulnerable group of all to nefarious influence."

Cattinson joined several other "detransitioners," as well as numerous therapists and medical professionals, to talk about their experiences in a film called *Affirmation Generation*, which aired in February 2023. The film was later renamed *No Way Back: The Reality of Gender-Affirming Care*, and was scheduled to premiere in select AMC Theaters in June 2023, but AMC backed out at the last minute. An organization called The Queer Trans Project had posted a campaign on social media to have the film canceled. It encouraged followers to reach out to AMC to complain and provided a sample letter for doing so. But *why* should a movie theater not feature a film that is designed to explore these sensitive topics? The film (which I have seen) tells the personal stories of individuals who have *themselves* gone through "transition." Why shouldn't The Queer Trans Project *want* people to hear these stories? The producers have stated publicly that The Queer Trans Project announced this campaign *without even having watched the film.* And in any event, if people associated with The Queer Trans Project didn't want to see the film, no one was going to make them go. Incidentally, The Queer Trans Project appears to provide "Build-A-Queer" kits (including breast binders) to anyone who wants them, as well as free flights for any "queer and/or trans" person who is seeking "gender-affirming care" and wants travel assistance to receive it. Its campaign worked, and AMC pulled the screening. The simple reason The Queer Trans Project does not want the public to hear these stories is because the stories contradict the mainstream liberal narrative that "trans" is natural and that "gender identity" is always something to be "affirmed."

Prisha Mosley has also started speaking out. Like so many others, she had a difficult childhood and suffered from numerous emotional and mental health struggles. She turned to the internet and found "trans." She says that at the onset of puberty at age twelve, she experienced "rapid onset gender dysphoria." She says, "I literally hated every aspect of who I was and what I was and what I looked like. I spent some time being a girly girl and being a tomboy and being a smart girl and being this [other] girl, but none of those different hats fit me. And so I was like, 'I guess I'm just not a girl.'" At fourteen, she was sexually assaulted by a twenty-year-old friend of a friend and at that point, she rejected womanhood entirely. Like the others, her parents were bullied and told that if they didn't agree, she would kill herself. She was given a prescription for testosterone after an hour-long appointment. She went on testosterone at fifteen and had a double mastectomy shortly after turning eighteen. She stopped taking the drugs a few years later and now understands that she is female. She says that she suffers from vocal cord pain and vaginal atrophy from testosterone. She knows that she will never breastfeed and doesn't know whether she is capable of conceiving.

Katie Lennon is a young woman who took wrong-sex hormones and had a double mastectomy at eighteen and a full hysterectomy at twenty-one. In April 2023, she testified in support of a parents' rights bill in New Hampshire. She said, her voice having obviously been harmed by testosterone: "I'm a detransitioner.... Like many children and teens today, I identified myself as transgender for years, and when I started to feel confused and ashamed about my developing body I asked everyone in my life to call me by a new name and use male pronouns to refer to me. So in other words, I went through a social transition from female to male. Everyone in my life immediately affirmed my new identity, either out of full support for it, or just to stay neutral and not cause any issues. But the constant affirmation, both active and passive, solidified me in my transgender identity. No one meant to lock me into an identity that would later leave me broken, ashamed, or more confused than before. They were really all just being nice. But the social transition eventually wasn't enough, and I soon felt I needed to take testosterone. And when that wasn't enough, I had a double mastectomy. And when that still wasn't enough, I had a total hysterectomy, including the removal of my uterus, cervix, fallopian tubes, and both ovaries. There is no point of contentment during a gender transition. We get fleeting moments of euphoria, but ultimately, one step leads straight into the next. I thought that in the end I could really become a man, but all I became was a mutilated and abused version of my old self."

Leigh Janet Marshall is an environmental scientist and a female "detransitioner." In April 2023, she spoke with radical feminist and birth worker Isabella Malbin on Malbin's YouTube channel *Whose Body Is It?* and stated: "I think transition is a soft form of suicide, which is why they use language like 'deadname.' And it's a soft suicide because you kill yourself. You kill the self that you were born into. And then once you transition, you die younger than you ever would have from the health complications—heart attack, stroke, blood clots, cancer. Or, if you don't live long enough to experience those side effects, it's likely because you have killed yourself. And you've killed yourself because of the chronic pain and the lack of erotic sensation. Going back to a very stark memory of mine that really pierced me to my core as a young person growing up in the Bay Area, I saw graffiti. It was a picture of a Glock, a stencil of a Glock. And the text next to it said 'the best thing you can do for the planet is kill yourself.' And I believed that. I believed that so much that I pursued my own sterilization. I was sterilized by 29. I wasn't, in my mind, courageous enough to do the job of killing myself, so instead I pursued self-harm. And I did so with an explicit intent to punish myself and to punish myself as a woman, as a woman with reproductive capacity."

A young woman known only as Layla Jane is suing her doctors for cutting off her breasts at age thirteen. Layla Jane suffered from severe mood swings, anxiety, and confusion about her sex. By age twelve, she was being given testosterone and puberty blockers. The next year, she had a double mastectomy. In 2023, she gave a statement before the California legislature, where she stated, "I was a mentally ill child and I was able to consent to removing my breasts permanently. And I also heard more people telling me I would regret this tattoo [points to tattoo on shoulder] than I would regret getting my breasts permanently removed at such a young age. So that is why I felt it necessary to speak. Thank you for hearing me out."

Jesse Pohlner is not a "detransitioner." She is a woman who claims to be a man. In 2021, she went to the Royal Women's Hospital in Melbourne to receive a hysterectomy as part of her "gender transition." She was confirmed for surgery ten days before the operation occurred. Because she claims to be a man, no pregnancy test was performed, even though hysterectomy is a procedure that can only be performed on people who have a uterus; that is, women, who might be pregnant. It turned out that she was four months pregnant without knowing it. The baby did not survive the procedure. These are the heartbreaking and dangerous results of pretending that sex isn't real or that it doesn't matter.

Our society, and our medical establishment, specifically, is harming these young women at the altar of a sick and twisted ideology that says that sex isn't real and that it is perfectly fine to remove healthy body parts. There are countless stories like Keira's, Luka's, Chloe's, Cat's, Prisha's, Katie's, Leigh's, and Layla's. Most of them are women, but there are plenty of male "detransitioners" too. Their stories are incredibly moving. There is an internet forum that is colloquially referred to as "detrans subreddit." It is intended to serve as a resource for people who underwent some form of "gender-affirming care" and now think that it was a mistake. When it was created in 2017, it had a few hundred members. By October 2023, it had over 50,000. But at the end of the day, no one really knows how many young people are out there who have been harmed by "gender-affirming care."

A 2022 study titled "Continuation of Gender-Affirming Hormones Among Transgender Adolescents and Adults" published in the *Journal of Clinical Endocrinology and Metabolism* reported that on average, 30 percent of people who took puberty blockers or opposite-sex hormones eventually went off them. The rates were higher among women who had taken them (36 percent). Twenty-six percent of minors who took puberty blockers and/or opposite-sex hormones eventually went off them. That is a much higher rate of "detransition" than is frequently reported in the media, and the rates are consistent with anecdotal evidence that children who take these drugs are more likely than adults to continue them. But still, no one can systematically track how many young people regret "transitioning" or how many are helped by it. A 2023 article in *The Archives of Sexual Behavior* titled "Transition Regret and Detransition: Meaning and Uncertainties" reported that "although recent data have shed light on a complex range of experiences that lead people to detransition, research remains very much in its infancy" and that there is "no guidance on best practices for clinicians involved in their care."

Heartbreakingly, the people who have come to regret their decisions to take life-altering hormones and have irreversible surgeries do not generally get support from the medical community (or from Democratic lawmakers). Typically, when a patient reports to his or her doctor that he or she regrets these decisions, the patient is simply ignored. In 2023, Texas Democratic lawmakers actively (and successfully) campaigned to kill a bill that would have required insurance companies operating in the state to cover healthcare associated with "detransitioning."

But all hope is not lost for "detransitioners." In May 2023, Cattinson launched a new nonprofit called Detrans Help, whose mission is to "raise the alarm on the current state of 'gender affirming care' and ensure detransitioners have access to the resources they need." Many "detransitioners" have spoken out about the importance of avoiding the use of words like "ruin" or "mutilation" to describe what has been done to them. Their argument is that if these young women and men are told that they have been "ruined" or "mutilated," they are *more* likely to continue to pursue self-harm than to accept what has happened to them and get the help they need to recover and go on to have happy and healthy lives. One male "detransitioner" refers to all the talk of "ruin" and "mutilation" as "trauma porn," and says it isn't helping anyone. In my view, all these young people (and the parents who were bullied into going along) are victims of a system that let them down. They deserve to have the support they need.

The Lie of "Trans Genocide"

An undercover video released in April 2023 by Project Veritas revealed that doctors in several states routinely prescribe puberty blockers to children as young as eight. Project Veritas said in its press release about the video that "The undercover investigation discovered hundreds of large health organizations admitting to advocating that children who haven't even hit puberty are mature enough to begin these life-altering, and often irreversible, treatments. After visiting 50 different clinics across eight states, *Project Veritas* discovered that puberty blockers were often made available for children as young as eight after only one prior consultation."

Doctors are on video saying that surgeries might be appropriate for children as young as ten.

But there is no evidence that any of this helps kids or young adults who are confused about their sex and a lot of evidence that it causes harm. A 2021 study published in the *Journal of Sexual Medicine* found that hormone interventions do not improve mental health and were likely to lead to an *increase* in the prescription of psychotropic drugs for kids with mental health problems. During a June 2023 Congressional hearing on the topic of "gender-affirming care," House Republican Daniel Crenshaw noted that the *British Journal of Medicine* had looked at sixty-one systematic reviews, concluding that "there is great uncertainty about the effects of puberty blockers, cross-sex hormones, and surgeries in young people." He asked a witness named Dr. Meredithe McNamara, who was there to testify in support of "gender-affirming care" to name a "journal that has done a systematic review that cites different evidence, that cites strong evidence of benefits from these therapies." She was unable to come up with a single one.

Meanwhile, state after state is passing legislation to prohibit the practice of subjecting minors to practices like these under the leadership of Republicans and with almost no support from Democratic lawmakers. The media mostly reports these developments with headlines like this one, from *CNN*: "GOP Lawmakers Escalate Fight Against Gender-Affirming Care with Bills Seeking to Expand the Scope of Bans." Parroting activists in lieu of reporting the news, they characterize these efforts to protect children as "trans genocide." One segment from *The Huntington News*, the paper of Northeastern University, reported in March 2023 about a gathering in Boston to "protest transphobia and trans genocide in the Transgender Day of Resistance March." It stated that "The protest comes after a wave of anti-transgender legislation in many states has raised concerns the United States is beginning a genocide of trans individuals, or the systematic eradication of transgender people. Among these pieces of legislation are bans in multiple states on gender affirming care for minors, and drag bans that could criminalize any kind of visible gender nonconformity." These are outright lies. Literally no one is calling for a genocide of people who claim to have a "transgender" identity or for the "systemic eradication" of any such people. And no state that I'm aware of is criminalizing non-conformity with sex stereotypes.

According to Article II of the U.N. Convention on the Prevention and Punishment of the Crime of Genocide, "genocide means any of the following acts committed with intent to destroy, in whole or in part, a national, ethnical, racial or religious group, as such: killing members of the group; causing serious bodily or mental harm to members of the group; deliberately inflicting on the group conditions of life calculated to bring about its physical destruction in whole or in part; imposing measures intended to prevent births within the group; or forcibly transferring children of the group to another group."

That's what genocide is. The term was coined in the forties in response to the Nazi policies of systematic murder of Jewish people during the Holocaust and to previous instances of targeted actions aimed at the destruction of particular racial, ethnic, or religious groups of people. Saving young people's lives by legally prohibiting their sterilization and/or mutilation is literally the opposite of that. The term "transgender" simply does not describe a coherent category of people who fit the definition of a "racial, ethnic, or religious group." And no one is calling for anyone who has a "trans" identity to be killed. The activists who claim that there is a "trans genocide," and the media that parrots them, are lying.

Things may be shifting. In 2023, the highly-regarded investigative journalist Gerald Posner announced the results of his six-month study into puberty blockers. Posner made the point that I have been trying to make throughout this chapter, that "The fashion for transgenderism has brought with it a new euphemism: 'gender-affirming care,' which means surgical and pharmacological interventions designed to make the body look and feel more like that of the opposite sex." He explained the dangerous effects of administering blockers and concluded that "Gender-affirming care for children is undoubtedly a flashpoint in America's culture wars. It is also a human experiment on children and teens, the most vulnerable patients.

Ignoring the long-term dangers posed by unrestricted off-label dispensing of powerful puberty blockers and cross-sex hormones, combined with the large overdiagnosis of minors as gender dysphoric, borders on child abuse."

Child abuse, indeed.

PART 3

THE PERPETRATORS

What will you do on the day of reckoning, when disaster comes from afar? To whom will you run for help? Where will you leave your riches?
–Isaiah 10:3 (NIV)

CHAPTER 4

THE QUEERING OF THE AMERICAN POLITICAL LEFT

I came into my political consciousness in the seventies. I learned all about Franklin D. Roosevelt and John F. Kennedy, whom I took to be historical heroes of the American political left (I later learned that both men were terribly flawed, but still). I learned all about the civil rights struggles of the sixties. I went further into my political consciousness in the eighties. At the time, AIDs was ravaging America and my father was the only doctor in the small town where I grew up who was willing to see HIV-positive patients. I grew into my political consciousness, in other words, when I understood that the Democrats were the party that cared about the working class, feminism, free speech, gay rights, and civil rights generally. Today, the American political left is letting men invade female-only spaces on the basis of their woman identities; harming children and young adults, including gay young people, with poisonous hormones and permanent surgeries; and stifling dissent. What the hell happened?

"Queer Theory": Subversion for Subversion's Sake

All "gender identity" flows from something called "queer theory"—a branch of philosophy whose essential tenet is that sex is a social construct that is not grounded in material reality. Following on a movement toward an embrace of postmodernism (sometimes referred to as poststructuralism) in academia, "queer theory" began to flourish in the nineties and is still with us today. Its creation is frequently attributed to French philosopher Michel Foucault, although Foucault was not alone in popularizing it. Gayle Rubin, another queer theorist, teaches at the Institute for Research on Women and Gender at the University of Michigan. Her research interests include "lesbian, gay, bisexual and transgender studies, ethnography of queer populations, urban sexual geographies, histories of sexology, and feminist theory and politics."

Perhaps the most well-known contemporary proponent of "queer theory" in the U.S. is Judith Butler, Distinguished Professor in the Graduate School and formerly the Maxine Elliot Chair in the Department of Comparative Literature and the Program of Critical Theory at the University of California, Berkeley. In 1990 (six years after the death of Foucault), she published a book called *Gender Trouble: Feminism and the Subversion of Identity*, which brought "queer theory" into the mainstream. Professor Butler's very extensive biography on the U.C. Berkeley website takes great pains to let us all know that she goes by "they/them" pronouns, as though she is some sort of academic committee all on her own. Meanwhile, in the land of material reality, she is an individual human being who is also a lesbian and in a long-term relationship with a woman, who is also an individual adult human female person (i.e., a woman).

Gender Trouble is a dense and tedious read, which is one of the reasons that the journal *Philosophy and Literature* gave it its annual Bad Writing Contest Award in 1999 for writing that contains "the ugliest, most stylistically awful" sentences. Bad writing aside, one of the primary aims of *Gender Trouble* is to challenge the institution of compulsory heterosexuality (society's expectation that all members partner with members of the opposite sex), which is undeniably a useful enterprise, whatever one thinks of the concept. Lesbian feminist scholars and activists have, for decades, been challenging the institution of compulsory heterosexuality and encouraging women to consider abandoning their male partners and centering women in their relationships (including both friendships and romantic relationships) instead. And for a time, it worked. As Ariel Levy recounts in her 2009 *New Yorker* article, "Lesbian Nation: When Gay Women Took to the Road," feminist Susan Brownmiller once described a "coming-out fervor akin to a tidal wave" and stated that she "was bewildered by the overnight conversions and sudden switches in overt orientation by many of the activists [she] knew."

But *Gender Trouble* is not limited to critiquing compulsory heterosexuality. It goes further by presupposing that the category "women" is an identity, as opposed to a coherent category of human beings. This presupposition follows naturally from the underlying assumption that sex *itself* is socially constructed rather than being grounded in material reality. For example, Chapter 1 of *Gender Trouble* is titled "'Women' as the Subject of Feminism," and includes this: "The very subject of women is no longer understood in stable or abiding terms.... [T]here is very little agreement after all on what it is that constitutes, or ought to constitute, the category of women." I was not paying too much attention to academic feminism when this book was originally published in 1990 other than to know that I was a feminist, but I am not at all persuaded that there is any truth to that statement at all. I do know that when I started college that year, I joined something called the "Women's Center." No one involved in that venture was confused about what the word "women" meant. We were concerned with things like campus sexual assault and protecting abortion rights; that is, matters that primarily concern women.

The even more insidious part of *Gender Trouble* is its political aims. Feminists in the sixties and seventies were interested in taking aim at gender itself and took the word "gender" to mean the social expectations that are imposed on both women and men on the basis of sex.[6] They wanted women to feel free not to conform to such stereotypes. That's partly why so many women abandoned their male partners in the seventies. But what Butler appears to be saying is that *subversion* on a personal level is what is needed, as opposed to any actual political activism. In her view, one can

[6] Butler would end up writing in a 2021 piece in *The Guardian* that opposition to gender constitutes "fascism." She provides zero evidence that anti-gender feminists are literal fascists.

subvert society's sex stereotypes but the entire system of gender cannot be brought down. She advocates for subversion for subversion's sake rather than for a political movement to revolutionarily change how society views women and men on the basis of sex.

Martha Nussbaum, a philosophy professor at the University of Chicago, took aim at Butler for this in a 1999 piece in *The New Republic* called "The Professor of Parody: The Hip Defeatism of Judith Butler." Nussbaum's main point was that feminists care about the material lives of women and girls and fight politically to improve them. We are not interested in "parodic performance," or subversion for subversion's sake. "Gender identity," on the other hand, is subversion for its own sake. It is an individual's declaration that he or she "is trans," and it does nothing to improve the material circumstances of anyone, let alone women. It is a contemporary version of a teenager giving her parents the middle finger and then running down the hall and slamming her door.

One outgrowth of "queer theory" on a global scale comes in the form of the Yogyakarta Principles, drafted in 2006 at Gadjah Mada University in Yogyakarta. These purport to be a "set of principles on the application of international human rights law in relation to sexual orientation and gender identity" and to "affirm binding international legal standards with which all States must comply." This is misleading, in that the Yogyakarta Principles are not binding on any single government entity, anywhere in the world.

The 2006 version sets forth twenty-nine principles, framed as "rights." They include several very basic and essential rights principles, including the right to the universal enjoyment of human rights, the right to equality and non-discrimination, the right to a free trial, and the right to be free from torture. These are all very universally accepted rights that everyone should enjoy on the basis of being included in the category of people known as human beings. Unfortunately, for anyone who cares about the material reality of biological sex, it asserts that "gender identity" is "integral to every person's dignity and humanity," where "gender identity" means "each person's deeply felt internal and individual experience of gender, which may or may not correspond with the sex assigned at birth, including the personal sense of the body (which may involve, if freely chosen, modification of bodily appearance or function by medical, surgical or other means) and other expressions of gender, including dress, speech and mannerisms." Readers, did you not realize that you have a "deeply felt internal and individual experience of gender?" Well, you do!

The problem with the principles is not that they explain basic universal human rights, which is a good thing, but that they declare that people have a human right not to be discriminated against based on some mysterious quality that is "deeply felt" but that does not actually exist in any real material sense. Should people be permitted to believe that they have an extra special gender essence? Sure, I guess so. But the principles stand for the proposition that everyone else has to go along with the idea that there are extra special gender essences. They essentially demand that everyone in the world have a right to legal recognition of their "gender identity," regardless of sex.

In 2017, there appeared on the scene something called YP+10 (Yogyakarta Principles + 10). These 2017 updates to the original Yogyakarta Principles add an additional nine principles, along with a list of "additional state obligations" (which are not actually obligations, but since the whole thing is based on postmodern nonsense, I guess reality shouldn't matter). The additional principles and state "obligations" maintain the central theme that "gender identity" must be legally protected at all levels of government.

One of the signatories of the initial Yogyakarta Principles was Robert Wintemute, a professor of human rights law in London. However, in 2021, Wintemute reversed course and went on record as saying that the international human rights community was mistaken to merge lesbian and gay rights with the idea of a right to have "gender identity" replace sex. He also said that women's rights were not considered during the original meeting where the principles were written and that the authors failed to consider the fact that men would seek to access female-only spaces based on their "female gender identity."

In January 2023, Wintemute was scheduled to give a talk at McGill University in Quebec, Canada. The topic of the talk was "The Sex v. Gender (Identity) Debate in the United Kingdom and the Divorce of the LGB from T." Over 200 protesters showed up. After throwing flour in his face and unplugging his projector, they succeeded in persuading university officials to cancel the event. The day before the scheduled event, a group of students posted an open letter to McGill administrators. In the open letter, the students said, "As much as McGill may try to absolve itself from blame by claiming its right to academic liberty, we must refute that argument by stating that the tolerance of intolerance ultimately results in the wiping out of tolerance. Would McGill give a platform to an openly misogynistic lawyer advocating actively for sending women back into the kitchen, under the guise of debate? No. Then why would McGill do the same, albeit to trans people? Undermining trans rights is a gateway towards enabling further attacks on people's bodily autonomy—especially for racialized cis women and intersex people, who do not fit the narrow mold of 'womanhood' that the so-called 'gender critical' movement dictates."

For the record, if a university gave a platform to an openly misogynistic lawyer who advocated actively for sending women back into the kitchen under the guise of debate, I would support that. I'm a feminist first, but a free speech advocate as well, and I think that misogynist men should absolutely be permitted to argue that women should be sent back to the kitchen. I would think that such a misogynist man is wrong, but I would defend his right to say it. Gender activists demonstrate every time that they are just not interested in critical thinking. What these students were saying is that if Wintemute even so much as had the opportunity to question whether "trans" falls into the same category as "lesbian, gay, and bisexual," then people will die. These are the lengths to which people will go to silence the voices of those who question "gender identity." We are told that we are responsible for the deaths of "trans people," despite there being no obvious definition of what the phrase "trans people" even means and no evidence whatsoever that advocating for the rights of women and girls, or lesbians, gay men, and bisexual people has ever resulted in anyone's death.

One of the signatories to the 2017 version was a man named Victor Madrigal-Borloz, who has served as the U.N.'s Independent Expert on Sexual Orientation and Gender Identity since 2017, the same year in which the Yogyakarta Principles were updated. In late 2022, he caught headlines after advising the Scottish Parliament to amend its "Gender Recognition Act" to allow for anyone to legally change their sex. Plenty of Scottish feminists expressed concern about what this would mean for women and girls, but the government completely overlooked them. According to Canadian feminist writer Eva Kurilova, "Madrigal-Borloz plays with language to ensure that he can't lose. By insisting that men who claim to be women are women, he effectively excuses himself from having to consider the harms that his position might cause to women and children. It's not even a blip on his radar."

Madrigal-Borloz has an office at Harvard Law school, where he serves as a Lecturer on Law and as the Eleanor Roosevelt Senior Visiting Researcher at the Harvard Law School Human Rights Program. In August 2022, he went on a tour of the U.S. at the invitation of the U.S. Mission to the U.N., during which he visited Washington D.C., Birmingham, Alabama, Miami, Florida, and San Diego, California. The official position of the U.S. under the Biden administration is that we support the mandate of Madrigal-Borloz to enshrine "gender identity" in the law and throughout society all over the world. In October 2022, the U.S. mission to the U.N. told Madrigal-Borloz that we "look forward to humbly reviewing [his] recommendations for the United States." As of writing, these recommendations have not been delivered.

No matter how you slice it, the Yogyakarta Principles (both the 2006 original and the 2017 updates) are an unmitigated disaster for women and girls and for anyone who cares about the material reality of sex. Its signatories, including Madrigal-Borloz, are pushing them all over the world, including at the U.N. and all the European governing bodies, and before individual country governments including the U.S. They are behind the push to redefine sex to include "gender identity" at all levels of government and they are having an influence on Democratic Party leadership.

The Democratic Party Elite

Democratic Party support for enshrining "gender identity" in the law at the expense of women and girls goes all the way to the top.

On August 9, 1990, a boy named Timothy Ryan McBride was born in Wilmington, Delaware. McBride first volunteered on a political campaign at the age of fourteen and went on to lead the Delaware chapter of Young Democrats by the age of seventeen. McBride would later work on Democrat Jack Markell's 2008 campaign for governor and as Beau Biden's "body man" (driver and aide) when he ran for attorney general in 2010.[7] In March 2011, American University announced that McBride had been elected student government president. The student paper, *The Eagle*, praised him, stating, "On paper, School of Public Affairs sophomore Tim McBride looks like the stereotypical Student Government president.... But there's more to him than meets the eye. McBride will take over the [Student Government] May 1, but says he's not going to be ruling from an ivory tower. He doesn't want to be the disconnected SG representative that many students envision.... McBride hopes to return to his home state to become a civil rights attorney after graduating in 2013." The following year, McBride "came out as transgender" in an op-ed in *The Eagle* called "The Real Me." In it, he claimed that he is a woman named Sarah and asked to be referred to using "she/her" pronouns. And with that, Tim became Sarah.

McBride is very close with the Biden family. As noted above, he worked on the late Beau Biden's 2010 attorney general campaign. McBride has claimed publicly that then Vice President Biden called him when he "came out" in 2012 to tell him that Beau was proud of him. As Sarah, he interned at the White House under President Obama. In January 2013,

[7] Beau Biden was President Biden's oldest son and he died tragically from cancer in 2015.

McBride joined the board of directors of Equality Delaware and led the lobbying effort for Delaware to enact a law to redefine sex to include "gender identity," successfully persuading Governor Markell and Attorney General Biden to publicly support the effort. In a speech in May 2015, Second Lady Jill Biden told Sarah's story, adding, "We believe young people should be valued for who they are, no matter what they look like, where they're from, the gender with which they identify, or who they love."

By 2016, McBride was serving as the National Press Secretary at HRC and spoke at the 2016 Democratic presidential convention. I happened to be at the U.S. Capitol one day in early 2019 with Kellie-Jay Keen and U.K. feminist Julia Long, and he was there to lobby for the Equality Act. Keen and Long asked him to explain why he hates lesbians, and he had no answer for them. He won a seat on the Delaware Senate in 2020 and visited President Biden at the White House for Pride month in 2021. McBride has been serving in the Delaware state senate ever since. He also served as a National Women's History Museum Predoctoral Fellow in Women's History between 2020 and 2022 (presumably McBride is entitled to hold such a position based on his woman identity). By 2023, he was running for a seat in Congress.

President Biden has been saying (at least privately) that "transgender discrimination is the 'civil rights issue of our time'" at least since 2012 (the same year that McBride "came out as transgender"). He frequently posts about it on social media. In January 2020, he posted: "Let's be clear. Transgender equality is the civil rights issue of our time. There is no room for compromise when it comes to basic human rights." He frequently trumpets support for the Equality Act. In his 2022 State of the Union address, he said: "For our LGBTQ+ Americans, let's finally get the bipartisan Equality Act to my desk. The onslaught of state laws targeting transgender Americans and their families is wrong. As I said last year, especially to our younger transgender Americans, I will always have your back as your President, so you can be yourself and reach your God-given potential." Notably, he didn't appear to have any concern for lesbian, gay, or bisexual people, despite referencing "LGBTQ+ Americans."

In October 2022, President Biden sat down with Dylan Mulvaney to discuss "trans rights" as part of a presidential forum hosted by *Now This News*. That might sound normal, unless you know that Mulvaney is a twenty-something man who claims to be a girl and is known for his "Days of Girlhood" series on TikTok (where he has around ten million subscribers). To the best of my knowledge, he has never done anything in his life that would warrant giving him a meeting with a sitting president. To open the interview, the host began with the premise that some states are banning healthcare for "trans people" and banning kids from playing sports (neither of which is true) and went on to explain that "to go deeper into this issue," there was Mulvaney, "who's welcomed us into her life by showing on social media her girlhood series." They showed a bit of Mulvaney's TikTok series, where he whined a bit about how during his "transition," he "tried not to let the internet's words hurt [him] or [his] spirit," before launching into the conversation, all while the U.S. president sat across from him, nodding along.

When Mulvaney asked the president whether states should have the right to "ban gender-affirming healthcare," the president responded, "I don't think any state or anybody should have the right to do that, as a moral question and as a legal question. I just think it's wrong. I was saying before we started that my deceased son used to be the Attorney General of the state of Delaware. He passed the broadest piece of legislation.... As attorney general he was able to convince the legislature to pass and the governor to sign...that dealt with all gender-affirming capability. I mean, there's a lot of...you know, sometimes they try to block you from being able to access certain medicines [camera cut to Mulvaney solemnly nodding], being able to access certain procedures, and so on. None of that should be available. I mean, no state should be able to do that in my view. So I feel very very strongly that you should have every single solitary right, including use of your gender identity bathrooms in public."

The president continued by saying that "It's really important that we continue to speak out about the basic fundamental rights of all human beings, and the idea that what's going on in some states...it's outrageous and I think it's immoral.... What they're trying to do to trans persons is immoral." He invoked the memory of his deceased son again and noted that his son had set up a foundation for abused children that raised millions of dollars to "educate parents as to what they should not be afraid of and to educate the community about what is just pure hyperbole. As I told you, I mentioned a young woman who used to be in his staff, used to be in my staff, who is now a state senator, and she's trans and she's a state senator in the state of Delaware." He was, of course, talking about McBride. Throughout this entire debacle, the president did not so much as utter a word of concern for women or girls (or for lesbians or gay men).

This was the President of the United States of America stating on the record, while pandering to a twenty-something man who is famous for nothing other than documenting his "transition" to "girlhood" on TikTok, that legislation to protect the rights, privacy, and safety of women and girls and to stop medical professionals from mutilating children is "immoral." And Now This News *reported it all as though this were totally normal.*

After undergoing what is known as "facial feminization surgery" (where doctors try to make a man's face look more like a woman's face), Mulvaney appeared at the 2023 Grammy Awards, where he gushed with *Entertainment Tonight* that it was his first awards show ever, talked about how he "felt like a princess" while getting dressed, and characterized himself as a "2023 Audrey Hepburn." He added that he was "stepping into [his] womanhood in a really exciting way" and talked about how "now the world gets to meet [him] in [his] true self," and how he was "on day 229 of girlhood" that day, "oh no 329, we're almost at 365! [gasp]" As readers have certainly discerned by this point, I think that all of "gender identity" is a monstrous, authoritarian, sexist, and homophobic horror show and a deadly serious matter. Still, sometimes you just have to shake your head, roll your eyes, and wonder if Audrey Hepburn is rolling in her grave.

March 13, 2023, marked Mulvaney's "365 Days of Girlhood" and he celebrated by going on Drew Barrymore's talk show to discuss it. Barrymore embarrassingly kneeled at his feet to congratulate him. On the same day, Kamala Harris, the vice president of the United States, sent him a letter on stationery from the vice president's office, stating, "Dear Dylan, I send you my warmest greetings as you celebrate your 365th day of living authentically. Thank you for courageously sharing your story and your journey. I appreciate your continued advocacy for transgender equality, including during your visit to the White House last year. Through your work as an activist and advocate for the LGBTQI+ community, you continue to break barriers and inspire young people across our Nation and around the world. While we have made incredible progress—from advancing marriage equality to enacting historic protections for transgender people—the fight is far from over. Our Administration stands with the LGBTQI+ community in the ongoing struggle for true equity and equality and against hate and discrimination in all its forms. I am grateful for your dedication and courage, and I hope you continue to use your platform to spread positivity and create change. I look forward to seeing all that you will accomplish in the future. Sincerely, Kamala Harris."

At no point did the vice president provide any indication of what she thinks marriage equality has to do with a young man donning a dress and pretending to be a girl, or why she thinks that objecting to Mulvaney's mockery of womanhood constitutes "hate." In the words of one X user: "No woman has ever received a letter from a VP congratulating her on being a woman. No, such privilege belongs to a man." By April 2023, Mulvaney, *who is famous for nothing other than mocking womanhood on TikTok*, had become a brand ambassador for Bud Light, Tampax, Nike, Maybelline, Olay, and ASOS wedding dresses. Anheuser-Busch lost over $20 billion in revenue and sales plummeted by nearly 30 percent as a result of a subsequent boycott because everyone knows Mulvaney is a man. They eventually cut ties with Mulvaney. In response, Mulvaney took to Instagram to whine about "transphobia": "For a company to hire a trans person and then not publicly stand by them is worse, in my opinion, than not hiring a trans person at all. It gives customers permission to be as transphobic and hateful as they want. I have felt a loneliness that I wouldn't wish on anyone." But Anheuser-Busch hadn't given customers permission to do anything—normal people just know that men aren't girls.

Admiral Rachel (Richard) L. Levine serves as the 17th Assistant Secretary for Health for the U.S. Department of Health and Human Services (HHS), after being nominated by President Biden and confirmed by the U.S. Senate in 2021. His nomination was supported by a group called the LGBTQ+ Victory Institute, which is funded partially by the Arcus Foundation (on whose board Maya Harris has served since 2017). Levine attended medical school at Tulane University where, according to the National Women's History Museum (which consistently refers to him as "she" and "her"), he "discovered a passion for pediatrics, specifically adolescent medicine, as she found teenagers both challenging and stimulating." I don't want to read too much into that characterization, other than to note that it is more than a little bit bizarre describe a doctor as "finding teenagers both challenging and stimulating." While at Tulane, Levine met and married Martha Peaslee, who is also a pediatrician. Together they had a daughter and a son. Levine became Rachel in 2011 and he and Dr. Peaslee divorced in 2013. Before joining the Biden administration, Levine served as the state Secretary of Health in Pennsylvania.

According to the HHS website, "[A]s Assistant Secretary for Health, ADM Rachel Levine fights every day to improve the health and well-being of all Americans." This is, of course, not true, as Levine supports so-called "gender-affirming care," which we know is harmful. In July 2022, Levine said, "Trans youth are vulnerable. They suffer significant harassment and bullying, sometimes in schools or their community.... So we really want to base our treatment and to affirm and to support and empower these youths not to limit their participation in activities in sports and even limit their ability to get gender affirmation treatment in their state." In other words, Biden's assistant secretary of health at HHS supports poisoning minors by giving them puberty blockers and wrong-sex hormones. He promotes this avidly and enthusiastically. He encourages schools to train teachers to teach "gender identity" to children. He gave a talk in a school in June 2023 in which he urged that medical care be based on "facts and evidence," and then went on to refer to "gender-affirming care" as "literal suicide prevention," despite the fact that not a single researcher has ever effectively demonstrated that such "care" prevents death by suicide.

But even though Levine talks a good game about how "gender-affirming care" is "literal suicide prevention," the think tank Capital Research Center revealed in September 2023 that most of the millions of dollars the administration spends on "trans" is actually spent to investigate the harms it causes. The Center said, "Despite the Biden administration's assurances that 'gender-affirming care' is safe enough to be performed on children, most of this money was spent by the U.S. Department of Health and Human Services (HHS) commissioning medical research on a variety of horrific mental and physical health conditions that plague transgender people both before and after transitioning. Some of these studies even examined catastrophic side effects from the hormonal and surgical transition procedures that the administration insists are supported by overwhelming medical consensus."

Levine also likes to talk about women (a category that he says includes him) breaking glass ceilings. In January 2023, during a meeting at HHS to prepare for women's history month in March, Levine was asked what it means to him for women to break glass ceilings. He responded: "I think women's history month is an opportunity for women to support each other. I think that we need to work to empower each other and provide mentorship and opportunities for success. So if someone opens a door, like we've been discussing, well then that door is open for more people to go through in the future. And that's what I hope that my appointment provides that sort of opportunity so that other women, other women who are part of the LGBTQI+ community, have the opportunity to follow their dreams and to maybe go beyond what they might have expected." When Levine refers to "women who are part of the LGBTQI+ community" here, I highly doubt that he's talking about lesbians or bisexual women. I suspect that he's talking about men who claim to have woman identities, like himself. His statements also shed light on the lie of acronyms like "LGBTQI+." Levine portends to be talking about women in this exchange. It never occurs to Levine, or to anyone listening, that there are no women in the G category.

The G in the acronym stands for gay men; women aren't involved in it at all. If anyone in any position of accountability would ever call this out, the entire acronym would fall apart. But they don't.

In 2023, the National Science Foundation started tracking data about the sexual orientations and "gender identities" of the doctoral students who receive funding from them. It had previously tracked information about students' sex and this new initiative was said to be necessary to ensure the participation of "LGBT" students in STEM fields. But did anyone at the NSF even consider for a moment the sensitive nature of potentially asking lesbian or gay students who may not be out of the closet to out themselves to the federal government? And what on earth does having a "gender identity" have to do with a student's ability to complete his or her doctoral work? And why is the National *Science* Foundation collecting data on the entirely *unscientific* concept of "gender identity" anyway?

In June 2020, the Supreme Court announced its decision in *Bostock v. Clayton County*, which held that discriminating against people on the basis of sexual orientation or "transgender status" in employment constitutes unlawful sex discrimination under Title VII. The Court could not be bothered to tell anyone what "transgender status" means, but never mind that for now. That was a bad decision for women and girls, but as bad as it was, things were about to get much worse under the Biden administration.

On his first day upon taking office, the president signed Executive Order 13988, officially titled "Preventing and Combating Discrimination on the Basis of Gender Identity and Sexual Orientation." The order announced a new federal policy: "All persons should receive equal treatment under the law, no matter their gender identity or sexual orientation," and ordered all federal agencies to promulgate rules redefining sex to include "gender identity" for all purposes under federal administrative law. The administration justified this based on a misrepresentation of both *Bostock* and the Constitution. The order states: "These principles are reflected in the Constitution, which promises equal protection of the laws." It is true that the Constitution promises equal protection of the laws, but it does not follow that anyone should be able to legally lie about their sex.

The order continues: "These principles are also enshrined in our Nation's anti-discrimination laws, among them Title VII of the Civil Rights Act of 1964.... In *Bostock v. Clayton*...the Supreme Court held that Title VII's prohibition on discrimination 'because of...sex' covers discrimination on the basis of gender identity and sexual orientation. Under *Bostock's* reasoning, laws that prohibit sex discrimination—including Title IX..., the Fair Housing Act, and section 412 of the Immigration and Nationality Act, along with their respective implementing regulations—prohibit discrimination on the basis of gender identity or sexual orientation, so long as the laws do not contain sufficient indications to the contrary." This is just categorically untrue, in two respects.

First, the Supreme Court did not mention "gender identity" once in *Bostock*, other than to include it a footnote, quoting an outside source. Second, the Court *expressly* limited its holding to the employment context. It said: "The employers [the defendants in that case] worry that our decision will sweep beyond Title VII to other federal or state laws that prohibit sex discrimination. And, under Title VII itself, they say sex-segregated bathrooms, locker rooms, and dress codes will prove unsustainable after our decision today. But none of these other laws are before us; we have not had the benefit of adversarial testing about the meaning of their terms, and we do not prejudge any such question today. Under Title VII, too, we do not purport to address bathrooms, locker rooms, or anything else of the kind. The only question before us is whether an employer who fires someone simply for being homosexual or transgender has discharged or otherwise discriminated against that individual 'because of such individual's sex.'"

Again, the Supreme Court didn't bother to tell us in its *Bostock* decision what it means for someone to legally "be transgender," but never mind that for now. The point here is that the Biden administration has repeatedly lied to the American people by saying that the Supreme Court enshrined "gender identity" in the law (it didn't) and ignored the Supreme

Court's express limitation of its own ruling to the employment context. The administration simply went ahead to annihilate the material reality of sex throughout U.S. federal administrative law. It did all of this without any prior notice or opportunity for public comment, as required by federal law.

In February 2021, the Department of Housing and Urban Development (HUD) issued a memo announcing that it will interpret the word "sex" to include "gender identity" throughout U.S. housing law, in accordance with the January Executive Order. That meant the end of any women-only housing, including domestic violence shelters and college dormitories, because the reach of the memo, which governs HUD's interpretation of the Fair Housing Act, covers "nearly all housing, including private housing, public housing, and housing that receives federal funding," according to HUD's website. The next month, the Department of Justice (DOJ) announced that Title IX's prohibition of discrimination on the basis of sex will be interpreted to prohibit discrimination on the basis of "gender identity," in accordance with the January Executive Order. That meant the end of women's and girls' sports at all federally-funded educational institutions, which is most of them.

In May 2021, the HHS announced that it had submitted a final rule to the Federal Register explaining that it would interpret the word "sex" to include "gender identity" in evaluating complaints of discrimination regarding the provision of healthcare under the Affordable Care Act (ACA). That meant that women will not be permitted to demand female healthcare providers for gynecological care in any healthcare facility that receives federal dollars. It also meant that such facilities cannot provide sex-specific healthcare to patients who claim to have a "gender identity" that differs from their sex. While all of this was going on, the administration just went ahead and decided to outright lie about what the law says—HHS claims on its website that the ACA *already* defines sex to include "gender identity." This is patently false. Whatever anyone thinks of the ACA (colloquially known as Obamacare), it was enacted in 2010 and did not include protection on the basis of "gender identity."

I'll explain in Chapter 9 about how some recent federal court decisions have addressed those blatant acts of administrative overreach. For now, it is enough to note that the Biden administration has been obliterating the material reality of sex since the first day of taking office, in blatant disregard of the rights, privacy, and safety of women and girls. In doing so, the administration appears to have the full support of the vice president, who frequently posts her support for "trans" and "gender identity" on social media. An example from 2022: "Transgender children in Texas and Florida should not be made to fear who they are. And transgender women of color should not have to fear for their lives. We must fight for a future where all people can live without fear." It is not difficult to find others. To the best of my knowledge, she has never said what she means by "transgender."

In March 2023, the White House celebrated International Women's Day by awarding an International Women of Courage Award to Alba Rueda, a man who claims to have a woman identity. Rueda is Argentina's Special Representative on Sexual Orientation and Gender Identity at the Ministry of Foreign Affairs. The White House, the First Lady herself, awarded a Women of Courage Award to a man on International Women's Day. That's how much the Democratic Party elite hates women.

In April 2023, the DOJ intervened in the case *L. W. v. Skrmetti*, where a bunch of kids (and their parents and doctors) are suing the state of Tennessee over a law that prohibits doctors from giving kids opposite-sex hormones and performing medically unnecessary surgeries. The crux of the DOJ's argument is that the law in question "denies necessary medical care to youth based solely on who they are" and that this violates the Equal Protection Clause of the 14th Amendment. The complaint states as a factual matter that "Gender identity refers to a person's core sense of belonging to a particular gender, such as male or female" and that "Every person has a gender identity."

But no one "belongs to a gender." Gender is sex stereotypes, not a category of human beings to which a person belongs. Further, the words "male" and "female" do not refer to "gender"—they refer to the two sex classes that exist within the species *homo sapiens*, the class *mammalia*, and to most beings throughout the animal kingdom (as well as to many plants). Every single human being on the face of the planet (all eight billion of us) is either female or male, regardless of a claimed identity. Even if none of that were true, the statement "every person has a gender identity," for which the complaint provides zero support whatsoever, is an obnoxious lie. Even if you believe in "gender identities," it is outrageous to claim that every person has one. I don't, and probably most readers don't either.

In June 2023, during what many have started referring to as "The Holy Month of Pride," the administration announced a set of "New Actions to Protect LGBTQI+ Communities." Having worked at a federal agency before, all the new "actions" sound to me like a bunch of bureaucratic gobbledygook that amount to nothing different from what the administration has already been doing for years. Incidentally, the words "lesbian" and "gay" do not appear anywhere in the fact sheet, even though it purports to be about protecting the "LGBTQI+ community."

The Democrats in Congress are no better. Here is an example of a post from Representative Nancy Pelosi from March 2022: "Trans rights are human rights. We see you. We love you. We value you. Today and every day, we are proud to stand with the trans and non-binary community in the fight to ensure you are accepted just as you are. #TransDayOfVisibility." This is what Senator Warren posted on the same day: "Trans and gender-nonconforming people have been trailblazers since the beginning of the modern LGBTQ+ rights movement. We look to their legacy on today's #TransDayOfVisibility as we fight back against right-wing extremists' hateful new laws." Neither of them has ever explained what they mean by "trans" or by the acronym LGBTQ+. To the best of my knowledge, not a single current Democrat in office anywhere in the federal government has had the courage to discuss the threats that enshrining "gender identity" in the law pose to women and girls, or to lesbians and gay men, even though they have been made keenly aware of them. In July 2023, Congressional Democrats simply walked out of a hearing on the harms of "gender-affirming care" rather than watch a video documenting the savagery of what it does to young people.

But even though Congressional Democrats talk a good game about "trans rights," it is clear that they understand the material reality of sex. In July 2023, Paula Scanlan (who went to school with Lia (Will) Thomas and was on the women's swim team with him) testified before Congress about how traumatizing it was to share a locker room with Thomas. Democratic Representative Steve Cohen said that he was sorry about what had happened to her and that the team should have put up barriers between Thomas and the women. *But if Representative Cohen thinks that barriers should have been put up, it must be because he knows there is a difference between Thomas and the women—what might that mysterious difference be?* I once asked Scanlan if anyone at Penn, at any point, even hinted at taking any action against Thomas. She, who had survived a sexual assault at sixteen, got tears in her eyes, said no, and talked about how the experience of having to share a locker room with him for two practices per day throughout an entire season gave her nightmares.

However, this goes far beyond Democrats in the federal government. It has permeated every Democratic office at every level of government all over the country. Numerous states have in place some form of erasing women and girls either in law or policy. For example, twenty-three states have laws on the books that list "gender identity" as a protected category and eight more have policies in place interpreting existing prohibitions on sex discrimination to include discrimination on the basis of "gender identity." These are overwhelmingly (but not exclusively) blue states. In April 2021, Texas Democratic Representative James Talarico announced during a hearing on a bill to protect women's sports that there are six sexes. *That's* how ridiculous Democrats are being.

Washington state law (under the leadership of Democrats) defines the word "sex" to mean "gender," which is outrageous from a feminist perspective. U.K. radical feminist Sheila Jeffreys calls gender "the foundation of the political system of male domination." Unlike sex, which is real and grounded in material reality, gender is purely a social construction that is loaded with various patriarchal roles, values, and expectations. For example, women are expected to be sweet, docile, and subservient to men, *because* we are women and *because* they are men. Expectations like these are imposed on the basis of sex. Accordingly, feminists call for the abolition of gender because from a feminist perspective, gender is a prison that keeps women in a position of subservience to men. For feminists, in other words, gender is a problem that is foisted upon us based on sex. To conflate sex and gender, as Washington state law does, is *itself* profoundly sexist.

In 2017, a man named Danica Roem made headlines as the "first out transgender person to be elected to the Virginia General Assembly" and the "first to both be elected and serve while openly transgender in any U.S. state legislature." As far as I can tell, what qualifies Roem to claim to have a woman identity is that he has long hair. As discussed above, a few years later, Sarah (Tim) McBride followed suit by being elected to the Delaware State Assembly. Stacie-Marie Laughton did the same in New Hampshire in 2020. Laughton would eventually face federal criminal charges of child exploitation after officials found more than 2,500 text messages between him and a teacher at a day care center that contained at least four sexually explicit pictures of children between three and five years of age. In 2022, a man who goes by the name Zooey Zephyr was elected to serve in the Montana State Legislature. Zephyr was born Zachary Raasch in Billings, Montana. He grew up in Montana and Washington state, and later studied at the University of Washington. In 2019, he announced his woman identity and in 2022 (on the night he was being elected to office) he flew to New York to have a vaginoplasty surgery. In 2023, he was expelled from the legislature after saying that legislators had "blood on their hands" for enacting a law to protect children from sterilization and mutilation and a mob of activists stormed the capitol to support him. Leigh Finke is another man with a woman identity who assumed office in the Minnesota House of Representatives in 2023 (and earned a Woman of the Year award from *USA Today* for it).

Roem, McBride, Laughton, Zephyr, and Finke are all Democrats. I am unaware of any other men who claim to have woman identities serving in the legislatures of any other states or of any men who claim to have woman identities serving as Republicans. I do know that there is one man, who does not claim to have a woman identity, who has been throwing women and girls and the material reality of sex under the bus for several years in California, and he deserves special mention. That man is named Scott Wiener and he serves in the California state senate.

As bad as Democrats are on this topic, all over the country, possibly the worst offender is Scott Wiener. He is so much worse than the others because not only does he support efforts to eradicate sex in the law, he has made it one of his signature issues. He is responsible for laws on the books in California that make it possible for men to be housed in women's prisons based on their woman identities (regardless of the charge of conviction), encourage vulnerable children to travel to the state to receive "gender-affirming care" without their parents' permission, permit the state courts to take custody of children (from California or otherwise) whose parents do not "affirm their gender," and get a parent's refusal to "affirm a child's gender" classified as child abuse. Journalist Abigail Shrier has argued that "On the grounds of making California more welcoming to LGBTQ youth, State Senator Scott Wiener is transforming the state into a haven for human trafficking." California Democratic governor Gavin Newsom generally signs every bill that Senator Wiener pushes through the state legislature that legislates sex out of existence, tramples on women's rights, places convicted murderers and rapists in women's prisons, and encourages the sex trafficking of children. This is what the left in America has become.

Traditionally "Progressive" Organizations

Organizations in the U.S. nonprofit sector that were once known for their leftist progressive values have become machines in promoting the regressive, sexist, homophobic, authoritarian regime that is "gender identity." Most rank-and-file Democrats who have profound respect for these organizations, based on the organizations' track record of actual civil rights advocacy, probably do not know this. Progressives all over the country probably continue to support these groups (including financially) without understanding that they have all been captured. I know that I did so for years before understanding what was happening.

The Arcus Foundation

The Arcus Foundation, founded by billionaire Jon Stryker, states on its website that it divides its giving into two categories: Social Justice and Great Apes & Gibbons. However, a quick glance at the list of 2022 grants on its website demonstrates that in fact, its Social Justice giving program provides grants only to groups that are advancing a "gender identity" agenda.[8] Every single Social Justice grant mentions advocacy on behalf of some form of "trans," "non-binary," "queer," or some version of the LGBTQIA+ acronym (none of them exclusively focused on lesbians, gay men, or bisexual people). The total comes to over $6.6 million from the Arcus Foundation to progressive groups to advance its "gender identity" agenda in a single year. And although it was not an Arcus grant, Stryker gave $15 million to the ACLU in 2021 to advance its "gender identity" agenda. That is an astonishing sum of money to go to a single nonprofit as a one-time gift. The Arcus Foundation (on whose board Maya Harris serves) clearly does not care about any type of "social justice" other than "gender identity," and it certainly has no regard for women and girls as a sex class.

The ACLU

The ACLU has been receiving funding from the Arcus Foundation at least since 2007, received $15 million from Stryker of the Arcus Foundation in 2021, and received another $100,000 from Jennifer Pritzker in 2021 to advance "gender identity" in Tennessee. It has also been doing a smashing job of pushing the "gender identity" agenda on everyone over the years.

---

[8] These are listed in the Appendix.

The ACLU, once a venerable institution that stood for freedom of speech and expression, women's rights, and public transparency, has become a shill for the "gender identity" industry. When I received my offer to work there in 2012, I was thrilled because I didn't know about any of this at the time. I was excited to work on its campaigns against mass incarceration and police militarization. I didn't know that it had already caved to "gender identity" ideology.

Founded in 1920, the ACLU initially focused on freedom of speech, mainly for anti-war protesters. It later expanded the scope of its priorities to include free speech rights for artists and striking workers, racial discrimination, police misconduct, and, during World War II, the unlawful internment of Japanese-Americans. Justice Ruth Bader Ginsburg founded its Women's Rights Project in 1972 and worked hard to secure equal rights for women and girls in the law before being appointed to the federal judiciary. It is hard to know when the ACLU really got going on its project to erase women and girls, as well as gay men, in the law; reading and examining some of the things the ACLU has had to say about its history of working on this topic gives one the feeling of being completely gaslit.

There is an undated post on its website titled "The Work of the ACLU: Linking Gender Identity and Gay Rights." The only clue as to when this might have been written is this: "The ACLU recently filed a friend of the court brief in the Brandon Teena case in Nebraska." This refers to a case brought by the mother of a lesbian named Teena Brandon. Brandon was born in 1972 in Nebraska and was sexually abused by her stepfather. Her mother did not accept her attraction to women. Brandon eventually moved across the state, called herself Brandon Teena, and passed herself off as a young man. At one point, though, she was arrested for forgery and held in the female unit of the local jail. Jail officials reported her by her real name and everyone found out that she was female. Eventually a group of vicious men would go on to sexually assault, rape, and murder her. In the case, Brandon's mother argued that county officials abused and failed to protect Brandon, and in doing so, bore some responsibility for the murder. I'm glad that the suit was brought and happy to report that JoAnn Brandon ultimately prevailed before the Nebraska Supreme Court in 2001, which found that the county's conduct was "extreme and outrageous, beyond all possible bounds of decency, and is to be regarded as atrocious and utterly intolerable in a civilized community."

What is most pertinent about the case to the topic of this book is that the ACLU's brief before the Nebraska Supreme Court includes this statement: "Hate crimes are crimes motivated by hatred of or bias against the victim because of the victim's race, color, religion, national origin, ethnicity, gender, sexual orientation, or gender identity." I have no doubt that countless crimes are motivated by hatred of or bias against victims because of race, color, religion, national origin, ethnicity, sex, and sexual orientation. But the inclusion of the phrase "gender identity" in this statement, apparently made at some point before 2001, surprised me.

The ACLU's brief cited two statutes as authoritative support for the statement that hate crimes include crimes motivated by "gender identity." But *neither of these statutes provides any support for the statement at all.* One law the ACLU cited is a federal statute that lays out the duties of the U.S. Sentencing Commission (a body that decides ranges of sentences that should be imposed in federal criminal matters). There is literally no mention of "gender identity," or even hate or bias crimes in the statute *at all.* The other one is a Minnesota law that addresses civil damages for bias crimes. So at least that statute concerns hate (bias) crimes. But it doesn't mention "gender identity" *either*. It defines a "bias offense" as "conduct that would constitute a crime and was committed because of the victim's or another's actual or perceived race, color, religion, sex, sexual orientation, disability, age, or national origin." It makes no mention of "gender identity" *whatsoever*. The ACLU appears to just be making all of this up. In any event, the ACLU's support for "gender identity" appears to date at least back to the early 2000s.

The timing of this is consistent with the emergence on the "gender identity" scene of a possibly even more insidious organization, HRC (discussed below). As mentioned above, by 2021, the ACLU was receiving $15 million donations from Stryker, a billionaire who is widely known to fund efforts to abolish sex all over the world. In 2000, Stryker founded the Arcus Foundation, which works to "ensure that LGBT people and our fellow apes thrive in a world where social and environmental justice are a reality." Stryker is also heir to the Stryker Corporation medical supply company fortune. Arcus has been called "the nation's largest LGBT funder."

There is another page on the ACLU's website called "ACLU History: Advocacy on Behalf of Transgender People," and it was last updated in August 2012. I was working there at that time, and none of this was on my radar at all. Even if it had been, I'm not sure I would have cared, because at that time, I had no idea about the threats that the ideology poses to women and girls. The ACLU has been working hard to erase sex in the law ever since. As far as I know, it has been involved in every lawsuit in the federal judiciary where *either* a male plaintiff is challenging a law or policy that protects single-sex spaces (and the ACLU is on the side of the man) *or* a female plaintiff is challenging a law or policy that obliterates single-sex spaces (and the ACLU is on the side of the law or policy). It went out of its way to intervene in WoLF's *Chandler* case, discussed in Chapter 2, on behalf of incarcerated men who want to be housed in the California women's prison.

Not only has the ACLU been working hard to advance "gender identity" throughout the federal judiciary, it has also been working hard to rewrite history to suggest that "trans" is a decades-old civil rights movement, trans-washing gay rights advocacy out of history. The ACLU has a page on its website called the "Trans Timeline." On its face, the timeline looks and reads like a typical timeline of a civil rights movement. But it is actually a series of misleading assertions and outright lies. This is all part of the "gender identity" industry's mission to persuade everyone that "trans" is a decades-long civil rights struggle. It is historical revisionism at its finest and it is blatantly homophobic.

The timeline begins, as these things so often do, with the 1969 Stonewall rebellion. It correctly states that on July 28 of that year, the police raided Stonewall, a gay club in Greenwich Village. But it also states that "trans and nonbinary individuals played a large part throughout the riots, including Marsha P. Johnson and Sylvia Rivera." In fact, Johnson was a gay man and "drag queen," who never claimed to have been present at the beginning of the riots. Rivera was also a "drag queen." Together, the two started the Street Transvestite Action Revolutionaries (STAR) group. Both have since died.

The first known use of the word "transgenderism" was in 1965, in the book *Sexual Hygiene and Pathology*, by psychiatrist John F. Oliven. But the term was not widely in use at that time. Feminist professor Janice Raymond warned us about it in her 1994 introduction to the reprint of her famous exposé *The Transsexual Empire*, and its use has grown with astonishing speed since the late nineties. It is unclear whether Johnson or Rivera ever referred to themselves that way, but the possibility seems very unlikely. It is much more difficult to find clues as to the origin of the term "non-binary" to refer to sex or gender. By all accounts, it evolved from the term "genderqueer," which was used in the eighties and nineties to refer to people who refused to conform to sex stereotypes. It is undoubtedly true that there were many people at Stonewall who refused to conform to sex stereotypes, but it defies reason to think that they were running around calling themselves "non-binary." In any event, the ACLU doesn't even bother to mention Storme DeLarverie, a lesbian who was definitely at Stonewall. DeLarverie was reportedly handcuffed and forced into a police car (after escaping several times) and was reported to have shouted "Why don't you guys do something?" at bystanders who were looking on, kicking off the rebellion. In other words, Stonewall was started by a lesbian, not by any "trans women."

Next it states that in 1967, the ACLU "Oppose[d] Ordinance Targeting Transgender People." In fact, the ordinance being referenced was a Los Angeles ordinance called Rule 9, a local rule that made it illegal for club performers to "impersonate by means of costume or dress a person of the opposite sex" without a special permit. It was essentially a rule against drag performance and it implicitly acknowledged that sex is real and that there are two of them. The rule did not mention, let alone target, "transgender people."

It goes on to state that in 1975, the city of Minneapolis became the "1st city to pass anti-discrimination law for transgender people." In fact, what happened was that in 1975, Minneapolis passed an ordinance prohibiting discrimination based on same-sex attraction and/or nonconformity with sex stereotypes. The ACLU insists that this ordinance was passed to protect "transgender people," but that is just obviously not true at all. The language of the ordinance said that it was meant to prohibit discrimination based on "affectional preference," where "affectional preference" meant "having or manifesting an emotional or physical attachment to another consenting person or persons," or "having or projecting a self-image not associated with one's biological maleness or femaleness." This ordinance *was* extremely progressive for its time, in that it appears to have been the first to protect lesbians and gay men from discrimination, and to protect anyone on the basis of nonconformity with sex stereotypes. Great! However, the ACLU is just lying when it says that it was the first to protect "transgender people." There is no indication whatsoever that the law was meant to protect some non-existent category of people for whom sex is irrelevant ("transgender people"). The law explicitly recognized that maleness and femaleness are biological.

The timeline claims that in 1985, Merissa Sherrill Lynn published a magazine called *Transgender Tapestry*. This lie is as blatant as it gets. *Tapestry* began as a newsletter rather than as a magazine and as far as I can tell, it started in 1978. The reason I say that is because the earliest edition I have found is referred to as *Tapestry Newsletter #7* and it is dated January 8, 1979. In it, Lynn refers to himself as a "cross-dresser by pleasure and inclination" and as a "transvestite philosopher." The newsletter morphed into *TV-TS Tapestry* (TV refers to transvestite and TS refers to transsexual) in June 1979 and then into *Tapestry: The Journal for Persons Interested in Crossdressing and Transsexualism* in 1985. Throughout the late seventies, eighties, and half of the nineties, it never pretended to be about anything other than cross-dressing and transsexualism. Lynn never claimed that he was interested in any of this other than for sexual gratification and philosophizing. This was a social club for cross-dressing fetishists, and there simply is no indication whatsoever that this social club for cross-dressing fetishists was holding itself out as a political movement. In 1995, it turned into *Transgender Tapestry*, ten years after the ACLU claims that a magazine with that title was created.

Some will say, "Who cares, Kara. Words change, so what?" And I get that. My point is that if the ACLU wants to take a social club for cross-dressing fetishists that started in the seventies and turn it into something different today, it should just say that it is doing that. Instead, it is blatantly lying to everyone by saying that this social club for cross-dressing fetishists was part of a decades-old political movement to secure legal rights for "transgender" people. Legitimate civil rights movements do not need to lie about their history or their agenda.

The next item is from 1986 and it states: "Louis Sullivan starts a local support group called FTM." This statement is true on its face. However, that group still had nothing to do with the contemporary movement to enshrine the words "transgender" and "gender identity" in the law. Lou Sullivan was born Sheila Jean Sullivan in 1951 in suburban Milwaukee. By all accounts, the person who would become Lou started wearing stereotypically male clothing in 1973. Sullivan referred to herself as a "female transvestite" in 1973 and as a "female-to-male transsexual" in 1975. She eventually moved to San Francisco, started taking testosterone, and had a double mastectomy and genital reconstructive surgery. Unlike many women who claim a "trans" identity, Sullivan was straight and wanted to be known as a gay man. She did start a group called FTM International, but it was more of a peer support group than a political movement, and I have been unable to find any indication that Sullivan spent any time at all engaged in grassroots organizing or political activism on behalf of "transgender people." To the extent that Sullivan was involved in political activism, it was gay rights activism, because she thought of herself as a gay man. None of her activism had anything to do with "rights for transgender people." Sullivan died of AIDS in 1991.

The timeline begins the nineties with the claim that in 1991, "[p]rominent trans rights and HIV activist, Connie Norman, starts her radio talk show." It is true that Norman did some great work in the fight against HIV and AIDS (he eventually died of it in 1996) and that he launched a radio talk show in 1991. It is not true that Norman was a "prominent trans rights" activist. Norman was a gay man who struggled with addiction as a teenager and ended up homeless on the streets of Hollywood. He would eventually become clean and live with his partner Bruce in Los Angeles. He underwent genital reconstruction surgery in 1976 and referred to himself as a "transsexual," but he also continued to refer to himself as a gay man. Nothing about his surgery changed that. Norman talked openly about gay rights issues and about other issues that specifically affected gay men and lesbians; there is simply no indication that Norman ever talked about "transgender" anything. He referred to himself as a gay man and also as a transsexual because he had his penis surgically removed. *But there is no evidence that he advocated that other men remove their penises or that he advocated for "transsexualism" more generally*. The ACLU simply has to refer to him as a "trans activist" in order to persuade everyone that he was part of a decades-long civil rights struggle for "trans." It is just not true. One has to wonder why the ACLU is so desperate to erase the sexual orientation of this prominent gay rights activist who appears to have wanted to do nothing other than improve the lives of gay men and lesbians. The ACLU is posthumously "transing" a gay man who died of AIDS, which is pretty revolting. His story is sad and, in my view, he deserves much more credit for his gay rights advocacy than the ACLU is giving him.

As explained above, the timeline includes an entry from 1975 stating that the city of Minneapolis became the "1st city to pass anti-discrimination law for transgender people." In fact, what happened was that in 1975, Minneapolis passed a very progressive ordinance prohibiting discrimination on the basis of same-sex attraction and/or nonconformity with sex stereotypes and had nothing whatsoever to do with "transgender people." The timeline also states that in 1993, Minnesota became the "1st state to pass [an] anti-discrimination law for transgender people." Apparently, the Minnesota Department of Human Rights appears to be under the same impression because its website states that in 1993, "sexual orientation, which includes gender identity in statute, was added as a protected class in the areas of employment, housing, public accommodations, public service, educational institutions, credit, and business discrimination."

This simply just isn't true. The actual law protects people from discrimination in employment because of race, color, creed, religion, national origin, sex, marital status, disability, status regarding public assistance, sexual orientation, familial status, and age. It protects people from discrimination in housing because of race, color, creed, religion, national origin, sex, marital status, disability, status regarding public assistance, sexual orientation, and familial status. It also protects people from discrimination in public accommodations because of race, color, creed, religion, national origin, sex, sexual orientation, and disability. It goes on to protect people from discrimination in public services and education based on similar categories. The words "trans gender" and "gender identity" simply do not appear in the law. The Minnesota legislature can add those words to the statute any time it wants to, but it hasn't done it (yet). Saying that it has (let alone that it did so in 1993) is just a blatant lie.

One entry states, vaguely: "1997: Supreme Court Strikes Down Online LGBTQ Restrictions." I believe, but can't be entirely sure, that this is a reference to the Supreme Court's 1997 decision in *Reno v. ACLU*, which did not, on its face, have anything whatsoever to do with "LGBTQ restrictions." Congress enacted the Communications Decency Act (CDA) in 1996. Its stated purpose was to prevent minors from gaining access to sexually explicit materials on the internet (a worthy objective, it turns out). The law prohibited any individual from knowingly transmitting obscene or indecent messages to a recipient under the age of eighteen. But nowhere did the act target any groups or individuals based on sexual orientation or other status.

The Court ultimately ruled that the act violated the First Amendment because the words in question were not sufficiently defined to give internet users a clear understanding of exactly which internet transmissions were prohibited. In coming to its conclusion, the Court posed this very reasonable question: "Could a speaker confidently assume that a serious discussion about birth control practices, homosexuality,… or the consequences of prison rape would not violate the CDA? This uncertainty undermines the likelihood that the CDA has been carefully tailored to the congressional goal of protecting minors from potentially harmful materials." In other words, the Court ultimately ruled that *because internet users could not reasonably be confident that conversations about certain topics, including homosexuality, would not be prosecuted under the law, the law unconstitutionally abridged such users' free speech rights.*

We are all free to think whatever we want to think about the outcome of the case. I know people who think the Court got it right and people who think that the Court got it wrong. But I do not think any reasonable person can honestly say that the decision "struck down online LGBTQ restrictions" *because the CDA contained no such restrictions.* If I have this wrong, and if the ACLU's timeline is referring to a different case, I hope someone will tell me (the ACLU also could have done us all a favor by simply providing the case name, but that would reveal its disingenuousness about what this case was about). I doubt that I am wrong about this. The ACLU is saying that the decision "struck down LGBTQ restrictions" because it serves its own narrative that "trans" and "gender identity" are a decades-long civil rights struggle. None of this should be surprising. The ACLU has been lying about a lot of things for a long time, including the notion that some men are women. In a recent court filing, it argued that there is no such thing as biological sex. There appears to be no end to its willingness to lie about anything to persuade Americans that they are advancing a legitimate civil rights movement.

Skipping ahead to the 2000s, the timeline states: "2003: Petra Leilani Akwai becomes the 1st transgender person officially welcomed to the White House." I have found zero evidence that this is even remotely true. What I have found is evidence that in 2003, the White House hosted a reunion of the Yale Class of 1968, which was all male. Akwai, who had had his penis surgically removed in 2002, happened to be present for it, and he bumped into President George W. Bush while there. Akwai states, "I was in the receiving line, I was dressed in an evening dress, and I was being escorted by a male friend from the Yale class of 1986. And I said, 'Hello, George.' And in order for him not to be confused, in case he hadn't been briefed, because our class was all male, I said, 'I guess the last time we spoke, I was still living as a man.'" President Bush graduated from the Yale Class of 1968. He invited his class to a reunion at the White House while he was president. He bumped into one of his former classmates, who had had his penis removed and was wearing an evening dress. That's it. For the ACLU to paint this as some sort of massive development in the history of the "movement for transgender rights" is completely disingenuous. There is just no evidence that Akwai was "officially welcomed" at all, "transgender" or not. All he had to do to get an invite to that reunion was be a male member of the Yale Class of 1968, which he was. If the ACLU wants to make a big deal out of the fact that this man had his penis removed, it can do that, but it shouldn't lie and say that this man was "officially welcomed" to the White House as some sort of statement about the "movement for trans liberation."

Starting in the 2010s, the ACLU's representations start to appear more true than they did in the 2000s, because it was during this decade that the ACLU and others started to succeed in their efforts to persuade public officials that it makes sense to obliterate sex throughout law and society by lying about material reality. The first entry in the 2010s is: "2011: *Fields v. Smith*." This, of course, tells us nothing about anything. However, a brief review of what the case was about tells us exactly how the ACLU manipulates facts and law. The ACLU's webpage about the case says that "[I]n 2005, the state of Wisconsin passed a law that barred prison doctors from providing transgender inmates medically necessary hormone therapy or sex reassignment surgery while in state custody." This is not true. The state law *prohibited the expenditure of public funds* for hormones or surgery. It did not *bar* prison doctors from doing anything, nor did it prohibit anyone from spending private funds on hormones or surgeries. It also did not bar anyone from doing anything that was medically necessary. Using hormones and surgeries to make a person appear to be more like the opposite sex is simply cosmetic surgery which, by definition, is not "medically necessary."

The upshot of all of this is that if "trans" were indeed a decades-long civil rights movement, the ACLU would not have to perpetuate these lies; legitimate civil rights movements do not need to lie about their history. Instead, it lies over and over in its attempt to get everyone to go along with the lie that sex isn't real. One of the ACLU's primary proponents of "gender identity" is Chase Strangio, who is on public record as saying that the North Carolina state legislature invented biological sex in 2016. Strangio evidently believes that a U.S. state legislature invented biological sex in 2016. One wonders how, if that's true, human beings all over the world have been procreating for all this time. The ACLU, in other words, has been working very hard to persuade the American people that sex is a social construct. This is patently absurd on its face.

The ACLU still cares about free speech, but only some. In November 2018, a professor named Dr. Nicholas Meriwether sued his employer, Shawnee State University (a public school), for disciplining him for refusing to use so-called "preferred pronouns" or opposite-sex titles when referring to students in class. He eventually won his case when the Sixth Circuit Court of Appeals ruled in his favor. In April 2022, the case concluded with a settlement in which the university agreed to pay $400,000 in damages and attorney's fees, rescind the disciplinary action, and affirm Dr. Meriwether's right to address students consistent with his beliefs. The ACLU was nowhere to be found.

And so much for transparency. In 2021, a woman filed a FOIA request, seeking to find out how many male inmates were being housed in Washington state's women's prison. For reasons that are completely unclear, the ACLU learned about her request and *sued to block it*. As far as I know, this is the only time the ACLU has ever moved to block a private citizen's effort to obtain what should be publicly available information.

On September 18, 2021, the one-year anniversary of the death of Justice Ruth Bader Ginsburg, the ACLU posted a quote about abortion rights from Justice Ginsburg's 1993 Supreme Court confirmation hearing, editing out all words that identified abortion as a right that pertains exclusively to women—that is, female humans, the only humans capable of getting pregnant. Justice Ginsburg's original statement read: "The decision whether or not to bear a child is central to a woman's life, to her well-being and dignity. It is a decision she must make for herself. When government controls that decision for her, she is being treated less than a fully adult human responsible for her own choices." The version that the ACLU posted read: "The decision whether or not to bear a child is central to a [person's] life, to [their] well-being and dignity.... When the government controls that decision for [people], [they are] being treated as less than a fully adult human responsible for [their] own choices." It is difficult to imagine a graver insult to one of the most prominent women's rights advocates in the history of the United States of America and the founder of the ACLU's own Women's Rights Project than to edit women completely out of one of her most famous quotes on the anniversary of her death.

In 2023, the ACLU lamented that the state of Florida had executed a man named Duane Owen. This is true, and I stand with the ACLU in opposing the death penalty. However, the ACLU's post about the matter complained that "The state of Florida never provided medically necessary gender-affirming care to Duane Owen—causing her enormous suffering and violating her right to be free from cruel and unusual punishment for the more than 30 years she was in state custody." But virtually every media outlet to report on the execution referred to Owen as the man that he was. Even though there were some minor indications that Owen wanted to be viewed as a woman, no one (including psychiatric experts) but the ACLU was buying it. And the ACLU could not be bothered to mention that Owen had been convicted of fatally stabbing a fourteen-year-old girl named Karen Slattery and then raping her corpse, and later raping a woman named Georgianna Worden in her own bed and bludgeoning her to death with a hammer.

The ACLU also fully supports "gender-affirming care" (i.e., life altering and possibly threatening medical experiments) for minors. It is not an exaggeration to say that the ACLU—once a bastion of civil rights and civil liberties—today is on a mission to destroy the lives of women and children. It has sued numerous times to block state laws that are designed to protect minors from the savagery of "gender-affirming care." The ACLU's capitulation to "gender identity" is rampant, complete, and possibly irreversible. Its social media posts feature content related to "trans" and "gender identity" more than any other topic. If any American who cares about the material reality of sex has any hope that the ACLU might be willing to take a stand for women and girls, for free speech, for children, or for transparency, now would be a good time to let go.

GLAAD

Like the ACLU, GLAAD has been trans-washing gay rights advocacy, including its own, out of history for several years now. Unlike the ACLU, GLAAD was specifically established to fight for the rights of lesbians and gay men. So as appalling as the ACLU's trans-washing of gay rights advocacy is, for GLAAD to do it is arguably even worse. Anyone on the political left who cares about the rights of same-sex attracted people should be disgusted by this.

GLAAD started out as the Gay and Lesbian Anti-Defamation League, but it soon had to change its name due to complaints by the Anti-Defamation League (ADL). It formally got going as the Gay and Lesbian Alliance Against Defamation in 1985 to protest against what it viewed as defamatory and sensationalized reporting on HIV and AIDS and on lesbians and gay men more generally. GLAAD did indeed do a good amount of work representing the interests of lesbians and gay men for several years. In 1987, for example, it persuaded the *New York Times* to use the words "gay" and "lesbian." At that time, a lot of people (including GLAAD) found use of the term "homosexual" offensive because it suggested that same-sex attraction is a deviant aberration from the norm and because it connoted the idea that same-sex attraction is a mental illness (the American Psychiatric Association classified it as such until 1973). Today, most of the lesbians and gay men that I know do not object to the words "homosexual" and "homosexuality," in part because same-sex attraction has become so much more accepted in society than it was back then. But in the seventies and eighties, removing the word "homosexual" from society's lexicon by getting it out of the *New York Times* was considered a pretty major accomplishment in the movement to protect the rights of lesbians and gay men.

In 1988, GLAAD persuaded NYNEX (an American phone company serving Maine, Massachusetts, New Hampshire, Rhode Island, Vermont, and New York from 1984 to August 1997) to list gay and lesbian organizations in the yellow pages under their own heading titled "Gay & Lesbian Services." This might seem like nothing today, but it was a big deal in terms of persuading society to accept same-sex attraction as legitimate in 1988. In 1990, its San Francisco chapter worked with the Bay Area Network of Gay and Lesbian Educators to launch Project 21—a California statewide effort to get the state Board of Education to include fair, accurate, and unbiased information about lesbians, gay men, and bisexual people in school curriculums. By November of that year, it had eleven chapters all over the country, from Boston and Chicago to San Diego, all of them working to advance the interests of lesbians and gay men.

In 1991, GLAAD persuaded Hallmark to end a ban on the use of the word "lesbian" on its cards. Later in the same year, it launched a series of ads and op-eds titled "The Bill of Wrongs," which listed ten basic rights that were denied to lesbians and gay men based on their sexual orientation. In 1993, GLAAD received an American Advertising Award for a billboard campaign that celebrated an expecting lesbian couple. In March of that year, it organized a turn-out of 106 same-sex couples to celebrate the first day of legal same-sex domestic partnerships in New York City. In May, it unveiled "Subway Shortstops," an ad campaign featuring lesbian softball players on display at the Yankee Stadium/161st St. subway station. In June, it coordinated the first Annual Day of Compassion, with daytime TV shows honoring people suffering from HIV/AIDS.

In 1994, the New York and Los Angeles chapters merged, creating a national organization with a board of directors, dedicated to championing the rights of lesbians and gay men. In 1995, GLAAD created an "Images" campaign to celebrate the Hawaii Supreme Court's 1993 decision ruling in favor of same-sex marriage. In 1996, it proclaimed October to be Lesbian & Gay History Month. In 1997, GLAAD coordinated a "Come Out with Ellen" campaign, coordinating over 1,500 house parties and hosting coming-out parties in New York City, San Francisco, Los Angeles, and Washington D.C. In 1998, GLAAD coordinated media outreach and vigils following the tragic death of Matthew Shepard, a gay university student who was brutally beaten to death in Laramie, Wyoming. GLAAD did a good job of amplifying the message that lesbians and gay men are at risk of being on the receiving end of horrific violence because of sexual orientation. This is all to say that at one time, GLAAD could credibly claim to represent the interests of lesbians and gay men. That would later change.

GLAAD changed its name again in 2013 from the Gay and Lesbian Alliance Against Defamation to, simply, GLAAD. It stated that its name change "brings with it a commitment from the organization to incorporate trans and bi people in their efforts to support the LGBT community in its entirety.... Our commitment to marriage equality, employment nondiscrimination, and other LGBT issues is stronger than ever, and now our name reflects our work on transgender issues as well as our work with allies." And with that, GLAAD publicly stated that it was no longer focused on representing the interests of lesbians and gay men exclusively. The same year, it gave an "Advocate for Change" award to former President Bill Clinton, which is odd, given the former president's anti-gay history. As president, Clinton signed the 1996 Defense of Marriage Act (which allowed states not to recognize same-sex marriages performed in other states and forbade the federal government from granting any of the over one thousand benefits to married gay couples that it provides to married straight ones) as well as legislation codifying the military's "Don't Act, Don't Tell" regulation barring homosexuals from serving openly in the armed services.

Also in 2013, GLAAD got a new co-chair of its National Board of Directors: Jennifer (James) Finney Boylan. James Boylan was born in Valley Forge, Pennsylvania, in 1958. In 2000, he decided that he was a woman named Jennifer and, in his words, "started the long and complex process of changing from male to female." There is, of course, no such thing as changing from male to female. At best, he likely would have started taking estrogen and possibly had some surgeries to make himself look slightly more like a woman than he did previously. A Google image search reveals that he is quite obviously a man with long blond hair. In a 2009 op-ed in the *New York Times* (six years before the Supreme Court legalized same-sex marriage), Boylan argued that there were already countless gay marriages in the U.S. because a lot of legally married straight people had "changed genders." What he was saying was that if a person in a legally married straight couple "changed genders," that instantly turned the marriage into a gay one. But this is pure obfuscation and it is part of why there is so much confusion today.

Like the ACLU, GLAAD has been trans-washing history and erasing what was a very successful movement for the rights of lesbians and gay men. It does this by simply adding the letter T to descriptions of events and developments that were, in fact, about gay rights advocacy. It states that in 1988, "LGBT activists form GLAAD chapters in Los Angeles and San Francisco," despite there being no evidence that "trans" had anything to do with it at the time. It also states that in 1990, it persuaded the Empire State Building to illuminate with lavender lights to "celebrate LGBT pride month," but at that time, there was no such thing as "LGBT pride month." A *Los Angeles Times* article from that year notes, accurately, that "The Empire State Building, which is illuminated with green lights every St. Patrick's Day and red, white, and blue for the Fourth of July, [was] awash in lavender [that] month to honor Gay Pride Weekend" and that "the building's managers agreed to the special display after six years of lobbying by homosexual rights groups.... Lavender is the traditional color of the gay rights movement."

It asserts that in April 1993, it endorsed a March on Washington for "LGBT equality." In fact, the event was called the "March on Washington for Lesbian, Gay, and Bi Equal Rights and Liberation." During the 1994 Olympics, it successfully campaigned to keep a volleyball match out of Cobb County, Georgia because the county had an anti-gay resolution on the books. Today, GLAAD claims that its advocacy concerned an "anti-LGBT resolution," but records from the time show clearly that it was (rightfully) complaining about homophobia. It encouraged ongoing activism, urging members to thank the Atlanta Committee for the Olympic Games and to "encourage them to continue to recognize the diversity of all participants including gays and lesbians." None of this had anything to do with "trans." GLAAD is just trans-washing *its own* venerable history of gay-rights advocacy out of existence.

In 2023, GLAAD complained that "For more than a year, the New York Times has published irresponsible, biased coverage of transgender people" by platforming "anti-LGBTQ activists who spread inaccurate and harmful misinformation about transgender people and issues." The same year, the organization posted a truck outside the *Times* offices in New York, displaying digital billboards "protesting the paper's slanted and inaccurate coverage of trans people and topics." What the *Times* had done to deserve these accusations was, in fact, print a few op-eds by feminist Pamela Paul who, to the best of my knowledge, has never said a single negative thing about lesbians, gay men, bi-sexual people, or about gay rights advocacy in general. What Paul did, in contrast, is argue that both the left and the right are erasing women and that "gender identity" is an enshrinement of sex stereotypes (both of which are true). The *Times* had also published a handful of articles questioning the safety of "gender-affirming care" for minors.

GLAAD lists a dizzying array of corporate partners on its website. Its top donors are Gilead (a biopharmaceutical company), Ketel One Vodka, and Procter & Gamble (one of the world's largest sellers of personal and consumer health products). In 2019, Gilead launched its "TRANScend Community Impact Fund," "under the advisement of community advocates and experts from Transgender-led advocacy and healthcare organizations." In 2021, it distributed $4.7 million to such organizations. In partnership with Procter & Gamble, GLAAD runs its "Visibility Project"—a campaign to "drive and to sustain LGBTQ inclusion in advertising and marketing, harnessing the power to accelerate LGBTQ acceptance so business can be a true force for good." But again, despite the use of the "LGBTQ" acronym, none of its work any longer focuses on lesbians, gay men, or bisexual people. Additional corporate partners include Netflix, Walt Disney, Comcast NBC Universal, Paramount, Warner Brothers, Sony Music Group, Amazon, TikTok, Tinder, American Express, Cover Girl, Hallmark Media, and the Hearst Media company.

In June 2023, GLAAD published an open letter calling on Instagram, Facebook, YouTube, TikTok, and X to "stop the flow of anti-trans hate and malicious disinformation about trans healthcare." The letter claimed that questioning the efficacy or safety of "gender-affirming care" constitutes "disinformation and hate" that "plays an outsized role in the sharp increase in real-world anti-transgender targeting and violence." It claimed that "misgendering" someone (i.e., referring to a person using accurate pronouns) constitutes "hate speech" and dramatically proclaimed that "True allies do not profit from anti-LGBTQ hate." Notably, although it purported to be concerned about "anti-LGBTQ hate," it did not provide a single example of any hate speech about lesbians or gay men that it was concerned about. It was only concerned about "hate accounts targeting transgender, nonbinary, and gender non-conforming people." Appearing to buy into the hysteria, hundreds of celebrities signed the letter.

Like GLAAD, a similar organization, GLSEN, was initially established as an advocacy group for lesbian and gay rights. Specifically, it formed in 1990 as the Gay & Lesbian Independent School Teacher Network (GLISTN). Its purpose was to promote acceptance of lesbian and gay youth in schools. In 1996, it changed its name to GLSEN (the Gay, Lesbian & Straight Education Network) to "more reflect the importance of straight educators in shaping safe schools." Its current website says, "As GLSEN was founded by a group of teachers in 1990, we knew that educators play key roles in creating affirming learning environments for LGBTQ youth," but there is no evidence that it had anything to do with "BTQ youth." This is simply another example of trans-washing. Today, it is mostly focused on pushing learning materials that center on "gender identity" in schools. In 2023, Target gave the group over $2 million to promote policies encouraging teachers and school administrators to hide students' "trans" identities from their parents. Perhaps unsurprisingly, Target's Vice President of Brand Management has served as an executive board member and treasurer at GLSEN since 2021 and as a board member since 2019.

PFLAG is no different. PFLAG has roots going back into the early seventies and it was formally incorporated as Parents and Friends of Lesbians and Gays in 1982. Like both GLAAD and GLSEN, it started out doing some great work on behalf of lesbians and gay men, but things started to change in the late nineties. In 1998, it added "gender identity, including transgender people" to its mission statement. It claims to be the "first national LGBT organization to officially adopt a transgender-inclusive policy, vowing not only to include transgender people in all of its work, but also never to support any policies or laws that are not trans-inclusive." Presumably, that means that PFLAG does not even claim to represent the interests of lesbians or gay men who do not wish to affiliate themselves with people who claim to have "gender identities."

HRC

A lot of people who work to protect sex in the law, including many TERFs and gay men, assume that HRC was once a legitimate gay rights organization that only took a dramatic turn toward protecting "gender identity" in the law after marriage equality was won in 2015 with the Supreme Court's decision in *Obergefell v. Hodges*. I know that I used to think that. Until, that is, I read *The 11th Hour Blog*'s outstanding reporting on HRC and how far back its insidious agenda of abolishing sex really goes.[9]

In 2007, Democratic political consultant John Aravosis published an article in *Salon* magazine titled "How Did the T Get in LGBT?" He lamented: "In simpler times we were all gay. But then the word 'gay' started to mean 'gay men' more than women, so we switched to the more inclusive

---

[9] Part I of a three-part series on the topic is available on its website: https://www.the11thhourblog.com/post/all-aboard-the-human-rights-campaign-and-the-making-of-transgender-industry-leaders-part-i.

'gay and lesbian.' Bisexuals, who were only part-time gays, insisted that we add them too, so we did (not without some protest), and by the early 1990s we were the lesbian, gay and bisexual, or LGB community. Sometime in the late '90s, a few gay rights groups and activists started using a new acronym, LGBT—adding T for transgender/transsexual. And that's when today's trouble started."

Aravosis's main issue was with the death of the Employment Non-Discrimination Act (ENDA), which would have protected people from employment discrimination based on sexual orientation. It was written and sponsored by openly gay Representative Barney Frank. For a while, it looked like it had a good chance of passing. But then a lot of people got mad because it only protected sexual orientation, not "gender identity." Advocates succeeded in getting "gender identity" added, but it looked like that would have killed it, so Representative Frank took the reference to "gender identity" out of the bill. And then, according to Aravosis, "all hell broke loose." He said, "Gay activists and 220 national and local gay rights groups angrily demanded that gender identity be put back in the bill, guaranteeing its defeat for years to come. Many of them, suddenly and conveniently, found all sorts of 'flaws' with legislation that they had embraced the previous twenty-nine years. They convinced House Democratic leaders to delay action on ENDA till later in October. They'd rather have no bill at all than pass one that didn't include the transgendered." The answer to Aravosis's question "How did the T get in LGBT?" is, in my view, relatively simple: HRC.

HRC was incorporated in Washington D.C. in 1982. It did have its origins in gay rights advocacy. Its original by-laws stated that its purpose was "to advance the cause of lesbian and gay civil rights by supporting and educating candidates for federal elective office." At first it did engage in a lot of gay rights advocacy and was hard at work fighting the AIDS crisis in the eighties. But this would all change by 2002. Today, according to *The 11th Hour Blog*, "HRC's allegiance is to the industry profiteering not only from the AIDS crisis but also from the carefully crafted phenomenon of the 21st-century 'transgender' human." I agree.

In 2002, HRC launched its Corporate Equality Index (CEI), which grades companies on a scale of 0 to 100 percent, according to various criteria, including whether the company "has a written non-discrimination policy covering gender identity and/or expression in its employee handbook or manual." Its 2002 CEI awarded a score of 100 percent to thirteen companies and gushed that "While many of these companies have had a long commitment to lesbian and gay employees, most achieved a perfect score by adding gender identity to their non-discrimination policies." It lamented that "Only 17 employers, or 5 percent, include gender identity and/or expression in their non-discrimination statements." The same year, 26 percent of employers scored 86 percent, and for eighty of the companies in this category, the factor they lacked was a policy prohibiting discrimination based on "gender identity or expression." By 2002, therefore, HRC was going all in for "gender identity."

In 2007, it added a Healthcare Equality Index to its CEI. In 2022, it proclaimed on its website: "In its 15th year, the Healthcare Equality Index (HEI) is the national LGBTQ+ benchmarking tool that evaluates healthcare facilities' policies and practices related to the equity and inclusion of their LGBTQ+ patients, visitors and employees." This is code for: any healthcare entity that does not immediately "affirm" a patient's "gender identity," is going to get a bad rating from us. The HEI 2022 evaluates more than 2,200 healthcare facilities nationwide. One of the HEI's early advisors was Mara Keisling, a man who claims to have a woman identity, founded the National Center for Transgender Equality in 2003, and was active in the fight to kill the ENDA if it did not contain the magic words "gender identity." Keisling had also attended an HRC forum "on transgender issues" in January 2003, according to HRC's spring 2003 quarterly report, *Building Equality*. By 2011, the HEI was funded by grants from Pfizer, Inc., and later by the Pharmaceutical Research and Manufacturers of America (aptly named PhRMA).

HRC long ago abandoned any commitment to actual gay rights advocacy. In 2015, the group Pride at Work, a labor-rights organization that works to protect "LGBT" people in employment, criticized HRC's CEI for praising corporations like Walmart that had CEI-approved policies in place but that in practice discriminated against actual gay people. The group issued a resolution that "calls upon all labor unions, labor federations, and labor-affiliated organizations to cease funding HRC at all levels until these matters are addressed in a manner that shows HRC stands in solidarity with all working Americans for a fair, just and equal society."

"Gender identity" is big business and today, rather than advancing an authentic gay rights agenda, HRC is all in for the cash and the destruction of healthy human bodies, including those of minors. HRC spent eighty-eight days in 2009 visiting President Obama's White House and $885,375 in lobbying efforts in 2022 and $685,000 in 2021. In 2019, then chair of the Democratic National Committee, Tom Perez, announced that Joe Solmonese, a former HRC president, would serve as CEO of the 2020 Democratic National Convention Committee. In doing so, Perez praised Solmonese for his "experience serving as the head of major organizations supporting causes typically allied with the Democratic Party, such as LGBTQ rights and abortion rights." It is not an exaggeration to say that HRC largely controls the Democratic Party's official policies regarding "trans" and "gender identity."

Planned Parenthood

I used to support Planned Parenthood consistently, using my words and my dollars. Today, Planned Parenthood has gone from being an essential provider of women's healthcare to being a drug distributor for confused young people. In 2023, it posted: "It's not just about abortion. Advocating for abortion goes hand-in-hand with advocating for gender-affirming care and birth control. Access to health care is a right, no matter what." Back in 2017, HRC put out a video called *Planned Parenthood Saves Transgender Lives*. It is about how Planned Parenthood, once a leader in women's healthcare and a champion of abortion rights, has become a dispensary for young women (and some men) who want to poison their bodies with dangerous hormones (Solmonese, the former HRC president discussed above, serves as the chair of the board). How did this happen?

In 2016, Planned Parenthood posted: "Menstruators in New York started to #tweetthereceipt celebrating the repealed tampon tax." The next day, it reported that "Purvi Patel [a woman who had been unlawfully imprisoned after suffering a miscarriage] has been released from prison, but people continue to be criminalized for their pregnancy outcomes." As everyone knows, only women have periods and/or pregnancy outcomes. What was with the use of language (going all the way back to 2016) that erased women? Why was Planned Parenthood doing this to women—the demographic most served by its facilities? None of this is a mystery. The same billionaire philanthropists are behind the "gender identity" push coming from all these traditionally progressive organizations. Jennifer Pritzker (the man who served in the military as James and only later became Jennifer), Jon Stryker and his Arcus Foundation, and George Soros's Open Society Foundation all donate to these organizations and are behind the erasure of language to describe women and girls.

In 2015, it was revealed that thirty-eight private companies and organizations provided the bedrock of Planned Parenthood's funding. Those companies and groups had something in common: one of their largest shareholders was a company called BlackRock. BlackRock is an investment firm whose global director of DEI (Diversity, Equity, and Inclusion) is a man named Erica (Eric) Seremeta. He has been at BlackRock for over twenty-five years, the first twenty of them as a man. He is still a man, but in 2018, he decided that he is a woman. In its 2016–2017 Annual Report, Planned Parenthood stated, "We're expanding access to care—from pioneering research on self-injectable birth control to offering new services for our transgender patients. Planned Parenthood has focused on expanding services to people who are too often overlooked by the larger medical community—including trans patients. 17 [sic] states now have Planned Parenthood health centers that provide hormone therapy." Today, Planned Parenthood claims to be the nation's second greatest provider of hormone "therapy."

In 2023, a bank called Alternatives Federal Credit Union partnered with Planned Parenthood to create the "TransAction Financial

Empowerment Program," which "provides access to funds to support gender affirmation, such as hormone therapy, vocal coaching, new wardrobes, legal documentation updates, and surgeries/procedures—without the risks of high-interest credit or predatory lenders." This can come in the form of a personal loan or a line of credit (up to $20,000). All that is required to obtain the loan or line of credit is a "referral letter from a medical professional." The letter does not need to come from a physician, nor does it need to contain a "disclosure of detailed medical care." Interested parties are encouraged to contact Planned Parenthood to obtain the referral letter.

None of this is a mystery either. On its website, Planned Parenthood lists the following corporate partners and sponsors: Akers Bioscience, Inc. (a biotechnology firm that merged with pharma giant MyMD Pharmaceuticals in 2021); Atlas Genetics, Inc. (a genetic research center); Becton Dickinson (which boasts of being "one of the largest global medical technology companies in the world"); Beckman Coulter (a biopharmaceutical company); Boston University Medical Center (which has "gender neutral" bathrooms on its campus and encourages the use of hormones in adolescents); Cepheid (a molecular diagnostics company); Genticel (another biotechnology company); Gen-Probe/Hologic (this one appears to be one of the few corporate sponsors that are not engaged in some form of biotech, genetics research, and/or pharma); HRA Pharma Laboratories; LIA Diagnostics (which makes flushable pregnancy tests); Merck (one of the biggest pharmaceutical companies in the world); Medicines360 (also pharma); Melinta Therapeutics, Inc. (also pharma); Meridian Bioscience, Inc. (a subsidiary of Pfizer); Novan (also pharma); Roche Molecular Systems, Inc. (molecular diagnostics); Temple University (I'm not sure what that one is doing there); University of California-San Francisco (home of Diane Ehrensaft, discussed in more detail in Chapter 6, who actively promotes the idea of "transgender children" and pushes hormones on confused young people); Watson Laboratories (pharma); and Xagenic (molecular diagnostics). These companies are all invested in advancing the idea that it is possible to change sex (including in children) and they carry out their agenda partially through Planned Parenthood, among many other former stalwarts of women's rights and reproductive health.

The Women's March

As readers know, the Women's March began in January 2017, the day after Donald Trump took office. It was meant to serve as a signal that women were not about to stand for a president who once bragged about sexually assaulting women. I was there in Washington D.C. It was the largest single-day protest in U.S. history. What I didn't know at the time was that the event organizers had invited a man who claims to have a woman identity, and who has publicly acknowledged sexually assaulting a woman, to speak. The original march eventually morphed into an entire organization that has been sacrificing women and girls at the altar of "gender identity" ever since.

The man at the center of the 2017 controversy is named Cherno Biko. In July 2016, he posted on the forum *Medium* a confession to having sexually assaulted a trans-identifying female person (i.e., a woman). In his confession, he stated that the purpose of the assault had been to impregnate the victim with "non-binary babies" and create a "holy trinity" family. He said, "I found the second piece to the holy trinity I wanted to create, complete with a black trans man and our black non-binary baby.... The first time we had sex I can barely remember, as it followed a night of drinking and smoking but I know that we broke two of the most important rules... consent and safe sex. When [she] told me that [she] felt used and violated, I immediately apologized." This was public knowledge in 2016 and it is difficult to believe that the Women's March organizers didn't know or that they didn't vet their speakers.

Another male abuser platformed by the Women's March is Andi Dier, another man who claims to have a woman identity. Dier had verbally abused actor Rose McGowan during a 2018 book launch event in New York. McGowan was talking about her personal experiences of recovering from assault. Dier was there and he suddenly began yelling, "We get raped *more often*. We go through domestic violence *more often*. Trans women are in men's prisons, and what have you done for them?" McGowan explained that women experience a unique oppression on the basis of sex, and that got her labeled "transphobic." Dier then did an interview with the magazine *Them*, titled "Rose McGowan Broke Down in a Transphobic Rage: And We Spoke to the Trans Woman Who Confronted Her." The Women's March posted that interview, stating, "Please read this interview with the activist who engaged with Rose McGowan last night. Transphobia and denying trans women's identities is never okay. The pain we feel does not excuse the pain we cause others."

While all of this was going on, it was being revealed that Dier has a history of harassing girls. Multiple women reported that he had sexually abused them as children and some noted that he shares child sexual abuse materials on social media. One woman said, "Andi Dier personally sexually assaulted me and two of my friends when we were 13 years old." Others wondered whether he was "still go[ing] to the mall every weekend to hang out with 13-year-old girls." Dier has stated publicly, "I like younger girls in the same way I like brunettes.... Age is an insignificant marker. I like cute girls, sometimes they happen to be a bit young" and "It's f-cked up for someone to tell me I don't deserve my freedoms because they feel uncomfortable. You don't mystically wake up one day with the ability to consent. You have it before you're 18." This is, of course, legally inaccurate. Age of consent laws do exist, regardless of what Dier thinks about them.

Dier was active on the web forum Reddit at the time. In a subreddit about rape fantasies, he posted a photo of himself with the caption, "trans lesbian r*pemeat needs to be f*cked straight." In a Reddit community for rape survivors, he wrote, "If a girl was obeying me after I said 'get on your knees,' I'd think she was consenting" and shared his sexual assault fantasies. He has been known to repost from accounts called "leggyteenfilms" and "teenobsessed." On X, he "likes" photos of underage girls and follows accounts that describe themselves as MAPs ("minor-attracted person"). The Women's March has never issued an apology or a retraction for platforming Biko at its inaugural march or for promoting Dier's perverted and pornographic writings.

In 2022, the Women's March posted: "Trans women are women. That's it. That's the tweet." Feminists were outraged and told them so. In response, the Women's March dug in its heels, posting: "Stay mad," with a cartoon image of a woman's face labeled "Little Miss Fuck the TERFs." On top of that, it posted, "We got some transphobes BIG mad the other day so let us spell it out for you: 'Women' is a term that encompasses cis & trans women. When we talk about 'people who can give birth,' it's because those people aren't all women! They're girls, trans men, & non-binary ppl." Needless to say, this is ridiculous. It is only women (and occasionally minor girls) who give birth. I don't remember exactly what I had to say to the Women's March about all of this, but the account ended up blocking me on X, so I can no longer see what they are posting. Eventually the iconic Women's March logo was edited to include a profile image of a man's face on top of the images of women's profiles.

Today, the mission of the Women's March is "to harness the political power of diverse women and their communities to create transformative social change." By "diverse women," they mean women as well as men who claim to have woman identities. It states further that it "is a women-led movement providing intersectional education on a diverse range of issues and creating entry points for new grassroots activists & organizers to engage in their local communities through trainings, outreach programs and events." By "intersectional education," it means advancing the causes of men who claim to have woman identities. Finally, it states that it is "committed to dismantling systems of oppression through nonviolent resistance and building inclusive structures guided by self-determinism." Dismantling systems of oppression is great, especially if we are talking about the system of male domination. But that is not what this is about. By "building inclusive structures guided by self-determinism," it means that it wants to create structures that permit men to claim to be women and to get away with doing anything they want to women and girls.

Incidentally, the National Organization for Women (NOW) and the National Abortion and Reproductive Rights Action League (NARAL) are no better than Planned Parenthood or the Women's March. Both consistently post things like: "Trans women are women. Trans women are women. Our fight for feminism must include trans women." NARAL posts things like "Gender-affirming care is reproductive freedom. Gender-affirming care is reproductive freedom. Gender-affirming care is reproductive freedom. Everybody should be able to access the care they need [image of a 'trans pride' flag]." All these organizations were established to serve the needs of women and girls. All of them have completely sold out women and girls by defining women and girls out of existence as a distinct sex class. I am still on these groups' mailing lists for fundraisers. Each time I get one of their mailings, I return the envelope with stickers proclaiming that a woman is an adult human female. I would encourage other American Democratic women to do something similar.

* * * * *

I could go on and on. Literally every single so-called progressive organization in this country has been completely captured by the idea that some men are women and that it's a good idea to poison young people with dangerous hormones and life-altering surgeries. Most of them are paid handsomely to do it. The others simply go along. The capture is so extensive that it is impossible to list every single "progressive" organization that has caved to this dangerous ideology because it is all of them. At this point, it is safe to say that the entire American political left has been "queered."

Starting with post-modernism and Judith Butler's insistence that sex is a construct; to the Biden administration's full-throated embrace of Sarah (Tim) McBride, Dylan Mulvaney, Rachel (Richard) Levine, and the Yogyakarta Principles; to literally everyone in Democratic Party leadership at the federal level; to the country's traditionally progressive organizations; the American political and cultural establishment left has completely lost the plot. Again, I say this as a leftist, a radical feminist, and a lifelong Democrat. It's time for the American political and cultural left to get a grip.

CHAPTER 5

MEDIA CORRUPTION AND SCHOOL INDOCTRINATION

There are two actors arguably more responsible for abolishing sex and betraying women and girls than the Democratic Party leadership and the traditionally leftist organizations—the media, because it should have been there to hold the Democrats to account, and American schools, which have been feeding young people a steady diet of lies that is rotting their brains.

Media Corruption

According to the ACLU, "The freedom of the press, protected by the First Amendment, is critical to a democracy in which the government is accountable to the people. A free media functions as a watchdog that can investigate and report on government wrongdoing. It is also a vibrant marketplace of ideas, a vehicle for ordinary citizens to express themselves and gain exposure to a wide range of information and opinions." I agree with the ACLU that these are important values. Unfortunately, the American media has been nothing like a "watchdog," a "vibrant marketplace," or a "vehicle for ordinary citizens to express themselves" on matters pertaining to sex and gender. The idea that the mainstream American media has given exposure to a "wide range of information and opinions" on matters pertaining to sex and gender is laughable. Instead, the media has mainly functioned as a mouthpiece for the "gender identity" industry (including the ACLU) and been an abject failure in holding the political left to account for terrorizing women and girls and condoning the slicing up of young peoples' bodies.

In some ways, this is understandable. The Associated Press (AP) Style Book is a style and usage guide on American English grammar created by and for American journalists. It guides journalists in their use of language and grammar. It has been called the "journalist's bible." I have a copy of the 54th (2019) edition, which includes a lot of guidance about discussions of gender. It encourages journalists to use the acronyms LGBT and LGBTQ (or LGBTIA, "where appropriate"), states that the word "transgender" is "an adjective that describes people whose gender identity does not match the sex or gender they were identified as having at birth" (it also encourages use of words like "cisgender" and "non-binary") and insists on the use of "preferred pronouns." The 2023 edition goes further by encouraging journalists not to refer to "transgenderism" as an ideology, denying that sex exists, insisting on the use of the phrase "gender-affirming care," and abandoning the concept of preferred pronouns altogether, preferring the use of phrases like "the pronouns they use," "whose pronouns are," and "who uses the pronouns." It is all Orwellian double-speak, and it is designed to obscure the material reality of sex out of existence.

But journalists are not *required* by any law to follow the AP Style Book. They can, and often do, buck the trend. I am not aware of the rules in place at any particular media outlet, and I think it is likely that most *do* require their journalists to follow the guide. Therefore, Americans have been treated to a steady diet of headlines and articles that obscure reality and gaslight readers into thinking that some men are women and that sex is not real.

Mainstream Legacy Liberal Media

In March 2023, the magazine *Mother Jones* ran a story with the headline: "Inside the Secret Working Group That Helped Push Anti-Trans Laws Across the Country: Leaked emails give a glimpse of the religious-right networks behind the transgender health care bans." This is an insane headline about an absolute non-story. The "story" talks about various email exchanges that occurred between some leftist feminists (myself included), some conservatives, and some apolitical medical professionals about a South Dakota bill to protect minors from harmful hormones and surgeries. There was no "secret group"; it was just a bunch of people emailing each other about public policy. We debated things like, "What should the penalties be for prescribing puberty blockers? Should there be criminal penalties? Withdrawal of medical licenses? Should there be a cause of action for young people who come to regret their decisions? If so, what should the statute of limitations be? 10 years? 20? 25?" These are all perfectly sensible questions for people to discuss in the context of drafting legislation to protect children. *Only in the world of "trans" can a reporter get away with publishing a "story" about a bunch of people emailing each other about public policy.*

Imagine the following scenario: It is 2019. A bunch of people, some political conservatives, some political liberals, some apolitical scientists, find that they have a common cause on which they generally align: saving the planet by curbing carbon emissions. Forget for a moment whatever you may think about climate change, and just imagine the scenario. It is perfectly plausible, right? These people probably disagree about a lot of other things, but on these they agree: Saving the planet is a worthy objective and imposing limits on carbon emissions is a reasonable way to do that. So these people decide to do something about it. One of them is a legislator in a state and he thinks it would be a good idea to introduce legislation in his state. The people start emailing each other about what the right approach might be. They debate things like "What are the right targets? Automakers? Other businesses?" "What are the right limits? How strict should the limits be?" "What should the consequences of violation be? Criminal penalties? Civil penalties? Loss of business licenses?" "How should the limits be framed, and what language should we use?" These would all be completely normal questions for such a group of people to discuss among themselves. The only reason this *Mother Jones* "story" saw daylight is because the topic is "trans." About no other issue would any reporter, regardless of political views, publish an article about people emailing each other.

As it happens, the *Mother Jones* reporter who broke this hard-hitting piece of investigative journalism about people emailing each other got the leaked emails from a man named Elisa Shupe. Shupe was born James, later decided that he was a "non-binary" person called Jamie, then decided he was a man named James again, then decided he was a woman named Elisa. He has publicly talked about having borderline personality disorder and autogynephilia. In addition to handing the emails to the *Mother Jones* reporter, he gave them to a male computer hacker named maia arson crimew. Crimew (who claims to be a woman) states on his blog that he is "gay, mostly for girls," and also that he is a "tiny kitten." He has been federally indicted on numerous charges related to computer hacking. He published all the emails on his blog on the same day of the *Mother Jones* piece and shortly thereafter, the hundreds of individuals who were involved in emailing each other to discuss public policy (gasp! A secret working group!) were bombarded with threatening email messages depicting graphic pornography and frequently racist imagery. I can't prove that the hacker was responsible for the threatening email messages, but it seems reasonable enough to wonder.

That Mother Jones *thinks it is a good idea to publish a "story" about a bunch of people emailing each other about public policy when the source of the emails is a known "trans woman" autogynephile with borderline personality disorder working in partnership with another "trans woman" who refers to himself as a "tiny kitten" and has been federally indicted on hacking charges tells us everything we need to know about the shoddy state of journalism among left-leaning media outlets when the topic is "trans."*

But the *Mother Jones* story was not an anomaly. Mainstream media outlets as a whole consistently refer to male perpetrators of crimes as if they were female, when the male perpetrator claims to have a woman identity. Here are some examples: "Woman gets 30 years for child sex abuse" was a 2021 headline in the *Massachusetts Eagle-Tribune* about a man named Jakob Nieves, who was convicted in August 2020 of two counts of sexual exploitation of children, one count of distribution of child pornography, and one count of possession of child pornography. Nieves claims to have a woman identity and calls himself Dakota. "Prosecutors: Woman Accused of Drugging Men, Stealing High-End Watches across South Florida" and "Woman Arrested After String of Watch Robberies: Police" were both headlines that ran in 2021 about a man named John Collins who was charged with multiple counts of robbery after allegedly drugging men and stealing their watches (and claims to "identify as a woman").

Media outlets also consistently refer to men as "she" and "her" when those men claim to have a woman identity. Take, for example, Nikki Secondino, a "transgender woman" (man) who has been accused of murdering his father and brutally stabbing his sister. This is how *Newsweek* reported on the story in December 2022: "A New York transgender woman has been arrested by police and is accused of killing her father and critically injuring her sister, according to reports. Nikki Secondino, 22, was arrested on Thursday night in connection with the attack that saw her father, Carlo Secondino, stabbed to death and her sister, Liana Secondino, taken to hospital in a critical condition."

The *Daily Mail* reported in 2023 that a "prominent Virginia Beach dentist" had been stabbed to death by his "trans daughter." The article stated that the man's "34-year-old daughter, Norah Horwitz, was arrested and charged with second degree murder and stabbing charges and is being held at the Virginia Beach Jail." It noted that "She appears in jail records as Michael and was said by police to be transitioning" and that "the Virginia Beach Sheriff's Office said they were monitoring her in the jail and that she had been placed on suicide watch." But the reason that the jail records him as Michael is that *his name is Michael.* Referring to him as "she and her" is completely disingenuous.

Stacie-Marie Laughton is a man who served in the New Hampshire House of Representatives from 2020 to 2022. According to Wikipedia, he was "the first openly transgender elected official in New Hampshire and the first openly transgender person elected to a state legislature anywhere in the United States." In 2008, he had been convicted of conspiracy to commit credit card fraud and falsifying documents and served four months in prison. He initially ran for office in 2012, but after some controversy about whether his conviction and sentence barred him from doing so, he abandoned the effort. He was charged in 2015 with making a false report of explosives but the charge was reduced to a misdemeanor. In November 2022, he was arrested and held in jail for stalking, then released. Then, in 2023, he was arrested and held in jail again on four felony counts of distributing child pornography. This is how one media outlet described the situation: "Laughton was initially charged with one count but then three more distribution charges were added later. She was held on preventative detention and was scheduled for arraignment in Hillsborough County Superior Court – South on Friday." This is another: "Detectives from the Special Investigations Division applied for and were granted a warrant for Laughton's arrest. She was arrested Thursday with distribution of child sexual abuse images. She was also charged with three additional counts of distribution of child sexual abuse images, Nashua police said."

Anyone reading these headlines and articles would understandably assume that these horrific crimes were in fact committed by women.

Most media outlets simply pretend that "trans" is real and expect readers to play along. Most likely, readers on the political left do. How would they know to question it? The only way that Americans on the political left would know to question "trans" is if they heard about the leftist critique of it. Which is precisely why the media never offers it. Radical feminists have been talking about the leftist critique of "gender identity" for years now, but most people would never know it because no mainstream media outlet will platform us, even though they *will* platform conservative organizations. I have a theory as to why: the "gender identity" industry thinks that it has a better shot at beating conservatives than it has of beating the TERFs, so it pays the media to ignore us. I think the industry is right—it *does* have a better shot at beating conservatives than it has of beating the TERFs, which is precisely why it needs to keep us quiet and out of the public conversation.

Matt Taibbi is a journalist who once wrote for *Rolling Stone* and considered himself to be on the political left. I don't know if he still considers himself to be on the left, but I don't doubt that regardless of who he votes for, he has his leftist values firmly intact. Taibbi interviewed me for his Substack in June 2022. Our interview primarily focused on the topic of men being housed in women's prisons based on their woman identities. In the piece that he published about it, he made an extremely important point: Radical feminist organizations are "full of people with decades-long track records as leftists or feminists, [who are being characterized] as not merely in temporary agreement with conservatives on trans issues, but actual converts to the entire conservative cause." It is an open secret among leftist feminists and our male allies that the legal media constantly either silences us or lies by calling us "right wing."

Since 2015, I have been called "right-wing," "far-right," "Nazi," "fascist," and/or a "tool for the religious right" more times than I can recall. In June 2022, the same month that Taibbi published his Substack interview with me, my own cousin took to X to call me a "far-right fascist bigot" for having the temerity to stand up for women and girls and then blocked me. Radical feminists are used to this and for the most part it doesn't bother us, because it is just stupid. I registered to vote Democrat in 1990, have only ever voted Democrat or Green (with one single exception), and have only ever worked for solidly progressive nonprofit organizations or government agencies. All of this is very inconvenient for the mainstream legacy media, which is desperate for word not to spread that there are leftists who oppose "trans." So they either silence us completely (the norm) or they paint us as "right-wing," knowing that we aren't (the very rare exception to the norm).

CNN is one of the worst offenders (although journalist Michael Smerconish has done some high-quality reporting on the topic). In 2023 alone, it ran the following headlines, among others: "Trans and Nonbinary Students Have Long Had a Place at Women's Colleges. Here's What They Want You to Know"; "Transgender Health Care Restrictions Hit Roadblocks in 3 States as Gender-Affirming Care Becomes Marquee Issue for State GOP Leaders"; "Understanding and Supporting the Transgender Community"; and "Republicans Ramp Up Attacks on Transgender People, in Statehouses and on the Campaign Trail." By "ramp up attacks on transgender people," CNN means that Republicans are advancing bills that acknowledge the material reality of sex, keep sports single-sex, and protect children from the harms of "gender-affirming care." And that's true. But as far as I know, CNN has not once acknowledged that there is a leftist feminist critique of "gender identity" at all.

CNN has been waging what I would call an all-out war on pronouns at least since 2019. It started innocently enough, with a 2019 heading reading, "Why it matters what pronouns you use to refer to people and what to do if you slip up." It ran a similar headline in 2021: "How to get people's pronouns right and what to do if you slip up." In 2022 it was talking about how "Tweens and teens explore the power of pronouns." By 2023, it was offering up "A guide to neopronouns, from ae to ze." This is not a news outlet; it's a mouthpiece for a movement that thinks you can abolish sex by using a particular pronoun.

NPR is similarly dreadful on this topic. In June 2021, it put out a "Guide to Gender Identity Terms," citing GLAAD. It regularly features people who push "gender affirmation" on teachers and parents and people who justify the housing of men in women's prisons based on their woman identities. I refuse to believe that no one at NPR is aware of the leftist feminist critique of "gender identity." They simply refuse to platform us. In 2014, Amy Goodman interviewed me on *Democracy Now*, which frequently airs on NPR, about the ACLU's report on police militarization, which I had overseen and written; there is no way Amy Goodman would even consider interviewing me today about the leftist critique of "gender identity."

Newsweek is considerably better. *Newsweek* will, for example, at least acknowledge that there is a critique of "gender identity" that is not coming from Republicans. For example, in 2022, it published an opinion piece that I wrote, titled, "The Global Abolition of Sex," about the Scottish Gender Recognition bill that passed in 2022 over the opposition of 70 percent of the Scottish population. It has also published commentary by Alexis Blake, a man who claims to be a woman, titled, "I Was Born a Man. Extreme Trans Activists Make My Life Harder." What Blake was arguing is that the most strident gender ideologues who deny the material reality of sex make life harder for those who, like him, pretend to be the opposite sex while at least acknowledging that sex is real. But *Newsweek* still runs headlines uncritically referring to Dylan Mulvaney as "she" and to people like Zooey Zephyr as "trans lawmakers," as though these men are not men.

This is happening globally. In March 2023, U.K. women's rights activist Kellie-Jay Keen went to Australia to host a series of Let Women Speak events. Keen makes no secret of her politics—she is from the political left and in favor of abortion rights, although recent developments regarding the championing of "gender identity" by left-leaning political parties in her country and elsewhere have made her rethink her stances on some topics. At one such event in Melbourne, a group of literal neo-Nazis showed up while the women were speaking and being surrounded and yelled at by trantifa (readers may recall that this term is a combination of "trans" and "antifa"). Trantifa activists sprayed women with water and liquid that smelled like feces, mimed slitting women's throats, and punched police horses to get past the police and attack the women. There is no evidence that Keen's group coordinated with the neo-Nazis or had any idea that they were coming. Yet Australian media pounced on the appearance of a neo-Nazi group at a women's rights event.

An Australian woman named Angie Jones whose X bio reads: "Gender Heretic. Woman. Leftie. Women's Rights Activist. Radfem" ("Radfem" is short for "radical feminist") helped coordinate the Let Women Speak event in Melbourne. After that event, Jones lamented the disingenuousness of the Australian media. She said that not a single journalist had contacted her group to ask who they were or what they were about. Not one of them watched the livestream or spoke to any of the women who spoke at the event. Not one of them attended the event to see for themselves what was going on.

The irony of it all is that the Nazis weren't even there to support Keen's group, and there is no evidence that Keen or any of the organizers had any reason to think they would be there. They just showed up, and from what has been reported, it seems as though the police allowed them to stand on the steps of Parliament. The Nazi group made statements saying that they were there because they didn't want the pushback against "gender identity" to be dominated by "radical feminist atheists." The Nazis were there, in other words, to protest against the "trans" activists, *but also against* the leftist women. The media will never be honest about this because they know the truth—if the general public could hear the arguments of rational, leftist, radical feminist women, the entire edifice of "gender identity" would come crashing down. So they subject us to a near total media blackout, and when they report about us at all—our concern for women's sex-based rights, our concern for the health and safety of children, or our concern for material reality—they paint us as "far right."

The reason for all of this, at least in the U.S., is simple: Mainstream legacy media in the U.S. has been entirely captured by "gender identity" because it is owned by it. As Jennifer Bilek states in "Media Conglomerates Marketing the Gender Identity Industry" on *The 11th Hour Blog*, "The propaganda that there is a subset of humanity that is not male or female, or who believe that they are something other than male or female and should be accommodated everywhere in society for this belief, has been like a distant media drumbeat in our lives. It is always there as backdrop noise, hypnotizing us with virtue signals and repetition." This is not an accident. The vast majority of major media outlets in our society are paid to advance this agenda.

Condé Nast Publications brings in $2 billion annually. In 2017, it announced a new arm called Condé Nast Health, which regularly courts advertisers from pharmaceutical companies, and stated that the new program would "offer our pharma advertising partners a next generation solution" and that it was "uniquely positioned to optimize and drive sales for our advertising partners through many custom, meaningful pharma programs and activations, rooted in our trusted editorial voice and in brand-safe environments." Thus, funded by pharma, Condé Nast magazines have run the following headlines, among others:

Allure: "Transgender Beauty Photos"
Architectural Digest: "The Leading LGBTQ+ Milestones in the World of Design"
Bon Appetit: "Give Your Money to LGBTQ Small Businesses"
Brides: "Amazing Honeymoon Destinations Welcoming to LGBTQIA+ Travelers"
Condé Nast Traveler: "Why I Chose Thailand for My Gender"
Glamour: "An Unforgettable Transgender Love Story"
GQ: "The Republican War Against Trans Children"
GQ Style: "Gender Euphoria: Ten Trans Britons on What Pride Means to Them in 2021"
GQUK: "Father Talks About Raising Trans Children"
The New Yorker: "I Didn't Need a Penis to Become a Man, but I Needed One to Be Me"
Vanity Fair: "Caitlyn Jenner: The Full Story"
Vogue: "Transgender Models"
Wired: "Trans Athletes Are Posting Victories and Shaking Up Sports"

A similar story can be told about Hearst Communications, a multi-billion dollar media conglomerate that owns *Car and Driver, Cosmopolitan,*

Country Living, Elle, Esquire, Good Housekeeping, Men's Health, Oprah Daily, Redbook, Seventeen, Town and Country, Woman's Day, and *Women's Health*, which have collectively run with the following headlines (among others): "Transgender," "20 Trans Actors Changing the Face of Hollywood," "How to Support Trans Youth in Texas," "Transgender and Non-Binary People Like Me Get Pregnant and Have Abortions Too." The mainstream lefty American media, in other words, works very hard to obscure the reality of sex, frame "gender identity" as a civil rights movement, and pretend that any objection to "trans" or "gender identity" is "right-wing" because it is paid to do so. Mainstream society can't get away from this inundation.

Scientific American magazine often publishes articles that are designed to make readers think that sex isn't real and to push the use of puberty blockers among minors. In 2021, it argued that boys should be able to compete on girls' sports teams based on their girl identities, completely denying the fact of male physical advantages in sports, which are known and well-established. On the same day in 2023, it published one piece titled "Here's Why Human Sex is Not Binary," which of course is not true, and one titled, "What Are Puberty Blockers, and How Do They Work?" arguing that puberty blockers are harmless and completely reversible, which is also not true. *Scientific American* is owned by Springer Nature, a subsidiary of the Holtzbrinck Publishing Group, which runs a program called "Queer@Holtzbrinck." Among its stated goals are "networking and empowerment of queer colleagues in the affiliated companies of the Holtzbrinck Group" and "strengthening the visibility and awareness of queer realities." Another way of saying that is that its goals are to gaslight everyone into denying the material reality of sex. In short, *Scientific American*, a part of this group, is anything but scientific. In 2023, Springer Nature announced its plan to retract a peer-reviewed paper reporting on parents who said that their minor children had suddenly announced that they "are transgender" out of the blue because a group of activists complained.

The mainstream liberal legacy media goes so far as to celebrate the "gender identities" of known child groomers in the interest of advancing its narrative that all opposition to "gender identity" is coming from the political right. In May 2023, *Rolling Stone* ran a piece titled "The Far Right Wants This LGBTQ TikToker Dead. They Say That's Only Making Them Stronger: With the release of their new book 'Take Your Own Advice,' viral TikTok star Jeffrey Marsh tells *Rolling Stone* that right-wing backlash won't stand in the way of their mission." In case readers are tempted to assume that the words "they" and "them" refer to multiple people, please don't be. *Rolling Stone* is using plural pronouns here to refer to a man named Jeffrey Marsh who does indeed make TikTok videos aimed at young people. In his videos, he wears a lot of makeup, talks about his "non-binary gender identity" and counsels children to break contact with their parents if said parents do not support the children's "gender identities." He encourages kids to message him directly and privately for additional advice. It is sick stuff and I know plenty of people across the political spectrum who think it is horrific, yet here is *Rolling Stone* calling opposition to it "Far Right." I don't know anyone who wants Marsh dead (although I know a lot of people who would like him to stop grooming children on the internet and magazines like *Rolling Stone* to stop singing his praises).

In March 2023, *USA Today* announced that it was giving a Woman of the Year award to Leigh Finke. Finke is a man who claims to have a woman identity and serves in the Minnesota state legislature. He sponsored legislation to make Minnesota a "refuge for trans youth," by which is meant a place for children to go if their parents do not want them to be fed puberty blockers or wrong-sex hormones. Finke had previously been involved in the production of books like the 2020 *Queerfully and Wonderfully Made: A Guide for LGBTQ+ Christian Teens*, which tells readers that parents who do not accept their children as "queer" are not acting in their children's best interests. After the book was published, Finke posted a photo of an excerpt on his Facebook page and stated "This chapter from my book is the most important thing I've ever written. Trans and non-binary and queer and gay and lesbian and bi young people: Don't listen to your parents!" Some women who received the award were actual women, including former First Lady Michelle Obama and former Supreme Court Justice Sandra Day O'Connor. Whatever one thinks about either of those two women, everyone should probably agree that this man who masquerades as a woman and tries to separate children from their parents does not deserve to be in the same category as them.

Reuters has occasionally published cautious critiques of the administration of puberty blockers and opposite-sex hormones in young people, which is good. But for the most part, in order to read any honest reporting on this topic, you have to pay close attention to lesser-known media outlets like *Reduxx* and *The Post Millennial*, both of which do an outstanding job of bringing attention to the topic (and both of which platform TERFs). Unfortunately, neither has as large of a following as any of the legacy media outlets.

One mainstream liberal legacy media outlet deserves special attention for being a mouthpiece of the "gender identity" industry and utterly failing in its responsibility to, in the words of the ACLU, "function as a watchdog that can investigate and report on government wrongdoing" and to serve as a "vibrant marketplace of ideas, a vehicle for ordinary citizens to express themselves and gain exposure to a wide range of information and opinions" (though there are indications this might be changing): the *New York Times*. The "newspaper of record." The Gray Lady. The *Times* has perhaps done more damage to women and girls—and to children generally—than any other mainstream liberal legacy media outlet and I hope it changes course.

Before 2022, readers of the *Times* could be forgiven for thinking that it was solely a mouthpiece for the "gender identity" industry. It routinely ran articles claiming that sex isn't binary and that all opposition to "gender identity" is "right wing." It consistently championed the idea that men should be allowed to compete in women's sports based on their woman identities. It completely denied the possibility of social contagion as an explanation for why so many young people were suddenly denying the reality of their sexed bodies. This is why I say the *Times* has historically been one of the biggest offenders in championing the sexist, homophobic, authoritarian "trans" machine, though that may be changing (slowly).

In February 2022, the *Times* ran an ad campaign encouraging people to "Imagine Harry Potter Without Its Creator." The point of this was basically to give Harry Potter fans permission to enjoy the books and movies while also erasing J.K. Rowling out of existence because she publicly questions the legitimacy of "gender identity." But just two months later, it ran a piece by conservative commentator Ross Douthat called, "How to Make Sense of the New L.G.B.T.Q. Culture War." That piece is a very careful and admittedly cautious attempt to offer three ways to make sense of the political discourse around "trans." Douthat doesn't come out and take a position about any of it, but he sort-of wonders out loud where mainstream liberals stand on the topic and acknowledges that there are feminist concerns "about the possible erasure of the biological sex differences that have traditionally been the basis of feminist analysis." He states that "This is a practical as well as a philosophical issue, manifest in the debates about whether transgender women belong in women's sports or women's prisons." Douthat also acknowledges that there exists a leftist gay-rights objection to the idea that sex isn't real.

Later in 2022, the *Times* ran an article by Michael Powell titled, "A Vanishing Word in Abortion Debate: 'Women'" with the subtitle, "Progressive groups and medical organizations have adopted inclusive language, which has led to terms like 'pregnant people' and 'chestfeeding.'" The piece is a stinging rebuke of the trend in progressive politics to pretend that women don't exist as a coherent category of people. In it, Powell quotes Ti-Grace Atkinson who is a staunch radical feminist from the second wave era. He describes her as being "wearied by battles over gender and language, which she said are pushed by transgender activists and eager progressives…distant from the urgent needs of women, who make up 50.8 percent of the population." He quotes her as saying, "I want to see material change. Taking away our reproductive rights is going to sharpen the battle. This is about women and our rights; it's not a language game."

A month after that, the *Times* ran an opinion piece by Pamela Paul titled, "The Far Right and Far Left Agree on One Thing: Women Don't Count." This piece presented harsh criticism of *both* the right *and* the left for erasing women. Paul states that "today, a number of academics, uber-progressives, transgender activists, civil liberties organizations and medical organizations are working toward an opposite end: to deny women their humanity, reducing them to a mix of body parts and gender stereotypes." In the piece, she describes TERFs as "women who publicly express mixed emotions or opposing views" and who "risk their jobs and their personal safety" for doing so.

In January 2023, the *Times* ran another article titled, "When Students Change Gender Identity, and Parents Don't Know: Educators are facing wrenching new tensions over whether they should tell parents when students socially transition at school." In June 2022, it had published an article titled, "The Battle Over Gender Therapy: More teenagers than ever are seeking transitions, but the medical community that treats them is deeply divided about why—and what to do to help them." For many of us who follow these topics, these pieces don't go nearly far enough because *of course educators should tell parents when their kid starts going by a different name and/or using opposite-sex pronouns, and, of course, we need to treat confused teenagers by helping them come to terms with their sex.* But still, even asking questions about these things, acknowledging that such questions exist and are legitimate, is a positive development.

The next month, the *Times* ran another opinion piece by Paul, this time in defense of J.K. Rowling. Paul asks why Rowling is often accused of being "hateful" and answers herself as follows: "Because she has asserted the right to spaces for biological women only, such as domestic abuse shelters and sex-segregated prisons. Because she has insisted that when it comes to determining a person's legal gender status, self-declared gender identity is insufficient. Because she has expressed skepticism about phrases like 'people who menstruate' in reference to biological women. Because she has defended herself and, far more important, supported others, including detransitioners and feminist scholars, who have come under attack from trans activists. And because she followed on Twitter and praised some of the work of Magdalen Berns, a lesbian feminist who had made incendiary comments about transgender people." Berns was a beloved U.K. lesbian radical feminist YouTuber who died tragically of a brain tumor in 2019. She was (and still is) famous among radical feminists for being a feisty, brilliant, and hilarious critic of "gender identity," but she isn't very well-known among the general populace, and certainly not in the U.S. For radical feminists all over the world, seeing her name in print in the *New York Times* was astonishing.

These very incremental developments in the *New York Times*, which do not go nearly as far as I would like, has made "trans" activists, who had grown quite accustomed to the *Times* accepting its narratives uncritically, very angry. In February 2023, two open letters appeared online. One was signed by a group of "trans" organizations and hard copies were hand-delivered to the *Times* offices by GLAAD, discussed in Chapter 4. It said things like "We have tried to educate you and your colleagues. We have sent emails, made calls, tried to help reporters source stories." It demanded that the *Times* "stop questioning science that is SETTLED" (an obvious lie). The other letter was signed by some *Times* contributors themselves who did not think that the *New York Times* should pose any questions about the validity of "gender identity." In response, the *Times'* editorial leadership sent an email (later leaked) stating that they would not be intimidated: "We do not welcome, and will not tolerate, participation by *Times* journalists in protests organized by advocacy groups or attacks on colleagues on social media or other platforms," the team said. In response to all of this, the ACLU's Chase Strangio was invited to appear on MSNBC to address it. The interviewer asked Strangio: "You have a room full of producers here, folks in the control room, thousands of people, hopefully, that are watching, what is your advice to journalists? How do we get this right?" *This is MSNBC, offering up its entire network to "trans" activism by asking a "trans" activist for advice on reporting*. It is as pathetic as it is outrageous.

The *Times* has run a few other pieces that seem to raise important questions about sex and gender, but then it seemed to reverse course again. In May 2023, it published an article titled, "How a Few Stories of Regret Fuel the Push to Restrict Gender Transition Care." It was essentially a hit piece on "detransitioners" (and on Chloe Cole, discussed in Chapter 3, in particular). It said that Cole "decided to detransition, returning to her female identity," despite the fact that "female," rather than being an identity, is a word to describe half the human population and half the populations of other species. It wrote that "Ms. Cole and fewer than 10 activists like her—people who transitioned and then changed course—have become the faces of the cause, according to a New York Times review of news coverage and legislative testimony." This paints "detransition" as rare, even though "detrans reddit" includes over 50,000 members. The piece then went into detail about the hard-hitting piece of investigative journalism in *Mother Jones* about people emailing each other and referencing Shupe, without bothering to note that Shupe is a known autogynephile with borderline personality disorder and without mentioning the involvement of a man who calls himself a "tiny kitten" and has been indicted on federal computer hacking charges. Plenty of us who fight the abolition of sex were pleased to see the *Times* cover the story about Jamie Reed blowing the whistle on the Washington University gender clinic in August 2023. A careful review of the piece shows that it really downplayed the significance of what Reed had uncovered and failed to communicate the very serious nature of putting kids on puberty blockers and wrong-sex hormones.

The *New York Times* also has a "Special Section for Kids," available in the Sunday edition once a month or online for $5.00. In April 2023, it ran "The Puberty Issue," the purpose of which was to teach kids ages eight to thirteen about puberty. It contained a special Editor's Note stating, "This section should not be read by grown-ups." The "puberty issue" contained information about normal things that kids go through, like periods, deodorant, acne, crushes, mood swings, mustache fuzz, and bras. But it also pushed "gender identity" in various ways. One page had cartoons filling in blanks after the phrase "The first time I...." Some of the entries were "got a zit," "suddenly got tall," and "realized I had B.O." But two others were "realized my gender identity" and "told people at school my pronouns." One article was headlined, "When It Doesn't Feel Right." It was all about "gender dysphoria" and instructed kids to seek help from teachers and school counselors and advised them to seek out a "supportive space with friends or a counselor" to "let you safely explore what feels best, like changes to your name, pronouns, or style of dress." Of course, there is nothing wrong with encouraging kids to get help if they are struggling, but pushing "gender identity" on eight-year-olds is another thing entirely.

I think the *Times* knows what it is doing. It knows it has been pushing the sexist, homophobic, regressive idea that sex isn't real for years now. It knows it is in the wrong. And it knows that Americans aren't having it anymore. It knows that if it publishes a leftist feminist critique of "gender identity," the entire edifice will come crashing down. I will be thrilled if I turn out to be wrong and if the *Times* does eventually come around to reporting factually on matters pertaining to sex and gender. But I'm not holding my breath. The mainstream lefty news media has been nothing other than a protection racket for "trans" and it is time for them to stop. Americans deserve the truth and journalists need to do their jobs.

Lefty Dudebro Media

Radical feminists often use the phrase "lefty dudebros" to refer to men on the political left who think of themselves as "feminists" or "feminist allies." They often talk a good game and claim to support women's rights. Then they ruin everything. Many of these men with large followings have been just dreadful when it comes to their complicity in the abolition of sex. In this section I'll describe the cast of characters I like to think of as the "lefty dudebros" in the media who regularly throw women and girls under the bus at the altar of "gender identity."

One of the best examples of this is Jon Stewart, former host of *The Daily Show* and then host of the Apple TV podcast *The Problem with Jon Stewart*. On Friday October 7, 2022, Apple TV released episode one of season two of *The Problem*, titled "The War Over Gender." I watched the whole thing. Unfortunately, many people have gotten the analysis wrong as to why the episode is so bad (which it is). The reason it is so bad is not that Stewart is confused or misinformed. The problem with Jon Stewart is that he knows better.

In it, Stewart argues that the question "What is a woman?" is "complicated" and then hosts a panel that includes two mothers who supported their children's "transition," ACLU attorney Chase Strangio, and a doctor who argues that child "transition" is safe. The episode ends with a disingenuous and manipulative interview with Arkansas Attorney General Leslie Rutledge. Viewers can come to their own conclusions, but in my view, the entire episode is completely disingenuous. Consistently, and repeatedly, Stewart uses the word "transgender" when he means either one of two things: differences of sexual development (DSDs) or non-conformity with sex stereotypes. These are actual real phenomena. The overwhelming majority of human beings (99.08 percent) are born with either XX or XY chromosomes. The rest (.018 percent) have some form of ambiguous sex characteristics or an abnormal chromosomal makeup (that's what a DSD is). There are also people (all of us, really, to varying degrees) who do not conform to the sex stereotypes that society imposes on us (also known as gender). Neither category has anything to do with the utterly meaningless concept of "transgender."

After the release, plenty of people took to X to complain that Stewart is uninformed and/or had not done his research. Those posts were meant to be critical of him, and supportive of TERFs, which is great. However, I would argue that there is approximately zero chance that Stewart didn't know exactly what he was doing. The problem with Jon Stewart, in other words, is not that he hasn't done his research. The problem with Jon Stewart is that he did his research and chose to lie about what is really going on.

On October 5, 2021 (exactly one year and two days before the release of the *Problem with Jon Stewart* episode), Netflix released Dave Chappelle's comedy *The Closer*, in which Chappelle discussed J.K.

Rowling, acknowledged that it is quite reasonable for women to object to the idea that men should be able to "identify as women," and announced that he is "Team TERF." Jon Stewart and Dave Chappelle are long-time close friends. Stewart defended Chappelle in the days after the fervor, saying that Chappelle's "intention is never hurtful" and described Chappelle as "good" and "decent." In classic dudebro fashion, he followed up with "I love that dude as a person."

During the COVID-19 pandemic, Stewart spent several months with Chappelle in the Ohio town where Chappelle lives, filming what would turn out to be an extremely touching story about how the town survived those long and terrible months by turning to comedy (the film is not freely available online, but I know that it's great because I saw it in 2021 at the Capital One Arena in DC). In 2022, Chappelle introduced Stewart when Stewart was awarded the Mark Twain Prize for American Humor at the Kennedy Center. It was a veritable lovefest.

In other words, there is no way that Jon Stewart does not know exactly what the term "TERF" means and the role that TERFs play in the gender wars. If he didn't know back in October of 2021, when *The Closer* was released on Netflix, he surely would have spent the next year studying the topic. He *knows* that we are leftist feminists who fight for the sex-based rights of women and girls and against the abolition of sex. He would *know* that all opposition to "gender identity" is not "right wing." He would know all of this, and even knowing this, he has chosen the side of those who want violent rapists and murderers to be housed in women's prisons. He has chosen the side that wants men taking over women's sports. He has chosen the side that wants to sterilize and mutilate children.

Jon Stewart is beloved on the American political left. He's also not stupid. Many of us spent the entire George W. Bush presidency glued to *The Daily Show*, laughing hysterically and shaking our heads while Stewart mercilessly mocked the likes of Dick Cheney and Donald Rumsfeld. So for many of us TERFs, Stewart's embrace of the industry-fueled, misogynist, and homophobic takeover of society that is "gender identity" is a terrible betrayal. He could have done the right thing. He could have interviewed leftist TERFs, gay rights activists, and biologists. I (naively, I guess) had hoped that he would not sell us out. And now Stewart is complicit. The problem with Jon Stewart is not that he doesn't know what he's doing. The problem with Jon Stewart is that he does.

Stewart is hardly the only example of this. Before becoming host of CBS's *Late Night*, Stephen Colbert hosted the satire program *The Colbert Report* on Comedy Central. In 2014, in that capacity, he had Janet Mock, whom he referred to as a "transgender activist" as a guest on the show in a segment called "Transgender Awareness." Mock had recently published his book *Redefining Realness: My Path to Womanhood, Identity, Love & So Much More*. The instant Mock sat down, Colbert addressed him as "young lady," while the crowd cheered. Colbert asked if "things are getting better for the trans community" and Mock waxed poetic about the fifty Facebook "gender markers" and whined that fifty was not enough.

Colbert has been championing the rights of the "transgender community" ever since. In 2016, the year that North Carolina was considering a statewide law to maintain single-sex public bathrooms, he quipped, "To all those lawmakers out there who are so obsessed with who's using what bathroom and what plumbing they got downtown, newsflash: You're the weirdos." I am not a lawmaker, so that comment is not directed at me, but I would like to state for the record that I do not think that women and girls are "weirdos" for not wanting men to use women's bathrooms. Polling shows that nearly all women (and men) across the political spectrum agree.

In 2018, after it was reported that Trump was instituting a "transgender military ban" (this was not true, the rule simply said that service members have a sex and that matters), Colbert did a monologue calling this "random cruelty." He went on to say that "they spun the wheel of discrimination and they landed on transgender" and that "gender is clearly a spectrum." By "wheel of discrimination," I assume that Colbert was referring to Trump's racist comments about Mexican people being rapists, his unconstitutional ban on Muslims entering the country, his horrific comments about women, and his immoral border policies. I agree—Donald Trump is a horrible person. But to suggest that those things are equivalent to acknowledging the material reality of sex in the military is pure science denial and woman hatred (please recall the servicewoman who is being forced to share a shower and a barracks with men who claim to have woman identities under the Biden administration).

In April 2023, Colbert returned to the topics of bathrooms, in a monologue accusing Republicans of being "obsessed with who's in the bathroom." Again, I don't think there's anything wrong with women and girls not wanting men and boys in our bathrooms, locker rooms, changing rooms, or spas, nor do the majority of Americans. He said, "My house *only* has gender neutral bathrooms." I'm happy to assume that is true, as it is true for families all over the world, but it ignores the fact that no one is talking about mandating single-sex bathrooms in private homes. The sole issue is with multi-stall public bathrooms.

The particularly interesting thing with respect to Stewart and Colbert is that it was not always this way. When they were both at *Comedy Central*, they appear to have gotten away with quite a bit of alleged "transphobia." In November 2013, a change.org petition was launched to encourage them to "reject transphobia and respect gender identity." The petition alleged that "By consistently making jokes at the expense of transgender people, Jon Stewart (*The Daily Show*) and Stephen Colbert (*The Colbert Report*) are using their bully pulpit to perpetuate transphobia. Consequently, they are contributing to the perpetuation of exclusion, harassment, and violence against transgender people."

Colbert was a brilliant satirist when he was doing *The Colbert Report*, and he did, indeed, say a few things that got him branded a "transphobe." Colbert is a pretty mainstream liberal, and *The Colbert Report* was generally a mockery of Republicans. But sometimes he went after liberals as well, particularly on this issue. He was once doing a segment on Lean Finely Textured Beef (LFTB, sometimes referred to as "pink slime beef") and quipped, "Yes! LFTB, because our beef now has so many hormones it's a member of the transgendered community. So I just want to get out in front of this and say that I, Stephen Colbert, apologize to any of my transgender bovine viewers that may have been offended." In another episode, as President Obama was preparing to take office, Colbert announced, "Nation, President Elect Obama is meeting every day with his transition team, or, in beltway lingo, trannies." Once, complaining about the sad state of the California Republican Party, he said, "I believe that 'The Man' is keeping the California Republicans down. And, being from California, 'The Man' is probably a tranny."

Stewart did similar things when he was hosting *The Daily Show*. He once did a bit mocking the idea of a "transgender woman" being named to the Supreme Court, shouting, "All rise for the honorable Justice Chick-With-Dick." In a segment about the 2006 U.S. Attorney firing scandal, he joked, "Here's a general rule of thumb I have: if you don't know whether you've made a particular mistake more or less than 50 times, that's not really a mistake. At that point, it's something you do. For instance, how many times have I accidentally picked up a tranny hooker at a truck-stop?" During a segment about protests in China concerning a new universal I.D. system, he remarked, "But Cow and Chipmunk are not alone! They are joined by Transvestite, who worries that her true gender will be revealed by this new system!" The camera then showed an image of a man pretending to be a woman, and a voiceover said, "I am afraid that when I lumber out of my apartment in a tight dress with my scrotum taped back and my large hands covering my Adam's Apple, somewhere, some bureaucrat will know I'm a dude."

In other words, at one point both Jon Stewart and Stephen Colbert had a sense of humor about all of this and weren't afraid to joke about the issue on *Comedy Central*. All of that has gone out the window as both have now chosen to throw women and girls and the material reality of sex under the bus at the altar of "gender identity." Today, I'm sure if they were called to account for their past "transphobia," they would hang their heads, apologize for offending the "trans community," and go right back to hating women and girls.

In 2015, on *Last Week Tonight with John Oliver*, Oliver announced that "this has clearly been a big week for the LGBT community," which was a reference to the Supreme Court's decision in *Obergefell*, before launching directly into a discussion about "the T part of that equation, from Caitlyn Jenner's Vanity Fair cover, to [various TV shows] to another milestone this past Friday." The reference to "this past Friday" concerned Madame Tussaud's decision to put a wax figure of Laverne Cox in its San Francisco wax museum (Cox is a man who claims to be a woman and who starred in the Netflix show *Orange is the New Black*). Oliver called this a "big step forward for transgender Americans." He then shifted to a local broadcast from Tempe Arizona where a man (a "transgender woman") had evidently been removed from a bar and the local weatherman said, "Let's bring it back to that last part. What is a transgender woman? What does that even mean now?" Someone off-camera said, "She used to be a guy," and someone else said, "but now is a woman." The weatherman appeared to have no idea what was going on (and I believe him), and exclaimed, "I can't even keep up anymore!"

Oliver mocked him mercilessly and then went on to attempt to provide some basic education. He stated that "transgender people" are "people who have a different gender identity from the ones that were assigned to them at birth," that "gender identity is who you are," and that "sexual orientation is who you love." Oliver ended the episode by referring to "gender identity" as a "civil rights issue" and suggested that if you don't support "transgender" people, you may as well be a racist or a Nazi. But it was all pure propaganda and indoctrination. In 2015, most Americans had absolutely no idea what "gender identity" is, or why they were supposed to support it. John Oliver certainly did his bit to change that by telling everyone that if they didn't, they were Nazis and racists.

In 2022, the same month that Stewart came out with his episode of *The Problem*, Oliver offered his own shallow and manipulative half-hour rant about "transgender rights." The episode begins right off the bat by talking about "LGBTQ rights." He makes a rather funny point about how in 1967, CBS News did a ridiculous broadcast about "the homosexuals," where Mike Wallace explained that "There is a growing concern about homosexuals in society, about their increasing visibility," and continued to talk about a twenty-seven-year-old man who was "unable to hold a job because of his inability to contain his homosexual inclinations." The man in question appeared on TV hiding behind a plant. I acknowledge that this is a ridiculous way to talk about lesbians and gay men and appreciate the point that Oliver appeared to be making. If the episode had been a celebration of how far society has come when discussing the rights and visibility of lesbians and gay men, that would be great. That's not what this was, however.

He continued to talk about how some "on the right" have "lost their minds about trans rights" and described state bills to protect the rights, privacy, and safety of women and girls and to protect children from being harmed as "anti-trans." He complained that "there are many on the left who seem reluctant to engage on this issue" (which is completely true) and, somewhat astonishingly, acknowledged that there are some on the left who are hostile to it and claim that the issue will cost Democrats elections. He lamented that former New York City mayor Michael Bloomberg said in 2019 that "If you go to the middle of the country, people would say that if your conversation during a presidential election is about some guy wearing a dress and whether he, she or it can go into the locker room with their daughter, that's not a winning formula for most people." Bloomberg did say that, and he was absolutely right. But all that Oliver had to say about it was "Michael Bloomberg can f*ck all the way off with that sh*t." Then he told the blatant lie that it is not Democrats who are talking about this issue, but rather Republicans. Someone needs to tell Oliver that the president talks about "trans rights" every chance he gets. The episode ends with Oliver stating that "We are working towards the goal of every trans kid knowing that they are loved, valued, and indispensable,... and never going back to a point where anyone feels that if they appear on TV, they have to hide behind a f*cking plant." It is, of course, critically important to ensure that all kids receive everything they need to live happy lives. I would argue that this includes the right to grow into healthy adults rather than having their puberty stunted. And, although the episode begins with a comedic riff about how gay people were painted in the media in 1967, the entire episode is in fact about "trans."

Trevor Noah replaced Jon Stewart as host of *The Daily Show* and has been relentlessly celebrating the abolition of sex and making women's and girls' justifiable fears a cheap target ever since. In 2016, at around the same time that Colbert was calling women and girls who care about the presence of men in our bathrooms "obsessed weirdos," Noah did a segment on the same topic. He was criticizing the argument that would-be sex offenders might take advantage of laws allowing men to use women's bathrooms to commit sex offenses. This is certainly *an* argument that some people make—the argument is that some men will "pretend to be trans" in order to assault women in the bathroom. Noah's rejoinder is that sex offenders are hardly waiting for laws to change to assault women in the bathroom, and he's right. Men who wish to sexually assault women in the bathroom often just go ahead and do it. That's true. But here's what people like Noah either don't get or refuse to acknowledge: *In a society where men are not permitted to enter women's bathrooms, women can always complain when they do.* If, in such a society, a man enters a women's bathroom and commits voyeurism, indecent exposure, or assault (or worse), he can be arrested and charged. Women's ability to complain about such things vanishes under laws that allow men to enter women's bathrooms based on their claimed woman identities.

In the same segment, Noah addressed the argument that women and girls need privacy from men and boys in the bathroom. This is what he said: "You know what? I understand that. Privacy. We all expect a certain level of privacy. And I've chatted to some of my friends who are parents of young girls and they go, 'Hey, I don't know if I'd be comfortable with my daughter being in the same bathroom as an exposed penis.' And I understand that. It's not like I don't understand that completely, because I'm not comfortable being in the bathroom with an exposed penis, and I'm a man.... In life, there are certain types of privacy we forego. It's one of the deals we make to be part of society. That's what we do. When I go to the gym, I have to accept the fact that in the changing room, there may be a man standing there blow-drying his balls." He concluded, "We're not comfortable with many things in society, but we've learned to get over it."

This is Noah literally making light of the likelihood that under laws that allow men to use bathrooms and locker rooms based on their woman identities, underage girls will be exposed to penises and testicles. He is not even bothering to pretend that "transwomen" are women who have had their penises and testicles removed (most men who claim to be women have not). *He is justifying indecent exposure of male genitalia to women and young girls.* He is saying that this is just a "deal" that we have to make. He is telling women and girls (and girls' parents) that if we don't want to see penises and testicles in a locker room, we all just need to "get over it."

In 2019, Noah interviewed a man named Jacob Tobia in a segment titled, "Promoting a 'Gender-Chill' Exploration of Identity with 'Sissy.'" Tobia (they/them, thank you very much) calls himself an actor, writer, producer, and author. What he really is, is a total creep whose constant presentation of himself in stereotypically feminine clothing and makeup makes a mockery of womanhood. In 2019, he published a book called *Sissy: A Coming-of-Gender Story*. Again, "sissy" refers to a type of pornography where men are basically hypnotized into perceiving themselves as sexually submissive and degraded women. It is frequently violent. In 2017, *Vice* magazine published a long piece in which Tobia and his fellow-they/them friend Alok Vaid-Menon whined that no one would date them (has either of them looked in a mirror?). During the *Daily Show* episode, Tobia was permitted to drone on about his "gender identity" and his "sissy" identification. No concern whatsoever was expressed for the rights, privacy, or safety of women and girls. When the Democratic Party champions "gender identity," and when the media platforms men like Tobia, this is what they are promoting—stereotypes, the mockery of womanhood, and porn.

In 2022, Noah took matters a step further and had as a guest on *The Daily Show* a man named Veronica Ivy (formerly Rachel McKinnon, formerly Rhys McKinnon) who claims to be a woman and who is permitted to compete in women's cycling based on his woman identity. In 2018, he became the first male women's world track cycling champion by placing first in the UCI Women's Masters Track World Championship for the women's thirty-five to forty-four age bracket. Incidentally, in 2012, he (as Rachel) published a thesis titled, "Reasonable Assertions: On Norms of Assertion and Why You Don't Need to Know What You're Talking About." A thesis arguing that you don't need to know what you are talking about when presenting assertions seems quite fitting for a man who lies to the world about his sex and steals championships from female athletes. In any event, Noah had him on *The Daily Show* and started by asking him to describe his "journey." McKinnon then talked about sport as a "human right." I agree with him that sport is a human right, but I also think that women and girls have a human right to compete exclusively with and against other women and girls. He explained his view that "white cis women's perceptions of femininity" are the problem and made women's sex-based rights out to be akin to racism. He claimed that he is biologically female (a blatant lie) and talked extensively about his woman identity. When asked if there are biological advantages to being male, he stated outright that there is no settled science on that question (which is flatly untrue) and made the claim that it is totally, completely, unambiguously fair for him to compete in women's sports. Noah mostly just nodded along in agreement.

Seth Myers hosts *Late Night with Seth Myers* on NBC and before that he was a cast member on *Saturday Night Live*. He was the head writer and anchor of SNL's "Weekend Update" from 2006 until he left in 2014. In 2016, he said regarding the bathroom controversy: "The most absurd impact of these kinds of bathroom bills is you're actually forcing transgender women, who *are* women, and transgender men, who *are* men, to use the wrong bathroom." This is, of course, not true, as no men are women and no women are men. He is reported to have said that bills to protect the rights, privacy, safety, and dignity of women and girls in bathrooms undermines "transgender people's concept of self," whatever that means. In 2017, after the federal government withdrew President Obama's previous guidance redefining sex to include "gender identity" for Title IX purposes, Myers did a segment called "Hey!," where he said to Trump, "Hey! What are you doing? As I understand it, you were elected to bring jobs back to the U.S. Now you don't want to let transgender kids use the bathroom of the gender they identify with? You think *that's* why the auto industry went to Mexico? For the *bathrooms*?... During the election, you told the LGBT community, and I quote, 'I will fight for you.' Did you not mean to include the word 'for'?" Whatever anyone thinks of the former president, Myers didn't even seem to understand that he was referring to a federal policy affecting female athletes. He didn't express a word of concern for women or girls at all. The same year, he also criticized the former president for what he referred to as a "transgender military ban" (which, again, never existed).

Readers may know that the actress Ellen (now Elliot) Page announced in 2020 that she is a "trans man." In 2014, Page had dramatically come out as a lesbian at an event at the Human Rights Campaign, where she said, "I am here today because I am gay." Page appeared on *Late Night* with Myers in 2015 to talk about how she was scheduled to receive a National Vanguard Award during an upcoming HRC convention because of her gay rights advocacy. The two discussed the speech she was going to give and Myers clearly referred to her as Ellen. In 2022, Page went back on the show and in introducing her, Myers said, "Please welcome back to the show Elliot Page, everybody!," completely ignoring the fact that when she had been on the show previously she was Ellen and that she was there to talk about being a lesbian and about receiving an award for having come out as such.

In the 2022 clip, Page sounds like she's been taking testosterone, but it isn't obvious. At that point, she still looked relatively healthy and strong. She had cut her hair short, but she was still unmistakably female, despite claiming to be male. Later in 2022, Page posted shirtless in the magazine *Esquire*, revealing the scars from her double mastectomy. By the end of 2022, Page would announce the cover of her upcoming memoir *Pageboy*, where she looks a bit gaunt and absolutely miserable. Tragically, in 2023, Page told the *Los Angeles Times* that she realized she was "transgender" when she started hearing and then talking to a voice in her head, following a psychotic episode in which she repeatedly punched herself in the face and head. Just a few days later, a doctor gave approval for her breasts to be removed. I have no idea why no one gave Page the help that she needed to accept herself as a lesbian. To the best of my knowledge, Myers has never said a word about the trauma Page has endured at the altar of "trans."

At some point between 2015 and 2023, someone at either *Late Night with Seth Myers* or YouTube edited the description of Myers's 2015 interview with Ellen Page, where she talked about coming out as a lesbian, to refer to her as Elliot. Perhaps even more sadly, Page had previously (in 2014) done an interview with Ellen DeGeneres, where she also talked about coming out as a lesbian. At some point between 2014 and 2023, someone at either *The Ellen Show* or YouTube edited the description on that video to refer to Page as Elliot too. This is the description on Page's interview with DeGeneres today: "After his impassioned speech at the HRC, Elliot Page was here to tell our host about his experience of coming out publicly as a lesbian." Ellen Page has effectively been completely erased.

The sex denialism from the lefty dudebro media does not stop there. MSNBC darling Chris Hayes from *All In with Chris Hayes* regularly has ACLU lawyer Chase Strangio as a guest, where Strangio says completely insane things like the North Carolina state legislature invented biological sex in 2016. He supports providing "gender-affirming care" to minors and in 2023 went on a bizarre rant about a Florida bill to prohibit it, where he addressed Florida governor Ron DeSantis and said that protecting children from harmful medical practices is "none of your g*ddamn business."

Cenk Uygur is a "progressive" political commentator and the founder of *The Young Turks*. Uygur is anti-gun and a proponent of gun control, but he has said that he makes an exception and encourages "trans people" to arm themselves with guns. As far as I know, he has expressed zero concern for the well-being of the women who are often targets of violent attacks at the hands of "trans" activists. In a strange turn of events, though, Uygur seemed to pivot in 2023, when he and co-host Ana Kasparian suggested some concern for children who are being harmed by "gender-affirming care." When he got pushback for doing so, Uygur posted, "If you can't tolerate any dissent from your maximalist position, are you sure you're a progressive? Is it left-wing to throw allies under a bus for the slightest disagreement? Probably not. I think some people on here are becoming the caricature the right-wing drew up of them." Kasparian went even further, appearing on the *Sitch & Adam Show* on YouTube to denounce "gender identity" and cancel culture generally. These are welcome developments and I look forward to seeing whether Uygur and Kasparian will stick to their guns or whether they will backtrack.

Hasan Minhaj is an American comedian, writer, and television host. He got his big start on *The Daily Show*, which he left in 2018 to host his own show, *Patriot Act with Hasan Minhaj*, which has won two Peabody awards. He has been included in *Time* magazine's list of the 100 most influential people in the world. He guest-hosted *The Daily Show* for a few weeks in early 2023, where he went out of his way to call for a wealth tax on people like J.K. Rowling. He said, "I've noticed one thing about a certain type of rich person. When they don't have problems of their own, they have to just make up problems just to make their lives interesting. Right? They're just like, sitting at home in the jacuzzi like, 'Hmm—what if I tweet about trans high school swimmers.' I can guarantee you, J.K. Rowling had zero opinions about trans people when she was on welfare. We need a wealth tax, not for infrastructure or schools.... Rich people, this is for your own good. The wealth tax is actually a shut the f*ck up tax." He was basically arguing that Rowling just made up all the problems facing women and girls at the altar of "gender identity" because she had nothing better to do and that she should just "shut the f*ck up."

Sam Seder is a lefty dudebro who hosts a YouTube channel called *The Majority Report*. He frequently hosts episodes complaining about TERFs with titles like "Understanding the 'Logic' of TERFs," "TERFs and Transphobes Are Miserable and They Want You to Be Too," and "TERF War on Misogynists Is Beyond Parody." In that last one, one of his co-hosts referred to me by name as an "infamous TERF writer" while an image of my book *The Abolition of Sex* appeared on the screen. This rather hilarious episode prompted a friend to send me a T-shirt with the words "Infamous TERF writer" on it. I don't know that I'm infamous, but I'm happy to publish books that argue in favor of the sex-based rights of women and girls and against the abolition of sex and even happier when lefty media sites accidentally give them unearned publicity.

These men are traitors to the progressive left and to the best of my knowledge, not a single one of them has ever expressed even a little bit of concern for women and girls in general or for the women and girls in their own lives. They care much more about a corporate-driven and authoritarian men's sexual entitlement movement than they care about the actual dignity of women and girls or the material reality of sex. They have done this for the benefit of their fellow men to perpetuate male domination.

There is one possible exception to this cadre of lefty dudebro media characters, and that is Bill Maher from *Real Time with Bill Maher* (formerly from *Politically Incorrect*). Like these guys, Maher is a lefty dudebro. Unlike them, however, he has spoken a lot of sense on this issue.

Maher has always been a bit unconventional. A die-hard liberal, he is not afraid to make liberals uncomfortable. All the way back in 2015, Maher was telling the "pronoun police" to ease up on people who mistakenly refer to Caitlyn (Bruce) Jenner as "he" because, he said, referring to Jenner as "she" will "take some getting used to." He also noted that some of the media coverage of Jenner had been a bit over the top. Maher said, "If she makes people accept people who are different, great then she's done a great thing. But let's not forget that this is a has-been from reality TV who got breast implants. This is someone who used to be Kim Kardashian's step-father now she's Kim Kardashian's step-mother. She's not Rosa Parks." That was a fairly moderate (and amusing) approach. Maher would honor the "preferred pronouns" while not insisting that others do so as well, and without fawning over Jenner as though he were some sort of civil rights hero.

But at that time, Maher still had a lot of learning to do. In 2019, Dennis Prager, a conservative radio host and writer, was a guest on the show. He told Maher and the rest of the panel that "It is a lie that some men can menstruate." Everyone, including Maher, laughed in response because the idea is so preposterous. Maher appeared never to have heard the absurd contention that men can menstruate and asked, "Wait, where did THAT come from?" Prager told him (accurately) that tampons were being handed out in the men's bathrooms at U.C. Berkeley and Maher mocked him, saying, "Dennis, I remember you in the old show, you were a little more reasonable." Maher could not, at that time, believe that anyone would argue that men can menstruate. Little did Maher know at the time that was *exactly* what the "progressive" left was saying and that Prager was exactly right. I don't know exactly when this started being said, but the earliest reference I can find to it is a 2016 article in *The Daily Beast*, titled, "Yes, Men Can Have Periods and We Need to Talk About Them." Later, in a 2022 segment, Maher said, "It's not my fault that the party of FDR and JFK is turning into the party of LOL and WTF," and added that there was now an "emoji for pregnant men" (which is true). He was basically mocking the idea that men can be pregnant. He had come a long way toward understanding what Prager had been trying to tell him back in 2019.

Toward the end of 2019, as the 2020 presidential primary season was heating up, he had some choice words for Democrats: "Stop acting weird." In a brilliant segment called "New Rule: Nowhere Else to Go," Maher scorched the Democrats, beginning with the statement, "Someone must explain to Democrats what 'binary' means." His main point was that we only have two political parties in America and that if the Democrats could just get it together, they would be assured of taking back the White House from Trump. And in making this point, he provided a list of incredibly dumb/insane things Democrats had said or done to make voters want to vote for Trump, including Elizabeth Warren's support for using taxpayer dollars to cover sex-change operations for "transgender prisoners" and Kamala Harris's "need to start off a recent town hall by saying, 'my pronouns are she, her, and hers.'" He lamented, "For some, I guess that makes her the Rosa Parks of pronouns, but there's a much larger group thinking, 'why is this important??'"

He also mocked candidate Julian Castro's support for abortion rights for "transgender women." Notably, Castro's support for "abortion rights for transgender women" shows just how insane this issue is. If you are someone who accepts that "transgender women" is a coherent category of people, you are also supposed to understand that they are male and therefore cannot get pregnant (and will never need an abortion). If you're on that side of "gender identity," you're supposed to understand that the relevant categories of people who need abortions are "ciswomen, transmen and some non-binary people." This is all, of course, ridiculous, but one would at least expect a Democratic candidate for president to get his talking points right. Maher understands this and pointed it out in his segment by saying, "They can't get pregnant! They don't have a uterus (unless they're in prison and Elizabeth Warren buys them one)!" His main point was this one that he made when addressing Democrats directly by saying, "Instead of trying to make the people on the far left double-dog like you, make some good people in the middle not HATE you." By the end, he was practically screaming, "THIS SHOULD BE EASY, JUST BE LESS CRAZY THAN DONALD TRUMP! ARE YOU GUYS SERIOUSLY STRUGGLING WITH THIS?"

By 2022, he was dedicating entire segments to the topic, criticizing Pride and taking on the speed with which the topic of "gender identity" has taken over society. But he was still saying things like "I'm happy we live in an age where LGBT people can live openly," still appearing not to understand that the conflation of the T with the LGB is *itself* part of the problem. By 2023, he was derisively and rightfully mocking the idea that people can be born neither male nor female, the argument that we should not separate sports by sex, and the notion that biology isn't real. I'm not convinced that Maher appreciates just how devastating the entire topic of "gender identity" has been for women and girls as a sex class, but he's come a long way since he was simply telling people to ease up on pronouns back in 2015. My hope is that he'll eventually get to the place where he's tearing apart "gender identity" for the tyrannical, sexist, homophobic, corporate behemoth that it is.

Conservative Media

With very few exceptions, conservative media isn't much better. For the most part, even conservative media outlets refer to men as "she and her," or say that "transgender athletes" are competing in women's sports instead of just calling male athletes men. Even *Fox News*, which notoriously leans conservative, uses opposite-sex pronouns to describe men, prompting *Not the Bee* (another conservative outlet) to publish an opinion piece titled "Dear Fox News: If you honor the transgender pronouns of a deranged child molester, you are part of the problem" (that piece concerned the story of James Tubbs, who decided that he was a woman named Hannah after being convicted of sexually assaulting a ten-year-old girl in a Denny's bathroom and was later convicted of manslaughter after bludgeoning a man to death with a rock and sentenced to fifteen years in prison).

Fox News regularly runs headlines like: "Alaska Education Board Urges State to Keep Trans Athletes Out of Sports Not Aligned with Birth Sex," "Biden's Transgender Sports Order is 'Heartbreaking,' Female Athlete Says," "California Lawmaker Introduces Bill That Would Require Schools to Notify Parents if Their Child Is Transgender," and "California Transgender Teen, Family, Hope to Be an Inspiration to Others." All of this perpetuates the idea that there is a coherent category of people, including children, called "transgender." It is a dangerous lie. According to a 2021 *Fox News* company handbook, employees are permitted to use the bathrooms that align with their "gender identity" and must be addressed by their "preferred name and pronouns" while in the workplace. The company offers "Workplace Transition Plans" for employees to "ease their gender transition at work." The handbook uses HRC's definitions of words like "cisgender," "gender transition," "non-binary," "transgender," and "LGBTQ." It might come as a surprise to readers that *Fox* has received a perfect score on HRC's Corporate Equality Index for years.

Other conservative outlets are no better. *The Daily Caller* publishes headlines like "Lawmakers Revive Bill Banning Child Sex Changes Last Minute After Volatile Debate," even though there is no such thing as a "child sex change." I understand that editors work hard to make headlines fit word limits, but the piece itself repeats the lie that there is such a thing as a "child sex change."

Headlines like these are infuriating to leftist feminists fighting the gender wars because they perpetuate the myth of "trans." There is no such thing as "trans athletes"; there are male athletes and female athletes. There is no such thing as a "transgender sports order." There is no such thing as a "transgender child" or a "child sex change." As enraging as it is, for liberal media outlets to suggest otherwise has become commonplace. For conservative outlets to do it is pathetic (for the record, I personally know conservative journalists who agree with me about this).

Perhaps the most notable exception to the trend of conservative media outlets using nonsensical language to describe men who claim to have a woman identity is Madeleine Kearns at the *National Review*. Kearns has consistently used straightforward and factual language since she started reporting on matters pertaining to sex and gender in 2018. I had the pleasure of meeting her in early 2019, at a public event at a library in Washington, D.C., when WoLF hosted a panel discussion about the topic. She posed the following question to the panel: "If the political left can't fix this, can the political right?" My favorite answer to that question came from WoLF founder Lierre Keith, who said, "It won't be the left, it won't be the right. It will be women, working together." I deeply appreciate Kearns's contribution to the national discourse about "trans" and "gender identity." Although I do not agree with its religious orientation, I also really appreciate the *Christian Post*'s reporting on this topic; it always reports accurately using correct-sex pronouns.

Another conservative-leaning outlet that has been refreshing in its candid publishing on these topics is the *Wall Street Journal*. It frequently publishes evolutionary biologist Colin Wright who writes articles with titles like "A Biologist Explains Why Sex Is Binary" and "When Asked 'What Are Your Pronouns,' Don't Answer: A Seemingly Innocuous Question Masks a Demand for Conformity with a Regressive Set of Ideas." In 2023, it published investigative journalist Gerald Posner's piece, "The Truth About Puberty Blockers," in which he refers to transgenderism as a "fashion," and calls "gender-affirming care" for children a "human experiment on children and teens" that "borders on child abuse."

The Economist has also been a very worthy contributor to public discussion on these matters. For example, it has exposed the fact that the U.S. is doubling down on "gender-affirming care" for minors, when other nations all over the world are putting a stop to it. Both the *New York Post* and the *Washington Examiner* also consistently report accurately on these matters (and both have published me before), although they also frequently fall into the trap of using opposite-sex pronouns.

Still, to date, virtually every single media outlet in the United States, and most media outlets all over the world, has served as the protection racket of an industry that denies the material reality of sex, invades women's spaces, and mutilates children. With very few exceptions, the only places to find clear, accurate reporting on "trans" are lesser-known outlets like *Reduxx* and *The Post Millennial*, independent blogs like *The 11th Hour*, and the private Substack pages of the few individuals willing to talk about it. Had the media challenged the narratives of the industry *at all* starting in the early 2010s, we wouldn't be where we are. Democrats never would have been allowed to enshrine "gender identity" in the law and "queer theory" would never have gone mainstream. From the *New York Times* and *Fox News* to *Mother Jones* and *The Daily Caller*, the media has a lot of apologizing to do.

One prominent conservative who refuses to go along anymore is Megyn Kelly. Kelly, a podcaster and former *Fox* newscaster started out accepting that "gender identity" has meaning and using people's "preferred pronouns." Over the course of 2022 and 2023, however, she changed her tune, and by June 2023, she decided that she had had it completely. She used her platform on YouTube to excoriate the "TQ" portion of the "LGBTQ" acronym and explained why she would no longer use "preferred pronouns." She did not mince words. She said she previously thought that "preferred pronouns" were harmless. She said, "I complied. I went along with it. I didn't see them harm." By 2022, she was asking herself why being "polite" requires denying material reality. In her 2023 video, she talked about Lia (Will) Thomas, Riley Gaines, Kellie-Jay Keen, and the "detransitioners." She thanked the women who had previously spoken out. Ms. Kelly, if you are reading this, thank you and welcome to the fight.

In early 2023, I was contacted by the producers of the forum American Public Square (APS), a Kansas City-based community organization "working to improve the tone and quality of public discourse by convening groups and creating space for respectful dialogue on important topics; educating community members about why engaging in this way is important and how to do it well; and engaging diverse segments of our society to ensure that multiple perspectives are explored." They invited me to join a panel of "experts" on the topic of "gender and identities." I had several very positive conversations with the producers, and I was excited to do it. The conversation was to take place in consultation with a local PBS affiliate, and I had nothing but positive interactions with the PBS representatives as well.

It was scheduled for September 26 and the other panelists were to be Jamie Reed (the Washington University gender clinic whistle blower), a black lesbian named Monica Harris who works with the Foundation Against Intolerance and Racism and blogs about feminism, a man named Justice Horn who serves as the head of the local LGBTQ+ Commission, and a young woman named Alex Pearson who uses they/them pronouns and founded something called Kansas Missouri Queer Law. On September 22, however, I was notified that Justice Horn and Alex Pearson had cancelled so they could not go forward with the program. I do not lay this at the feat of APS; they did what they had to do. I lay this at the feet of Justice Horn and Alex Pearson who were apparently so afraid to discuss issues of "gender and identities" with a bunch of people they view as TERFs that they chickened out at the last minute.

This is why the media generally silences TERFs. If we can be heard, we will win.

School Indoctrination

To readers who are parents of school-age children: I beg you to put this book down immediately and do one of two things: (1) if your children are nearby, please ask them if they have heard the word "transgender" in school; or (2) if your children are not nearby, go to your computer, find the names of your school board members, and email them demanding to know what your children are being taught regarding matters related to sex and gender. Or, if you are not ready for (2), send an email to your children's teachers (it can be about anything). If the email comes back with pronouns in the signature know that the school has already been infected. By the time the school turns away from "gender identity" (if it ever does), your kids will already have aged out and been indoctrinated. Another good thing to do is read the Substack of the group Parents with Inconvenient Truths about Trans (PITT). Their stories about how their kids got sucked in are both breathtaking and devastating. Regardless of how you choose to approach this, you might be astonished by what you learn. I hope you will finish this book eventually, but at the moment, nothing is more important than protecting your children from being indoctrinated by "gender identity" at school.

In 2021 and 2022, a group of volunteer women at Women's Declaration International USA got to work on a FOIA project to see what they could learn about what our schools are teaching children about "gender identity."[10] It turns out that our schools are teaching children *a lot* about "gender identity," none of it good or grounded in science. What the team found is terrifying. Our schools are setting an entire generation's worth of kids up for a lifetime of confusion about the material reality of sex. According to WDI USA, "Millions of children across the United States are being taught the regressive ideology that everyone has a 'gender identity.' This ideological curriculum starts in the earliest school years, and is appearing in red and blue states, big city and small-town schools. Children are inundated by gender identity ideology from all sides, over and over again, as though 'gender identity' were real, and as though it is more important than the material reality of biological sex."

---

[10] All information discussed here is available at https://womensdeclarationusa.com/gender-identity-indoctrination-in-our-schools/.

Most of the school districts that responded to the team's FOIA requests reported that they teach some version of "The Genderbread Person" in school. I don't know exactly how many U.S. schools teach about the Genderbread Person. I do know that when I attended a meeting in 2019 at the U.S. Department of Education to discuss Title IX with the Office for Civil Rights, every wall on the first floor of the Department building was plastered with posters of it.

The Genderbread Person is a cartoon drawing of a gingerbread man cookie with a big smile on its face. Around the drawing are labels and arrows. It labels the cookie's brain as "identity," its heart as "attraction," its genitals as "sex," and its entire body as "expression." It is, of course, not true that biological sex is only located in genitalia. We are all either female or male, down to every last cell in our bodies. Underneath the cartoon drawing are a bunch of words that purport to explain what's going on. It asks kids to check boxes for "Sex Assigned at Birth," where the options are "Male," "Female," and "Intersex." This is ridiculous for several reasons. First, sex is not "assigned at birth." It is observed by medical professionals (or by ordinary individuals) and usually recorded. It is accurate approximately 99 percent of the time. Second, "Intersex" is not a "third sex." It is a medical condition that occurs in approximately .018 percent of the population. Third, many kids with intersex conditions don't know it until puberty. These kids appear to be unambiguously boys or girls, but when they hit the typical age of the onset of puberty, they do not experience the physical developments expected of their apparent sex. Fourth, even if kids with intersex conditions knew they had them, *on what planet do educators think it is a good idea to ask them to disclose that information*? Young people with intersex conditions (and their parents) often struggle to understand what is going on with them, medically. This is a matter for young people, their parents, and their doctors. Teachers should unequivocally not be asking for this information unless it is relevant to some aspect of protecting a child while at school.

Underneath that, it says that "Gender Identity" = "Woman-ness" or "Man-ness"; "Gender Expression" = "Femininity" or "Masculinity"; and

"Anatomical Sex" = "Female-ness" or "Male-ness." Note the subtle use of the phrase "anatomical sex." As mentioned, sex is not only anatomical; it is biological and it runs through every cell of our bodies. When teachers present this false information to students, they are either lying or they are ignorant about the material reality of sex. Finally, underneath all that, it talks about being sexually and romantically attracted to others. It says that people can be either attracted to "Women and/or Feminine People and/or Female People" or attracted to "Men and/or Masculine People and/or Male People," and it says the same for romantic attraction. This is pure obfuscation. Every single person on the face of the planet is either attracted to members of the same sex, members of the opposite sex, or members of both sexes. Young people who are just beginning to explore sexuality and who may experience same-sex attraction often have a difficult time navigating that experience because of society's expectation of heterosexuality. Obscuring the material reality of sex is just cruel to young people just beginning to explore the world of sexuality, especially those who are experiencing same-sex attraction. The Genderbread Person, with its lies, obscurations, and obfuscations, has no place in our schools, in children's study materials, or in the U.S. Department of Education.

When the WDI USA team reached out to the Oregon Department of Education, it sent them to the Department's Office of Equity, Diversion, and Inclusion (EDI), which has a page called "Supporting Gender Expansive Students: Guidance for Schools" and provides a link to download the guidance. The page states that the guidance is "grounded in the civil rights of students to be free from gender identity-based discrimination when pursuing their education." The office also released a set of "supplemental resources aligned to the strategies and recommendations outlined in the LGBTQ2SIA+ Student Success Plan," which "outline recommendations, best practices, and resources for districts to consider as they develop policies and programming to support gender expansive students."

Under "Tools for School Staff," the EDI Office provides links for downloading resources related to "affirming a student's gender":

"Gender-Affirming Schools Action Plan"; "Affirming Gender, Names, and Pronouns in Student Information Systems"; and "Gender Expansive Individual Education Program." The main document, "Supporting Gender Expansive Students: Guidance for Schools," was issued in January 2023 and builds on the agency's 2016 guidance titled, "Creating a Safe and Supportive School Environment for Transgender Students," which was "one of the first statewide guidance documents in the nation to help *K–12 schools* synthesize state law, federal law, and best practice in order to support transgender students" (emphasis added). Since 2016, Oregon has been telling its school teachers and administrators that children as young as five might "be transgender." According to the Director's Introduction, "National data demonstrates the impact of anti-transgender legislation on nonbinary youth, in addition to ongoing racist, transphobic, and homophobic harm experienced by LGBTQ2SIA+ youth of color in the United States." Oregon has gone from teaching about the existence of five-year-old "transgender" kids in 2016 to talking about "non-binary youth" and "LGBTQ2SIA+ youth of color" in 2023. The Introduction concludes: "It is our responsibility to move beyond mere tolerance and inclusion toward respectful, affirming, and celebratory school communities where all students belong and succeed." The action plan instructs schools to "consistently use affirming language, including student-asserted names and pronouns" and says that "gender expansive students and staff should be given the opportunity to offer affirming language recommendations, in order to support cultural and regional relevance."

I want readers to really think about what this document is saying. We know that "affirming gender" means encouraging kids to think that sex isn't real, or that they might be "born in the wrong body." It often means going along with opposite-sex pronouns, puberty blockers, wrong-sex hormones, and/or surgeries. But according to Oregon, it is not even enough to "tolerate" or "include" students who go through these processes. It is now our collective responsibility to "celebrate" the denial of the material reality of sex in *schools*.

In Princeton, New Jersey, Thomas Foley and Jen Simon teach middle school teachers that sex isn't real. Foley is a school counselor at Princeton Unified Middle School, where he co-advises the school's Sexuality and Gender Alliance and "leads professional development related to creating inclusive classrooms for students in the LGBTQIA+ community." Simon is his co-advisor at the Alliance and a special education teacher. What the WDI USA team learned through FOIA is that they regularly offer a training program to middle school teachers and administrators called "Supporting our LGBTQIA+ Students." They teach that in addition to being lesbian, gay, or bisexual, a middle school student can be "transgender" ("MtF, FtM, Sometimes an umbrella term") or "queer."

They share a lot of statistics about the experiences of "LGBTQIA+ students" and promote the lie that kids are likely to commit suicide if the people around them do not "affirm their gender." They admonish teachers to "respect students' desired names and pronouns," avoid using the words "boys" and "girls," and "add your pronouns to email signature, syllabus, and website." They teach that "transgender pre-school aged children do exist." They expressly conflate non-conformity with sex stereotypes with "transgender," suggesting that if a child plays with toys typically associated with the opposite sex, that child *actually is* the opposite sex. They promote "universal bathrooms" (by which they mean mixed-sex). They insist that everyone respect students' preferred pronouns and share some information about a 2018 report by HRC titled, "LGBTQ Youth Report." It exclaims that "Calling Trans Youth by Chosen Name Can Drastically Reduce Chance of Suicide." In other words, this is bullying teachers into thinking that if they don't go along with a student's insistence that his or her name is something other than what it is, the student is likely to commit suicide.

In another presentation, the same presenters direct teachers to an organization called AMAZE. According to its website, AMAZE "harnesses the power of digital media to provide young adolescents around the globe with medically accurate, age-appropriate, affirming, and honest sex education they can access directly online—regardless of where they live or what school they attend" and "strives to assist adults—parents, guardians, educators, and health care providers around the globe—to communicate effectively and honestly about sex and sexuality with the children and adults in their lives." This is all very nice language, but I want to encourage readers to think very critically about what it means to "provide young adolescents around the globe with…affirming and honest sex education they can access directly online."

First, I hope that readers understand by this point what "affirming" means, but also, why does this organization think it is appropriate to provide sex education to kids that they can "access directly online?" AMAZE videos (all available on YouTube to anyone) are quite obviously aimed at kids younger than adolescence. They are animated shorts that cheerfully talk about everything from "Can a Doctor Tell if I'm a Virgin?" to "Does STI Testing Hurt?" to "Why Do I Smell Down There?" to "Condom Negotiation." There is also one called "Range of Gender Identities," which is being shown in seventh-grade classrooms. AMAZE's goal is to reach kids globally and it has numerous resources for educators on its website, including "Educator Toolkits: Ready to Use AMAZE Videos in Your Classroom?" and "3Rs: Lesson Plans that Incorporate AMAZE Videos." Regardless, AMAZE videos are available to anyone with a WiFi connection and its YouTube channel places no age restrictions on its content or makes any age-related recommendations.

The WDI USA FOIA team uncovered similar lesson plans in jurisdictions in California, Colorado, Illinois, Minnesota, Rhode Island, Texas, Virginia, and Washington. A particularly egregious example comes from Seattle. The District's "K-5 Gender Book Kit Background Information and Teacher Guide" states: "An estimated 10 to 12% of our students identify as gay, lesbian, bisexual, transgender or non-binary. More and more students are recognizing at young ages who they are and how they want to express their gender identities. To support these students, their peers, their families and friends, Seattle Schools offer support groups, referrals to professionals in the community, and curriculum materials that reflect the gender diversity we see every day in all of our schools. Educational research points to the importance of making school relevant to students' lives by reflecting their lived experiences in the classroom. In addition, the silence and invisibility caused by ignoring, erasing or leaving out portions of history, or their lived experiences, causes confusion, isolation, and alienation. As a result of this invisibility and erasure, a lack of engagement and increased disconnect from the educational experience can occur. Teachers, students and families have been seeking materials that address the needs of this often vulnerable and marginalized population. Seattle Public Schools is proud to offer this K-5 Gender Book Kit to teachers to help build more welcoming and inclusive classroom environments." The teacher guide also provides "Answers to Common Questions about Gender, Gender Expression and Gender Identity." In July 2023, *The Post Millennial* reported that Seattle schools are literally referring children *directly* to "gender affirming" clinics without informing parents *at all.*

The New York State Education Department posts guidance from the University of the State of New York (with the help of the New York Civil Liberties Union) titled, "Creating a Safe, Supportive, and Affirming School Environment for Transgender and Gender Expansive Students" and provides it to schools throughout the state. The guidance defines "gender identity" as "one's innermost concept of self and how one perceives and identifies themselves, including, for example, male, female, trans, transgender, queer, nonbinary, gender non-conforming, and gender expansive. Gender identity can exist on a spectrum where some individuals feel entirely male, some entirely female, and some somewhere in-between. Gender identity is a mental, emotional, and spiritual state that is not determined by a person's anatomy." It instructs schools to hold a planning meeting when a student "comes out as a trans or gender expansive," *whether or not the student's parents attend.* It emphasizes that "schools will want to adopt a flexible approach, given that transgender students may not feel comfortable or safe being their authentic selves in all contexts" (by which they mean at home, with their parents). But a 2023 poll of New Jersey parents revealed that seventy-seven percent of parents want to know if their school children are starting to "identify as a different gender" at school, and presumably New York parents are not too different.

The indoctrination of our entire education system never ends. A University of Arizona nursing school teaches future nurses that three-year-olds can "know they are transgender" and to start asking kids about their "gender" at the age of three. In 2023, a teacher's union in Colorado told teachers to have kids conduct "gender" questionnaires using pencil and paper and to then get rid of the evidence.

But things are slowly starting to change. Parents all over the country are suing schools over policies that either encourage or require teachers and school administrators to "affirm" a student's "gender identity" without informing them that their children are going by new names, being referred to using opposite-sex pronouns, and/or using opposite-sex bathrooms. In California, two teachers have sued their school districts arguing that requiring them to withhold such information from parents violates *their own* rights (specifically, their First Amendment rights to freedom of speech and religion). In September 2023, a federal district court agreed that the teachers have a religious freedom right not to withhold such information from parents and declined to rule on the freedom of speech question. Some states have enacted laws permitting teachers to ignore students' "preferred pronouns." Also in September 2023, a federal court of appeals ruled that the First Amendment prohibits public schools from compelling students to use language they disagree with, including language that hews to "gender identity."

According to the Code of Ethics for Educators at the National Education Association (one of the most powerful progressive labor lobby groups in the nation), "The educator, believing in the worth and dignity of each human being, recognizes the supreme importance of the pursuit of truth, devotion to excellence, and the nurture of the democratic principles. Essential to these goals is the protection of freedom to learn and to teach and the guarantee of equal educational opportunity for all. The educator accepts the responsibility to adhere to the highest ethical standards." Our nation's educators are failing woefully to adhere to these principles. This is all happening with the support of the National Education Association *itself*, which tells teachers to teach a book called *Gender Queer* in their classes. The American Federation of Teachers (AFT) is no better. It held a conference in July 2023 where members were taught how to inject the topic of "gender identity" into classrooms. One of the conference sessions was called "Affirming LGBTQIA+ Identities in and out of the Classroom." Another was "The TBNCNB [transgender, gender nonconforming, non-binary] Inclusive School and Classroom." Readers can be forgiven for having trouble keeping up with the shifting acronyms.

Our society is teaching children that sex-stereotypes are innate and that "gender identity" overrides the material reality of biological sex. Our society is teaching an entire generation of confused children that sex isn't real, that it is possible to be born in the wrong body, and that if they are confused about sex then it is perfectly fine to block puberty, take wrong-sex hormones that cause sterility and other long-term health problems, and it is maybe even okay to change your genitals if doing so helps you align with the sex you think you are. Schools are "transing" kids and they are doing it without parental knowledge. This is unforgivable and educators should be unabashedly ashamed of themselves for promoting this toxic poison by teaching it to children.

CHAPTER 6

PHARMA AND THE GHOULS IN THE MEDICAL ESTABLISHMENT

Who benefits from putting an entire generation of children on a lifetime's worth of hormones?

In 2023, the journal *Qualitative Research in Health* published a paper titled "Medical Uncertainty and Reproduction of the 'Normal': Decision-Making Around Testosterone Therapy in Transgender Pregnancy." It argued that women who claim to identify as men should not only be permitted to ingest testosterone during pregnancy and nursing, but that they should be *encouraged* to do so to persuade society to reframe what we think of as "normal pregnancy outcomes." These authors were literally arguing that even if we know that exogenous testosterone harms fetuses and infants, we should give it to pregnant women anyway because insisting on healthy babies is rooted in a problematic desire to "protect offspring from becoming anything other than 'normal'" and "reflects historical and ongoing social practices for creating 'ideal' and normative bodies."

What is going on here?

Many people who have been examining and critiquing the abolition of sex for several years now understand that it is being driven by a vicious industry that is intent on medicalizing otherwise healthy human bodies.

As far back as February 2018, independent journalist Jennifer Bilek was writing about how "Exceedingly rich, white men (and women) who invest in biomedical companies are funding myriad transgender organizations whose agenda will make them gobs of money." She published that year in the conservative publication *The Federalist*, even though she is not conservative, because no more mainstream or left-leaning media outlet would listen, even though Bilek was writing about a massive capitalistic industry driving what was being framed as a "civil rights struggle." This should have been a scandal a long time ago. The reason it wasn't was because its main perpetrators were on the political left and very few people wanted to expose it. Bilek states, "This ideology has taken the bullet train of post modernism to the juncture we are at now."

So-called "gender clinics" are all over the country. Thanks to the Gender Mapping Project, we know that ten years ago there were only a handful. By 2023, there were over 400 in North America, most of them in the U.S. and Canada. One example is the Cincinnati Children's Hospital's Transgender Clinic. Chris Cicchinelli, the CEO of a sex toy company, gave it $2 million in 2018. Countless "detransitioners," discussed in Chapter 3, have told stories about how they were referred to these clinics and given prescriptions for puberty-blocking and/or cross-sex hormones on the first day or within weeks of referral. In June 2023, *The Daily Wire* reported that at one such clinic, the Juniper Center, intake workers were just making up diagnoses of "gender dysphoria" to cash in on insurance money. Dr. Erica Li, a pediatrician at Washington State, says that what is happening amounts to "postmodern medicine." I'm not a doctor, but given what I know about postmodernism, she certainly seems to be right. A deep dive into the history of "gender identity" in the medical establishment reveals the extent to which it has always been this way.

I'm sure that countless doctors have innocently referred patients to "gender clinics" on the assumption that the "gender clinics" were the medical experts, not realizing that they were unwittingly contributing to what is surely going to become the biggest medical scandal in modern history. But not everyone in this story is innocent. There is a cast of characters—organizations and associations, clinics, and individuals—at the center of this horror show who need to be called out by name.

Organizations and Associations

WPATH

The World Professional Association for Transgender Health (WPATH) started out as the Harry Benjamin International Gender Dysphoria Association (HBIGDA), founded in 1979 by a man named Paul Allen Walker. At its origins, WPATH was basically a merger of the Janus Information Facility (JIF), described as a "referral service for transsexuals affiliated with the University of Texas" in Galveston Texas, the Harry Benjamin Foundation, and the Erickson Educational Foundation (EEF), a non-profit philanthropic organization funded and controlled by Reed Erickson (a woman born Rita Mae Erickson, sometimes referred to as Rita Alma Erickson, who had undergone what was then called a "sex-change" operation conducted by Harry Benjamin himself). The HBIGDA became WPATH in 2007. Its current president is a man named Marci (Mark) Bowers. Bowers brags on his website that he is a "pioneer in the field of Gender Affirmation Surgery," that he has performed more than 2,250 vaginoplasties and 3,900 "gender-affirming surgeries" overall, and that he has been named the "Transgender Surgery Rock Star," the "Georgia O'Keefe of Genitalia," and the "Beyonce of Bottom Surgery." He has also served on the board of GLAAD.

Throughout the sixties, seventies, and eighties, there emerged a growing field of research in the U.S. into what was then termed "transsexualism." Earlier in the twentieth century, doctors in Europe had been experimenting with the idea that people could "change sex." In her 2021 book *Trans: When Ideology Meets Reality*, Helen Joyce tells the story of Einar Wegener, a man who very much wanted to be transformed into a woman, and Magnus Hirschfeld, the doctor who operated on him. Hirschfeld had already been performing genital surgeries, but Joyce explains that for

Wegener, Hirschfeld wanted to try something more ambitious: a transformation of body chemistry as well as genitals. Joyce discusses how the doctors involved in all this seemed to believe that it was possible to "change sex." By the 1960s, however, the American sexologists mentioned above who were looking at what they termed "transsexualism" knew there was no such things as "changing sex." For them, it was always about medicalizing identity.

A lot of this is grounded in the work of Dr. Alfred Kinsey, who is known for research on child sexuality. Hirschfeld (the European doctor who operated on Wegener) knew Harry Benjamin, and it was through Kinsey that Benjamin would become interested in what he referred to as "transsexualism." By the late 1960s, Benjamin was working directly with Dr. John Money, who ran the Johns Hopkins University Gender Clinic, where he somewhat famously performed surgery on a male infant named David Reimer to make the child appear to be female, when in fact the child had undergone a botched circumcision. Reimer would eventually learn the truth that he was male when he did not experience female puberty (because, of course, he didn't), and after a tumultuous young adulthood, he tragically took his own life at the age of thirty-five.

It is unclear exactly how much money the EEF contributed to all of this work on "transsexualism," but the EEF claims that Erickson's businesses eventually developed into a personal fortune estimated to be over $40 million. That is a lot of money today and was a lot more in the sixties and seventies. According to the EEF's website, the foundation "funded many early research efforts, including the creation of the Harry Benjamin Foundation, and the opening of the first North American gender clinic at Johns Hopkins." The EEF sponsored public addresses, educational films, radio and television appearances, and newspaper articles bringing "transsexualism" to the attention of the public. In addition, the EEF also published informative quarterly newsletters, educational pamphlets, and books. "Trans" is, and has always been, big business.

Walt Heyer is a man who spent eight years claiming to be a woman named "Laura." He had been treated by Paul Walker (WPATH's founder), who approved him for cross-sex hormones during his first counseling session. Heyer states: "On the strength of his saying I was a candidate for 'gender reassignment' surgery, I divorced my wife and traveled to Trinidad Colorado, in April 1983." There, Dr. Stanley Biber (who had completed 3,000 surgeries before Heyer's) performed his surgery. Heyer explained that when he later decided to accept himself as male and applied to change his birth certificate back to male because of his male sex, he reached out to both doctors who had "treated" him. He states: "The document that Biber and Walker signed and submitted to the Superior Court testified that no gender change took place. They said I was male with 'neutered' genitalia and 'mixed' outward appearance. Their document provides proof that 'gender change' is a fraud and a scam and the 'treatment' of hormone therapy and gender surgery is ineffective to change genders—and doctors know it." Heyer has been an outspoken advocate on behalf of "detransitioners" and against "gender-affirmative care."

I have been unable to track down the original WPATH Standards of Care from 1979. However, we know that there has been a total of eight versions since then. The most recent is Version 8, which seeks to provide "clinical guidance to health care professionals to assist transgender and gender diverse (TGD) people in accessing safe and effective pathways to achieving lasting personal comfort with their gendered selves with the aim of optimizing their overall physical health, psychological well-being, and self-fulfillment." Optimizing physical health, psychological well-being, and self-fulfillment sound great, but what does it mean to "achieve lasting personal comfort with one's gendered self"? I don't know what it means to have a "gendered self." Probably most of us don't. One hundred percent of human beings are either female or male, and all of us have some ways of presenting in society either in conformity with sex stereotypes or outside of them. That should be completely fine. But if we know, as everyone does, that it is not possible to "change sex," why should any of that be medicalized?

The previous version of the WPATH Standards of Care (Version 7, 2012) had set forth recommendations for young people who wish to "transition." My own opinion is that all people who struggle with matters pertaining to the material reality of sex should receive the mental health care they need to accept themselves as they are. But still, the WPATH Version 7 Standards of Care *at least* urged caution when it comes to young people. It recommended a cautious and staged approach with the full involvement of parents. It contained disclaimers to the effect that long-term outcomes of administering hormones on children and adolescents were not really known. And Version 7 was explicit about surgery: Genital surgery should not be carried out until a patient has reached the legal age of majority and "lived continuously for at least 12 months in the gender role that is congruent with their gender identity" (whatever that means).

Version 8 lifts all these recommendations. Currently, WPATH does not recommend *any* age limit for hormones or genital surgeries on minors. Version 8 also, for the first time, advances the idea that "eunuch" (referring to a man or boy who has had or wishes to have his genitals removed) is a "gender identity." This is in large part thanks to a man named Thomas W. Johnson, a retired professor at California State University in Chico (CSUC), who helped form a body modification fetish website called The Eunuch Archive. According to *Reduxx*, the Eunuch Archive "hosts over 3,000 pieces of fictional child pornography that detail the rape, torture, and killing of children. In some narratives, children with stunted puberty are raped by doctors. In others, children are castrated by force as part of a sadistic sexual torture ritual." Johnson has also been involved in research on the topic of castration as a fetish. In 2022, he co-authored an article titled "Castration for Pleasure: Exploring Extreme Castration Ideations in Fiction" in the journal *Archives of Sexual Pleasure*. That article is included in the National Library of Medicine on the NIH's website.

After WPATH announced Standards of Care Version 8, a group of "mental health professionals, public health scientists, and allied organizations and individuals" announced a declaration called "Beyond WPATH." The crux of the effort is to state that these professionals "have grave concerns about the damaging physical and mental health impacts of the current Standards of Care.... We hold that WPATH has discredited itself." I view this as a very positive development.

The early sexologists were focused exclusively on "transsexualism" among adults. Whatever anyone thinks about that, they did not appear to concern themselves with the concept of a "transgender child." The 2012 version of the WPATH Standards of Care, although it recommended the administration of hormones under limited circumstances in children and adolescents, at least urged caution among medical practitioners when working with such kids. But the seeds of change had already been sown. The concept of a "transgender child" had been introduced and WPATH went right along with it. Most people had probably never heard of the idea of a "transgender child" before 2020 or so. But by then, it had become impossible to ignore. WPATH is one of several organizations that have concretized the idea in society that medicalizing identity is healthy and safe for all people, including children, and it continues to double down on its position to this day. It is paid handsomely to do so.

The Biden administration supports all this. In November 2022, HHS Secretary Xavier Becerra submitted written testimony before the House Committee on Education and Labor stating, "The Biden-Harris Administration supports the upcoming release of the World Professional Association for Transgender Health (WPATH) Standards of Care Version 8 and believes that all children and adults should be afforded life-saving, medically necessary care. Payers, both public and private, should cover treatments which medical experts have determined to be medically necessary." This is the nation's top medical chief calling for taxpayer dollars to fund the administration of hormones and surgeries to otherwise healthy children and young adults.

In response, Republican Representative Nancy Mace wrote to the Department: "The Biden Administration appears to be encouraging any child, who does not conform to perceptions of masculine or feminine stereotypes, to alter his or her body through potentially irreversible medical or surgical intervention. Instead of funding these life-altering drugs and procedures, our government should be promoting policies to protect vulnerable children—who cannot consent. In light of these concerns, I am requesting documents and information to understand whether, and to what extent, taxpayer dollars are being used to promote and/or fund these potentially harmful practices." I agree with her completely.[11] Americans deserve to know how the Democrats in power are spending our money and whether our tax dollars are funding medical practices that harm children. WPATH has a lot to answer for.

The AAP

One early reference to the concept of a "transgender child" is the 2008 publication of *The Transgender Child: A Handbook for Families and Professionals* by Stephanie Brill. Brill founded the group Gender Spectrum, which "works to create gender sensitive and inclusive environments for all children and teens." In 2015, a man named Julian Gill-Peterson published a dissertation titled *Queer Theory Is Kid Stuff: A Genealogy of the Gay and Transgender Child*. For that, he received a PhD in Philosophy from Rutgers University. From then until 2021, he was an Assistant Professor in the English Department of the University of Pittsburgh, with a secondary appointment in Gender, Sexuality, and Women's Studies. His "New Faculty Profile" on the University of Pittsburgh's website names him as Julian and refers to him using he/him pronouns. In 2018, he published a book called *Histories of the Transgender Child*, arguing that "transgender children" existed in the early twentieth century and that they "not only existed but preexisted the term transgender and its predecessors, playing a central role in the medicalization of trans people, and all sex and gender."

---

[11] Incidentally, Representative Mace has called on her Republican colleagues to soften their stance on abortion and in 2023, introduced a bill to increase over-the-counter contraceptive options for women. Regarding abortion, she has said, "We've buried our head in the sand. We're afraid to talk about it. Because we're afraid, we want to go to the extreme corners of this issue. But that's not where the vast majority of Americans are right now. And we've got to show compassion, especially to victims who've been raped." If her Republican colleagues would follow her lead on this, I know plenty of women who would vote for them.

Today, Julian is Jules and "she" teaches in the History Department at Johns Hopkins University.

All this was fairly obscure at the time, but in January 2017, *National Geographic* announced that there had been a "Gender Revolution" in an issue featuring a cover image of then nine-year-old Avery Jackson. Avery is a boy whose parents "socially transitioned" him at the age of four and refer to him as their daughter. His mother gave a public talk where she stated that Avery "transitioned, which means she changed her outward appearance from male to female and started living full time as her true gender when she was four. Until that point, she was quite a rough-and-tumble little boy with a buzz cut and a shark-tooth necklace. But when she was three, she asked her dad and I if we could buy her a princess dress." Then she went on for a bit about how Avery liked "bright and sparkly things." This is what is so frustrating for feminists and gay rights activists who fight the abolition of sex—so much of this is grounded in sexist stereotypes. Why not just buy the poor kid a princess dress and accept that your son likes bright and sparkly things and might grow up to be gay? Why insist that kids who wear princess dresses and like bright and sparkly things are actually girls and then put them on the cover of a major national magazine? This is not a "gender revolution." It is rank sexism, homophobia, and child abuse.

By September 2018, the American Academy of Pediatrics (AAP) had announced its first "policy statement to provide guidance for parents and clinicians through a gender-affirming approach." The statement was published the following month in Volume 142, Issue 4 of the prestigious journal *Pediatrics*. At around the same time, the AAP published an article called "Advancing the Practice of Pediatric Psychology with Transgender Youth" in the journal *Clinical Practice in Pediatric Psychology*. Its primary author was Dr. Diane Chen, who is an active participant in the NIH study concerning the administration of wrong-sex hormones in young people, discussed in Chapter 3. And that very same year, the Johns Hopkins University's History Department posted Gill-Peterson's *Histories of the Transgender Child* on its website. And with that, the concept of the "trans child" was cemented by two of the most prominent and well-regarded medical institutions in the U.S., as well as the Johns Hopkins Department of History.[12]

If all this sounds a bit bizarre, it is important to understand the entire concept of a "transgender child" has been invented by the industry itself. In 2019, British feminists Heather Brunskell-Evans and Michele Moore published an anthology called *Inventing Transgender Children and Young People*. It is a collection of essays written by doctors, psychologists, sociologists, teachers, parents, and "detransitioners" about how "transgender" young people are *invented* in different contexts: "gender identity" medical and mental health services, lobby groups, school resources, social media, and the media at large. None of this is to say that these children and young people are not themselves real; it is to say that all children (and adults) have a sexed body and the idea that a person can be the opposite sex (or "born in the wrong body") is simply a lie.

The AAP's 2018 policy statement is titled, "Ensuring Comprehensive Care and Support for Transgender and Gender-Diverse Children and Adolescents." It begins: "As a traditionally underserved population that faces numerous health disparities, youth who identify as transgender and gender diverse (TGD) and their families are increasingly presenting to pediatric providers for education, care, and referrals. The need for more formal training, standardized treatment, and research on safety and medical outcomes often leaves providers feeling ill equipped to support and care for patients that identify as TGD and families." It is true that kids who claim to have a "trans" identity need care and that this is a matter of tremendous concern in our society—a concern that the AAP played a role in *creating*.

The policy encourages "gender affirmation" and puberty suppression in confused kids. On the topic of surgery, the policy states: "Although current protocols typically reserve surgical interventions for adults, they

---

[12] I attended Johns Hopkins as an undergraduate, majored in political science, and took some courses in the History Department.

are occasionally pursued during adolescence on a case-by-case basis, considering the necessity and benefit to the adolescent's overall health and often including multidisciplinary input from medical, mental health, and surgical providers as well as from the adolescent and family." All this has created a cohort of kids whose bodies have been altered and who may or may not ever have functioning sexual or reproductive systems. It has also created an entire community of parents who have been manipulated and devastated.

The policy statement includes a table of definitions for explaining how it uses various terms. They bear a remarkable similarity to HRC's definitions. For example, the AAP defines sex as "an assignment that is made at birth, usually male or female, typically on the basis of external genital anatomy but sometimes on the basis of internal gonads, chromosomes, or hormone levels." HRC states that sex is "sex assigned at birth—The sex, male, female, or intersex, that a doctor or midwife uses to describe a child at birth based on their external anatomy." The real definition of sex is relatively simple. A quick Google search brings up these results: "Either of the two main categories (male and female) into which humans and most other living things are divided on the basis of their reproductive functions." "The members of either sex considered as a group." "The fact of belonging to either the male or female sex." Merriam-Webster defines it as "either of the two major forms of individuals that occur in many species and that are distinguished respectively as female or male especially on the basis of their reproductive organs and structures." In my 2021 book *The Abolition of Sex*, I defined it as follows, with the help of a friend who is a doctor: "Sex: The differentiation between male and female, determined by whether an X-bearing sperm or a Y-bearing sperm fertilized the X-bearing ovum, which determines the type of sexual and reproductive organs that develop, and the biological differences between females and males."

Surely the AAP must know what sex is. Its website has an entire section devoted to gynecology that advertises policy statements with titles like "Diagnosis, Management, and Treatment of Female Genital Mutilation or Cutting in Girls" and "Menstruation in Girls and Adolescents: Using the

Menstrual Cycle as a Vital Sign." Surely it knows what it means by the word "girls" in these titles. But although the AAP's website says that it is "dedicated to the health of all children," a simple Google search for aap.org brings you straight to its shop. One wonders if the AAP cares more about selling products than about the health of girls and boys.

The AAP defines "gender identity" to mean "A person's deep internal sense of being female, male, a combination of both, somewhere in between, or neither, resulting from a multifaceted interaction of biological traits, environmental factors, self-understanding, and cultural expectations." HRC defines it to mean "one's innermost concept of self as male, female, a blend of both or neither—how individuals perceive themselves and what they call themselves. One's gender identity can be the same or different from their sex assigned at birth." The definitions that appear in the AAP 2018 policy statement are *activist* definitions that have no place in a policy statement being put out by a reputable medical professional association whose mission is to help doctors provide ethical care to minors. There is not perfect overlap between the AAP's definitions and HRC's, but the similarities are striking.

For years now, a pediatrician in Oregon named Julia Mason has submitted proposal after proposal for revising this policy at the AAP's annual conventions. For years, the AAP has ignored and silenced her. The AAP is also ignoring concerned parents and "detransitioners" who have requested systematic reviews of its policies. In October 2022, a group of parents called Our Duty held a rally at the AAP's annual convention. The participants held signs that said things like "Democrats Against Puberty Blockers" and "No One Is Born in the Wrong Body." They offered packets of materials to conference participants, but the AAP reportedly instructed participants to avoid them. According to Erin Friday writing at the online magazine *Human Events*, concerned parents sent 121 letters after the rally to the AAP's president, Dr. Moira Szilagyi, and the president elect, requesting a systematic review. The letters were sent from twenty-seven states and signed mainly by registered Democrats or by parents who had left the Democratic Party because of this issue. No one received a response.

Another letter went out in December 2022, imploring the AAP to conduct a systematic review. That letter emphasized the social contagion aspect of girls suddenly announcing that they are "trans" and referenced a statement of concern by an FDA investigator involved with approval of Lupron regarding use of the drug to block puberty. It also included reference to a change.org petition calling for a systematic review. That letter got no response either. The following year, they sent the AAP a petition put forth by the Women's Liberation Front, calling for a policy reversal. Nothing.

A lot of people who stand up for the material reality of sex often say, "there is no such thing as a transgender child." I agree with that statement, and I think it is vitally important that our society take steps to protect children from medical interventions that result in sterilization and sometimes the removal of healthy body parts. However, I also think that part of the reason there is no such thing as a "transgender child" is that "gender identity" is a lie that denies the material reality of sex, whether we are talking about children *or* adults. Regardless, our society is grappling with a generation of "transgender children." This generation of "transgender children" exists at least in part because the AAP, among others, created it.

By August 2023, however, the AAP started suggesting that it might reverse course. In a policy statement, it said it would continue with its 2018 policy (over the known objections of countless parents), but it *also* said that it would commission a systematic review of medical research on "gender-affirming care" for its effectiveness in adolescents. A lot of people who are concerned about children's safety and the material reality of sex worry that the AAP is going to try to quietly walk back its 2018 policy and fail to acknowledge the harms they have been perpetrating. We cannot let that happen.

The Endocrine Society

The Endocrine Society, an international professional association with over 18,000 members in 120 countries, touts itself as being "at the forefront of hormone science and public health" for one hundred years. In 2017, it put out a clinical practice guide providing "Gender Dysphoria/

Gender Incongruence Guidelines Resources." It is all about suppressing natural sex development. It *does not* (yet) recommend puberty suppression in pre-pubertal children, but it *does* recommend puberty suppression in girls and boys at the onset of puberty. It encourages the administration of "gender-affirming care" for those with a diagnosis of "gender dysphoria" or "gender incongruence."

In 2020, the society updated its policy in its position paper declaring that: "There is a durable biological underpinning to gender identity that should be considered in policy determinations" and that "medical intervention for transgender youth and adults (including puberty suppression, hormone therapy and medically indicated surgery) is effective, relatively safe (when appropriately monitored), and has been established as the standard of care." It called for increased funding for pediatric "transgender health research." But why is an organization whose purpose is to provide information to practitioners about internal hormones taking the political position that "there is a durable biological underpinning to gender identity that should be considered in policy determinations"? It strikes me as incredibly irresponsible to state that "medical intervention for transgender youth and adults…is effective [and] relatively safe (when appropriately monitored)." It is "relatively" safe? What about all the teenagers who don't follow up for monitoring? Researchers literally have no idea how many young people have showed up at a clinic to receive "gender-affirming care," started a course of hormone "treatment," and then simply not followed up. No one knows how those young people are faring.

The American Medical Association has no trouble with any of this. In June 2023, its House of Delegates passed the Endocrine Society's "resolution to protect access to evidence-based gender-affirming care for transgender and gender-diverse individuals." In doing so, it announced that "The AMA [is] committed to opposing any criminal and legal penalties against patients seeking gender-affirming care, family members or guardians who support them in seeking medical care, and health care facilities and clinicians who provide gender-affirming care."[13] I am not aware of any individual, organization, or lawmaker who supports any criminal or legal penalties against *patients* who seek out these hormones or surgeries, nor am I aware of anyone who supports any penalties against anyone who helps patients seek out actual medical care, so the statement seems disingenuous at best. By now, the point is fairly clear: Medical associations in the U.S. (and internationally) are pushing an agenda to medicalize the healthy bodies of people (young people and adults) who are confused about the material reality of their sex. What is even more interesting is what is fueling all of this.

The Endocrine Society has a Corporate Liaison Board (CLB), which "forges a partnership between the Endocrine Society and senior executives in industry. It is a unique consortium of thought leaders and stakeholders assembled to discuss ideas and goals for the future of endocrinology.... *Through participation in the CLB, members have a forum to share their perspective with the Endocrine Society leader representatives on issues, such as clinical education, healthcare legislation, or patient education. Additionally, members have access to an array of benefits while showing leadership within in their fields*" (emphasis added).

The society lists numerous corporate partners as members of the CLB, among them: AbbVie Inc. (which makes and markets the drug Lupron, the primary drug used to suppress puberty, even though the FDA has not approved the drug for that use), Amgen, Inc., Ascendis Pharma Inc., AstraZeneca, Boehringer Ingelheim Pharmaceuticals, Inc., HRA Pharma, Ipsen Biopharmaceuticals, Inc., Merck & Co., Inc., Pfizer, Inc., Regeneron Pharmaceuticals, Inc., Strongbridge Biopharma, Takeda Pharmaceuticals, Ultragenyx Pharmaceuticals, Vertex Pharmaceuticals,

[13] My profession is no better. In August 2023, the American Bar Association announced two new resolutions: one encouraging the use of wrong-sex pronouns within law schools, during the bar admission process, the legal profession, and the justice system generally; and another urging all law schools and bar admission entities to include self-reporting options for wrong-sex pronouns, honorifics, and so on.

and Xeris Pharmaceuticals. All biopharmaceutical companies. The AAP lists several of the same companies as "corporate donors to [its] Friends of Children Fund." The Pediatric Endocrine Society works closely with the Endocrine Society, focusing on matters pertaining specifically to pediatric hormonal health. It lists as its Mission Alliance Partners: BioMarin Pharmaceutical, Inc., AbbVie, Endo Pharmaceuticals, Pfizer, Ascendis Pharma, and Lumos Pharma. In July 2023, twenty-one leading experts on "gender-affirming care" for minors from eight countries published a letter to the editor of the *Wall Street Journal*, expressing disagreement with the Endocrine Society's policies. It remains to be seen whether the society will respond or take any action to protect young people.

In other words, these organizations, each of which actively promotes "gender-affirming care" among their members and publicly, works hand in hand with Big Pharma, which profits from the medicalization of healthy human bodies. Is it any wonder, then, that after the state of Florida announced a ban on "gender-affirming care" for adolescents in 2022, the Endocrine Society (speaking also for the Pediatric Endocrine Society) and the Florida chapter of the AAP both opposed the move? These are by no means the only medical organizations or associations that have been captured by "gender identity," and this section has only scratched the surface of the damage they have done. They are just some of the worst offenders.

Clinics

Boston Children's

Boston Children's Hospital boasts that it specializes in "providing comprehensive care to gender non-conforming children, adolescents, and young adults." In my view, comprehensive healthcare should be a universal human right, including, of course, for people who do not conform to sex stereotypes, which is presumably what is meant by "gender non-conforming." So, this is about providing care for common colds, strep throat, and more serious medical problems, right? That could only be a good thing. It does do that, to a point. It states that it provides wellness checkups and preventive care, immunizations, same-day visits for illnesses and other concerns, services and support for children with special healthcare needs, and mental and social support. Great! But that's not really what all of this is about.

The Boston Children's Gender Multispecialty Service (GeMS) was "the first major program in the U.S. to focus on gender-diverse and transgender adolescents." It states that it provides "individualized, safe, and affirmative care to gender-diverse and transgender individuals and their families." Its Center for Gender Surgery states that "gender dysphoria occurs when there is a conflict between the gender you were assigned at birth and the gender with which you identify. This can create significant distress, and you may feel uncomfortable in your body." As I said earlier, I know there are people who are sincerely confused about their sex and I understand that that *does* indeed cause distress. How could it not? The problem here is that in order to address this psychological problem, instead of helping them, the Center puts these confused young people on hormones and removes their healthy body parts. Boston Children's director Dr. Jeremi Carswell once stated that the hospital hands out puberty blockers to kids "like candy," while also acknowledging that they cause sterility. This is what "gender-affirming care" *is* and how the industry makes its money.

The center states that it offers "vaginoplasty, metoidioplasty, phalloplasty, chest reconstruction, breast augmentation, facial harmonization and other gender affirming surgeries to eligible patients." It is "guided by the World Professional Association for Transgender Health (WPATH) standards and other criteria to surgically treat people who are stable in their gender identity and have documentation of persistent gender dysphoria." Remember that WPATH recommends no age limits for the provision of puberty blockers, opposite-sex hormones, or surgeries in connection with the administration of "gender-affirming care." It goes on to state that "All genital surgeries are only performed on patients age 18 and older." That may very well be true, but this suggests that it *does* provide non-genital surgeries (including double mastectomies, facial harmonization, and other "gender-affirming surgeries") to minors under the age of eighteen. We know that some children have in fact had double mastectomies. Chloe Cole, discussed in Chapter 3, is one example. She had it at fifteen. Also, is it true that the center only does genital surgeries on patients age eighteen or older? It says this, but it also says that it is "guided by" the WPATH standards of care, which no longer make any recommendations regarding age limits. Which is it? The hospital once boasted on its website that it provides vaginoplasties to boys as young as seventeen, but then it deleted the reference, so we don't know for sure.

Boston Children's also has a Transgender Reproductive Health Service that "provides inclusive reproductive health care for people of all gender identities and anatomies." By "reproductive health care," it means the management of gynecologic problems for women on testosterone (a pretty candid acknowledgment) and hysterectomies for women who claim to be men. It also includes fertility preservation including egg freezing, sperm banking, or ovarian tissue cryopreservation (removal of the egg-producing portion of the ovaries). Debates rage in society about the ethics of fertility preservation and I think there are good arguments on either side. Regardless of what anyone thinks about that, we should all understand that the purpose of these procedures for people who want to "affirm their gender" is so that they can eventually reproduce, even having had hormones altered and body parts removed—an explicit acknowledgment that "gender-affirming care" causes sterility.

Children's Hospital of Los Angeles (CHLA)

CHLA is home to the Center for Transyouth Health and Development. Like Boston Children's, CHLA "is dedicated to providing affirming care for transgender and gender diverse children, adolescents, young adults, and their families." Their team is also "dedicated to partnering with young people and their families as they navigate their gender journey [and] uncover their gifts while helping to remove any institutional barriers blocking their path to achieving their authentic selves." One wonders how taking puberty blockers to block natural puberty and sterility-inducing wrong-sex hormones, or removing healthy body parts, helps one achieve his or her "authentic self." What makes CHLA different from other "gender clinics"? According to its website, its clinic "rejects the gatekeeper model of care and focuses on how to help [its] patients and families in the least restrictive environment possible. [It] focuses on gender-affirming care and strives to make [its] patients and their families feel welcomed and understood." In other words, they reject the entire concept of gatekeeping or even questioning whether hormones or surgeries might be appropriate for some patients and just get right to it.

Beyond these vague statements about "affirming gender" and rejecting gatekeeping, there is shockingly little information on its website about what it actually does. It simply, and vaguely, states that it provides following services:

- Gender-affirming medical treatment and mental health services
- Family support services and linkage to outside resources
- Case management services, including assistance with legal name and gender marker changes
- Peer Support groups
- Sexual health education including groups, one-on-one navigation services, and HIV/STD (Sexually Transmitted Disease) screening and treatment
- Access to PEP (Post Exposure Prophylaxis) and PrEP (Pre Exposure Prophylaxis) for HIV prevention
- Voluntary participation in ground breaking research

Regarding the reference to "voluntary participation in ground breaking research": this center was one of the participants in the NIH study discussed in Chapter 3 (the study in which the NIH funded four "gender clinics" to observe young people—some as young as twelve—as they pursued their "gender journeys," and in which two study participants were known to have committed suicide without the study's researchers intervening to ask why). Its director is Dr. Johanna Olson-Kennedy, discussed further below.

Lurie Children's Hospital of Chicago

Lurie Children's Hospital has a Gender Development Program that provides outpatient services "aimed at supporting the physical, mental and social health of patients and their families as youth progress through gender identity development." The language being used here is interesting, in that the program seems to assume that "gender identity development" is something that all youth "progress through."

The program divides its patients into three categories: gender expansive or gender non-conforming children, gender-questioning youth, and transgender and gender-fluid youth. The first category of kids are literally just children who don't conform to sex stereotypes. This would, presumably, include boys who like pink and sparkly things, girls who like trucks and mud, and adolescents who are exploring same-sex attraction. The Lurie Hospital thinks that these children should be medicalized and given hormones and possibly surgeries to change their healthy bodies. And it says so explicitly. The second and third categories of kids are almost entirely a creation of the industry. This is an industry that tells young people that if they are questioning or uncomfortable with their actual sex, then they must undergo permanent medical changes. This industry is telling children and their parents that such fantasy and identity exploration is a medical condition that must be "treated" with hormones and/or surgery. It is the equivalent of changing that little girl's body to make her seem more like a fairy or changing that little boy's body to make him seem more like a cat.

Like the others, the program at the Lurie Hospital offers "gender affirming" "services" to minors who defy sex stereotypes, are confused about their sex, and/or are exploring same-sex attraction. Regarding "gender-affirming surgery," the program simply states: "Gender affirming surgery refers to a wide range of surgical interventions, including chest surgery, surgery involving reproductive organs, and surgery on facial structures. We work closely with several surgeons who are experienced in this type of care and can provide more information and referrals for patients seeking these services."

All these clinics go instantly to the "affirmation" approach to addressing non-conformity with sex stereotypes or confusion about sex. It does not have to be this way though. There are other approaches. Some practitioners, for example, use an approach called "watchful waiting," which essentially entails working with young people who are confused about sex to help them accept their sexed bodies. Such practitioners have demonstrated that this works, and that many young people will go on to "desist" (i.e., stop thinking that they are the opposite sex). But these practitioners are often driven out of the field.

Dr. Kenneth Zucker is one such practitioner. He is a psychologist who served as the clinical lead of the Child Youth and Family Gender Identity Clinic (GIC) at the Center for Addiction and Mental Health (CAMH) from 1982 to 2015. He also headed the Sexual and Gender Identity Disorders group in 2008 for the fifth edition of the *Diagnostic and Statistical Manual of Mental Disorders* (DSM-5) and is a member of WPATH. He is a controversial figure in that he *both* opposes any form of "transition" in pre-pubescent children but *also* supports it under certain circumstances for adolescents. Either way, he is a proponent of "watchful waiting." But critics of his approach labeled it "conversion therapy" and succeeded in getting him fired from the CAMH in 2015. Two years later, he was scheduled to speak at the annual conference of the U.S. chapter of WPATH, but a group of men who claim to be women protested and the conference cancelled his talk.

Rick McCarthy is a marriage and family therapist and a member of the California Association of Marriage and Family Therapists (CAMFT), which publishes a magazine called *The Therapist*. When he realized what was going on, he wrote a letter to the editor, calling attention to the dangers that "gender-affirming care" pose to young people and they published it. That prompted a petition to get him kicked out of CAMFT and get his license revoked for "hate speech." CAMFT removed his letter from the online edition of the magazine and published a subsequent issue apologizing to its membership for having the temerity to publish a letter raising important questions about "affirmation."

Stephanie Winn is a marriage and family therapist who hosts a podcast called *You Must Be Some Kind of Therapist*. She states that her professional goals are to restore integrity to the profession of psychotherapy, end childhood sexual mutilation, and promote justice and healing for those who have been harmed by "gender-affirming care." She was an associate producer of the 2023 film *Affirmation Generation* (later renamed *No Way Back: The Reality of Gender-Affirming Care*), a highly recommended feature-length film about the ethics of "transition." As discussed in Chapter 3, the film included the voices of twelve experts and six "detransitioners" and discussed forty-five medical articles in support of the "watchful waiting" approach. The film's producers describe themselves as life-long, West Coast, liberal Democrats. There are many others in the field, many of whom appear in *No Way Back*. We don't have to harm children. There are better ways to deal with a young person's confusion about sex.

Individual Actors

So, if all these medical institutions have been captured by the "gender identity" industry, who are the individual doctors carrying out their work? There are several, but a handful deserve special mention.

Dr. Johanna Olson-Kennedy is the Medical Director and Attending Physician of the Center for Transyouth Health and Development (CTHD) in Los Angeles. When she joined the team in 2006, the center was intended to serve young people with HIV. The CTHD became recognized as a "gender identity clinic," separate from the HIV clinic, in 2012. The move was not circumstantial. Olson-Kennedy is a firm believer in "innate gender identities" who pushes "gender affirmation" on children and their parents. She is also partnered with a woman who claims to be a man named Aydin.

In 2016, she may have become one of the first practitioners to advocate for WPATH to lower its recommendations regarding age limits for genital surgeries. That year, she posted on the WPATH Facebook page:

"Hi friends, wondering if WPATH SOC 8 might be changing guidelines around genital surgery in trans young women younger than 18? Here's the issue: these girls are blocked at early puberty, so by high school they having [sic] been living and presenting as their authentic selves, but are forced to navigate high school with 11 y/o 'male' genitals until 18. I have a handful of girls (many more coming up) whose lives are on hold because of this. They are ready, their parents are ready to support after care, they have strong mental health support, but the insurance won't cover because of the WPATH recs. Thoughts?" This is what she was saying: She has intentionally arrested the natural puberty of some number of boys and essentially created a cohort of young men whose penises and testicles have not been allowed to develop and now, having created this cohort of young men with undeveloped genitals, it was necessary for WPATH to reduce its recommended age limit so that she could have these young men's genitals removed entirely.

Young men are not her only victims. She openly promotes the pre-pubescent administration of puberty blockers and cross-sex hormones for both boys and girls and for the removal of girls' breasts during adolescence. At a 2018 conference of the group Gender Spectrum (founded by Stephanie Brill, the author of the 2008 book *The Transgender Child: A Handbook for Families and Professionals*), when asked about this, Olson-Kennedy stated, "If you want breasts at a later point in your life, you can go and get them." This is a medical doctor advocating for the removal of healthy breast tissue in adolescent girls and cavalierly dismissing any concerns that this might raise as a minor problem with the very easy solution of later having plastic surgery to create fake breasts. In 2023, she told participants at a training session for mental health workers for the California Association of Marriage and Family Therapists that puberty blockers are "as reversible as a new clothing style and haircut."

At the February 2017 conference of the U.S. chapter of WPATH, Olson-Kennedy was asked if it is possible to get courts to intervene in cases where one or both parents wanted to hold off on "transition." She said: "I can say that the stickiest situations I've had is where one parent is supportive and one isn't and they share medical custody. And so we work really hard to bring both parents in and bring them both on board. Because even if you get a court order, the most protective factor for a good outcome is parental support. So it's not my first line to go to court to get somebody what they need. But it is my second line and I will do it. We've been pretty successful in 5 or 6 situations where we really had a recalcitrant parent that we just could not bring along." That's right, parents. If your kid is confused about his or her sex and wants to "transition," but you would rather protect your child's body and health, Olson-Kennedy is happy to get a court to force you to go along.

Diane Ehrensaft is not a medical doctor. She's a developmental and clinical psychologist who "specializes in gender-affirmative care for transgender and gender-expansive patients; assessment and psychotherapy for children; and support for parents and children in families created through assisted reproductive technology." She has a PhD in psychology from the University of Michigan and serves as the Mental Health Director of the Child and Adolescent Gender Center at the University of California San Francisco.

In December 2018, she co-authored (with Jack Turban) an article titled "Research Review: Gender Identity in Youth: Treatment Paradigms and Controversies." The article concluded: "The field of pediatric gender identity has evolved dramatically. Emerging data suggest that these patients' high rates of anxiety, depression, and suicidality appear to be improved with affirmative protocols, although future longitudinal data are needed." Like Ehrensaft, Turban works at the University of California San Francisco (though unlike her, he has a medical degree). Turban is a big proponent of the concept of "transgender youth" and of "gender-affirming care." In January 2022, Stanford University published a study by Turban called "Access to Gender-Affirming Hormones During Adolescence and Mental Health Outcomes Among Transgender Adults." That study was funded in large part by the companies Arbor Pharmaceuticals and Pfizer, both of which produce hormones that are used in "gender-affirmation care."

In April 2021, Ehrensaft led a Zoom training titled "Fertility Issues for Transgender and Nonbinary Youth." As reported by the parent-rights group 4th Wave Now, one theme being addressed was that "Future reproduction is pretty much foreclosed as a possibility for children who have been puberty-blocked, but the 'benefits outweigh risks' to move the child from, as Ehrensaft puts it, 'gender dysphoria to gender euphoria.'" As 4th Wave Now points out, it is pretty outrageous to acknowledge knowing that puberty-blockers cause sterility and *also* claim that the "benefit" of "gender euphoria" outweighs the risks. Ehrensaft is listed as one of the authors of the NIH study on the administration of wrong-sex hormones to young people discussed in Chapter 3; in 2016, she also contributed to the HRC's publication *Supporting and Caring for Transgender Children.*

There are so many medical professionals who could be named here, including Diane Chen and Robert Garofalo, both of whom are *also* participants in the NIH study and hold leadership positions at Lurie Children's. However, in the interest of brevity, I will conclude the chapter by discussing one doctor who deserves her own special mention.

Dr. Sidhbh Gallagher is a plastic surgeon with a practice in Miami, Florida. In addition to performing breast augmentation, lift, and reduction; tummy tucks and liposuction; labiaplasty and "mommy makeovers"; and "non-surgical facial rejuvenation and lip enhancement with injectables"; according to her website, she performs a range of "gender confirmation" procedures. Gallagher openly admits to performing "top surgery" on minors and advertises her services on TikTok, where she has around 270,000 followers. In her TikTok videos, she is always smiling warmly and playing catchy music. She brags in them about "yeeting the teets" ("yeet" is a slang word that means to throw with forcefulness and a lack of concern for the thing being thrown). She refers to double mastectomy surgeries as "teetus deletus" and to herself as "Dr. Teetus Deletus." In other words, she openly encourages young women to "throw with forcefulness and a lack of concern for the thing being thrown," their healthy breasts. On TikTok.

She once posted a TikTok video posing the question, "How is the pain after Top surgery (Teet yeet)?" She answers her own question by saying

"Not too bad! Most of our patients rate their pain 4/10 in the first two days (which are the worst)." Then she goes on to say that she has "yet to meet a patient who says it's worse than wisdom teeth." This is highly unlikely. Many women experience pain after having a mastectomy. It is common enough that there is a condition called post-mastectomy pain syndrome (PMPS), whose symptoms can include pain and tingling in the chest wall, armpit, arm, and/or shoulder, as well as numbness, shooting or pricking pain, or itching. In 2023, Gallagher started promoting the eunuch "gender identity," citing the guidelines by WPATH discussed above, which were devised with input from men in an online forum that hosts sadomasochistic pornography about castrating and raping children. Of all the people in the medical industry pushing this stuff, Gallagher might just be the most ghoulish of them all.

These medical experiments are harming many people, including many of our loved ones. In 2021, the *British Journal of Cancer* reported a case of a "serous borderline ovarian tumour in a transgender male adolescent (a female)," noting that "this is the second report of borderline tumour in a transgender individual and the first in an adolescent, an age group in which borderline tumours are extremely rare," and that "the effects of testosterone therapy on the ovaries is incompletely understood with conflicting data in the literature."

In January 2023, Ontario, Canada opened its first vaginoplasty post-op clinic to treat male patients who were experiencing complications with vaginoplasty. A review of the first eighty patients seen at this new clinic showed that common concerns were pain (53.8 percent), dilation concerns (46.3 percent), and surgical site/vaginal bleeding (42.5 percent). ("Dilation" refers to the practice whereby these men have to "dilate" their fake vaginas to prevent them from closing up.) In February 2023, the American College of Cardiology announced a study finding that people taking opposite-sex hormones face a substantially increased risk of serious cardiac events, including stroke, heart attack, and pulmonary embolism. The same study also found that both estrogen and testosterone, administered exogenously, increase blood clots.

The most important thing to note about all this is that the harmful effects of puberty blockers in young people *have been well-known for decades*. In 2010, when the Tavistock Gender Identity Development Service (GIDS) in the U.K. launched a trial of puberty blockers for children in their early teens, neither the drug manufacturers nor the British government had certified them as safe or effective. The director of the center itself is on record as saying, "The question is, if you halt your own sex hormones so that your brain is not experiencing puberty, are you in some way altering the course of nature? The debate revolves around the reversibility of this intervention—physical and also psychological, in terms of the possible influence of sex hormones on brain and identity development."

Meanwhile, the lawsuits are piling up. In 2023, Chloe Cole announced that she was suing the clinicians and corporations that subjected her to permanent harm. Her complaint begins, "This case is about a team of doctors (i.e., the Defendants) who decided to perform a mutilating, mimicry sex change experiment on Chloe, then a thirteen-year-old vulnerable girl struggling with complex mental health co-morbidities, who needed love, care, attention, and regular weekly psychotherapy, not cross-sex hormones, and mutilating surgery." It noted that "there is no other area of medicine where doctors will surgically remove a perfectly healthy body part and intentionally induce a disease state of pituitary gland function based simply on the patient's wishes."

Later that year, Layla Jane (also discussed in Chapter 3) announced that she was doing the same thing. Her attorneys sent a Letter of Intent to Sue to the Permanente Medical Group and Kaiser Foundation Hospitals alleging gross negligence and accusing Kaiser of allowing "radical, inadequately studied, off-label, and essentially experimental treatment to occur on minors." It alleges that Layla's doctors medically "affirmed her gender" without meaningful evaluation, failed to adequately explain the health risks associated with the hormone treatments she was given, and emotionally manipulated her parents by telling them that if they did not consent, she would commit suicide.

Prisha Mosley, who has been left with irreversible scars, a deep voice, body and facial hair, pain in her neck and shoulders, and a damaged vagina, and who will not be able to breastfeed even if she is ever able to become pregnant, is doing the same thing. Her complaint states that her doctors "lied when they told [her] she was actually a boy; they lied when they told her that injecting testosterone into her body would solve her numerous, profound mental and psychological health problems; they lied by omission, withholding critical information from her about the long-term adverse health consequences and permanent damage these treatments would cause her, and failing to inform her of alternative courses of treatment for her psychological problems."

They are not the only ones. Soren Aldaco is suing the doctors who put her on testosterone at seventeen and botcher her double mastectomy the next year. She says they should have treated her for depression and anxiety instead. As of November 2023, there were eleven lawsuits filed by "detransitioners" making their way through the judiciary, alleging claims of fraud, conspiracy to commit fraud, misrepresentation of material evidence, deceptive trade tactics, civil rights infringement, breach of fiduciary duties, battery and more. All the medical organizations, associations, clinics, and physicians, and all the politicians who are furthering this agenda, have blood on their hands. In March 2023, Dr. Susan Bradley, a Canadian psychiatrist who once pushed "gender-affirming care," came out against it. She had founded a pediatric "gender clinic" in 1975 and in 2000 started prescribing puberty blockers to kids. She said, simply, "We were wrong. They're not as reversible as we always thought, and they have longer term effects on kids' growth and development, including making them sterile and quite a number of things affecting their bone growth."

"We were wrong," she said. Where are the rest of them?

CHAPTER 7

THE ACCOMPLICES

The GOP

In January 2022, I told Tucker Carlson (on television) a story about an abortion-rights rally I had attended. In December 2021, on the day that the Supreme Court was hearing oral arguments in the case of *Dobbs v. Jackson Women's Health* (the case that would eventually overturn *Roe v. Wade*), I and several feminist friends went to rally in support of abortion rights. Naturally, there were two camps at the Court that day: those who wanted *Roe* to remain good law, and those who didn't. Police had divided the camps, and for the most part, everyone stayed on their sides. We were there to chant TERFy things like "ABORTION IS A WOMEN'S SEX-BASED RIGHT" and "ONLY WOMEN NEED ABORTIONS." We got some opposition from the pro-*Roe* camp (for being TERFs, not for supporting *Roe*), but we also got a lot of interest from pro-*Roe* women who wondered what we were talking about and learned a lot about feminist opposition to "gender identity" that day.

But then we did something different: We took our pro-*Roe* TERFy chants to the anti-*Roe* side. We got a lot of the typical opposing chants: "WITCH!" "BABY KILLER!" "YOU'RE ALL GOING TO HELL!" Okay, sure, whatever. We expected all that, having been in the abortion rights trenches for decades. But then we heard something that we hadn't expected: "TRANS RIGHTS START AT CONCEPTION." None of us had heard that before. It was a take on "HUMAN RIGHTS START AT CONCEPTION," a common anti-abortion slogan. But here were some people in the anti-abortion camp chanting for "trans rights." That was new.

When I first told Carlson this story, he understandably laughed and called them silly people who were just there to be annoying. But then he reflected a bit and acknowledged that I was making an important point. My point was that having fully colonized the political left, the "gender identity" industry was coming for the political right, or, as Carlson phrased it, the right was prime "political real estate." It turns out I wasn't wrong. The Republican Party has so far failed to stop the abolition of sex, despite purporting to be against it. I know this both from my own observations and from listening to the grumblings of some Republican friends who are just as sick of their party as I am of mine.

In the past few years, several Republican Members of Congress have introduced legislation at the federal level to preserve the material reality of sex. Many of these bills are quite good, but they rarely get very far. I assume the reason the bills don't advance is that until January 2023, Democrats controlled both chambers of Congress and the bill sponsors probably assumed it wasn't worth their effort. But really, why not? Even if the bills stood no chance of getting out of committee, why not use the opportunity to raise the issue and highlight rank-and-file Democratic support for the bills, force the issue in the media, and shame Democratic leadership for failing to protect women and girls? I think Republican members of Congress are missing opportunities when they fail to advance such bills and when they fail to highlight rank-and-file Democratic support for them. The Republicans in the House have gotten *much* better in recent years about having female athletes and "detransitioners" testify, which is great, but the media can still frame the discussion as partisan—Big Bad Christian Right on one side and "poor marginalized community" on the other. It would be much more effective for Republicans to platform leftist feminists on these issues. TERFs are better than anyone at shaming our Democratic

Party leaders for throwing women and girls under the bus at the altar of "gender identity."

One such bill is the Women's Bill of Rights (WBOR), which is based on a model bill co-authored by the Women's Liberation Front and the Independent Women's Forum. This bill was introduced in both the 2021 and 2023 Congressional sessions by Republican Representative Debbie Lesko and Senator Cindy Hyde-Smith. It is a very straightforward bill to confirm the material reality of sex in federal law. It is great that this bill has been introduced, and I hope it advances. It has the strong support of Women's Declaration International USA. Both the House and the Senate versions have been referred to their respective Judiciary Committees. Republican Greg Steube introduced the "Protection of Women and Girls in Sports Act" in both 2021 and 2023. This is a very strong, clean, and straightforward bill that would make it a violation of Title IX for recipients of federal funds to allow male athletes to participate in women's sports. It also defines sex biologically. It also has the strong support of Women's Declaration International USA. While it passed in the House, it hasn't advanced in the Senate. Similar Republican-sponsored bills have languished at the federal level. Again, this is mainly because Democrats controlled both houses of Congress until January 2023. But still, I wish Republican members of Congress and conservative organizations would do a better job of platforming leftist feminist Democrats who support their bills.

At the state level, nearly every bill that has been introduced to protect the sex-based rights of women and girls in sports or to prevent the sterilization of minors has been introduced by a Republican. Republicans have introduced various versions of the WBOR in several states, and numerous states have passed legislation to protect minors from sterilization and mutilation and/or to protect women's sports. Some of these bills advance, while others languish. These lawmakers deserve credit for doing the right thing, and some of them have worked very hard in doing it. For example, Idaho became the first state to protect women's sports in 2020 after Republican Representative Barbara Ehardt worked hard to get the

Fairness for Women in Sports Act to the governor's desk, where it was signed in March of that year and is now the subject of litigation brought by the ACLU.

Not all state level Republicans are as committed, though.

In an ominous move, in December 2022, New Jersey Democratic governor Phil Murphy nominated a man named Allison Myers to serve as the head of the state's Civil Service Commission. Much ado was made of the nomination, with local media outlets announcing that Myers "used to apply makeup and change her clothes in her car after work, hoping her co-workers wouldn't catch her with mascara in hand. In her office, she wore masculine clothes, and colleagues saw her as a man." Probably his colleagues saw him as a man because he is one. Fast forward to June 2023, when the New Jersey Senate Judiciary Committee and then the entire state senate voted to confirm the nomination *unanimously and without asking a single question.* Four of the eleven members of the New Jersey Senate Judiciary Committee are Republicans. Of the forty members of the state senate, fifteen are Republicans. This is a commission whose mission is to "advance NJ government with fair and efficient human resources responsive to the needs of the Civil Service workforce." Of course, the real onus of this falls on the Democratic governor of the state, but really—could not a single Republican on the committee or in the senate bother to ask a single question about whether *a man who lies about his sex is competent to serve in this position?*

Texas governor Greg Abbott found himself in some hot water with the establishment left in February 2022, after ordering the state's Department of Family and Protective Services to investigate the provision of "gender-affirming care" as child abuse under existing state law. A family sued (anonymously, and represented by the ACLU), arguing that the governor's directive violated state procedural law and various statutory and constitutional laws. They succeeded in obtaining a temporary restraining order blocking the directive from taking effect statewide (that was later limited to blocking the directive as applied only to the family itself).

In its complaint, the ACLU stated that "After the Texas legislature failed to pass legislation criminalizing well-established and medically necessary treatment for adolescents with gender dysphoria, the Texas Governor, Attorney General, and Commissioner of the Department of Family and Protective Services have attempted to legislate by press release." The ACLU is right that the state legislature failed to pass what I would call legislation to criminalize child sterilization and mutilation during the eighty-seventh legislative session. Why? Why would legislation to ban "gender-affirming care" for minors fail to pass in blood-red Texas? After all, the Texas Republican-led legislature had no trouble passing (and Governor Abbott had no trouble signing) SB 8, which bans abortion after six weeks of pregnancy without exceptions for rape or incest in 2021. Why the resistance to banning "gender-affirming care," in light of its zeal to ban abortion? The resistance to legislatively banning "gender-affirming care" in blood-red Texas didn't come from Democrats, who do not control the legislature or the governor's office. It came from Republicans.

The state's eighty-seventh legislative session occurred in 2021–2022. Six bills were introduced during that session to ban "gender-affirming care" for minors. The governor was silent about all of them. Four of the six died in the House Public Health Committee, chaired by Republican Representative Stephanie Klick. Eventually, Senate Bill 1311 cleared the Senate and was awaiting a vote in the House Public Health Committee when Republican House Speaker Dade Phelan recessed the House for three days, right before the deadline for bills to be considered in the House. None of the bills passed. Governor Abbott, Lieutenant Governor Dan Patrick, House Speaker Phelan, and Representative Klick—all Republicans—had received donations from a political action committee (PAC) called Friends of UT Southwestern Center, some going as far back as 2015. UT Southwestern Center refers to the Children's Medical Center at the University of Texas, which operates the GENder Education and Care, Interdisciplinary Support (GENECIS) program. That program was shuttered to new patients in November 2021 because of legal and political pressure, and it started accepting new patients again in May

2022. Its director is Dr. Ximena Lopez, who also serves as co-chair of the Transgender Health Special Interest Group of the Pediatric Endocrine Society and who contributed to the 2016 publication of the HRC's *Supporting and Caring for Transgender Children*. In short, these Texas Republicans failed to advance important legislation to protect children because they were paid by the "gender identity" industry not to.

Tracy Shannon lives in Texas and has become something of a champion in fighting the "gender identity" industry in her state. Shannon describes herself as conservative, having moved to the right politically after witnessing libertarian indifference to the harms of "gender identity" ideology. When she started getting active in state legislative advocacy, she says she thought that in speaking with Republicans she would find like-minded legislators who understood the importance of biological reality, protecting children from medical predation, and protecting the rights of women in sex-segregated spaces. What she didn't realize was how hard it would be to convince them.

I asked her what first made her notice that something might be "off" with respect to Republicans' hesitation in taking this on. She said: "In 2019, I noticed that Governor Abbott had tweeted about the case of James Younger whose mother had been transitioning him from an early age. [James's] parents were locked in a custody dispute over this issue. When the Governor tweeted that he and the Texas Attorney General were 'looking into the case of James Younger,' I honestly believed that this young boy and his father would be spared more abuse by Texas Family Courts and their complicity with the gender industry. But as time passed I realized this poor father was left with no help from our state as he battled for his son. It felt familiar. I felt very alone as I waged a battle not many years before to save my own children from the jaws of the transgender movement when transgender activists funded my ex's attempts to take my children away."

I asked her to list a few things that Texas Republican lawmakers could have done to enact legislation to protect women and children but didn't and she gave me a few examples. In 2017, Republicans could have protected female-only spaces but they didn't. In 2019, Republicans in

Texas could have passed a ban on pediatric gender modification as they were aware of what was happening with James Younger. In 2021, Texas Republicans had a chance to stop pediatric gender modification. Some of them denied it was even happening. The legislators claimed they simply ran out of time in 2021 to pass the bill. The governor called three special sessions and did not include a ban on pediatric gender modification in any of them. In 2021, Republican Valoree Swanson told her that grassroots activists simply hadn't done the work and needed to "make more calls." Shannon says this assertion that the grassroots didn't do the work is an insult to the thousands of Texans who worked on the platform in 2020.

The 2021 session came to a close without passing a ban on pediatric gender modification and it was then that Shannon learned that the top Republicans in the state were taking millions of dollars from PACs that are affiliated with "gender clinics." All these Texas Republican leaders who were in a position to pass legislation to criminalize child mutilation chose not to, having received campaign contributions from a PAC whose aim is to advance the goals of one of the largest "gender clinics" in the American south. The committee *finally* advanced a bill to protect children from harmful hormonal and surgical procedures in April 2023 and another to protect women's sports later that year, but it sure took its time doing so, and one wonders how many women and kids were harmed while the Republican majority in the Texas legislature and the governor failed to act to stop it.

In January 2023, the conservative-leaning magazine the *National Review* published a scathing article titled, "How Gender Ideology Conquered South Dakota." It criticized many Republican South Dakota officials, including Governor Kristi Noem and several state legislators, for opposing bills that would protect minors from "gender affirming" abuse, maintain single-sex sports and bathrooms, and prohibit people from changing their sex on their birth certificates. Noem did eventually sign a single-sex sports bill, but only after having vetoed a different one the previous year. In February 2023, Noem signed a bill that outlaws the prescription and administration of puberty blockers, wrong-sex hormones, and "gender affirming" surgeries for minors. But those moves came after years of caving to pressure from groups and lobbyists associated with the South Dakota-based Sanford Research Center, Sanford Health, and the Transformation Project, a local advocacy group that supports "gender identity" ideology. The *National Review* piece highlighted a January 2023 event called the "Third Annual Gender Identity Summit," which was being hosted by all three of those groups in the state. The summit was to take place one month after Noem announced that the state was terminating a contract it had entered into with the Transformation Project. For years, South Dakota Republicans in the statehouse and the governor's office with deep connections to the "gender identity" lobby failed to do anything to protect South Dakota's women and children.

In February 2021, Arkansas Republican Representative Robin Lundstrum introduced HB 1570, the Save Adolescents from Experimentation (SAFE) Act, which prohibited doctors from providing "gender confirming" hormones or surgery to minors. The bill passed in both houses, but then Governor Asa Hutchinson (a Republican) vetoed it. The legislature eventually voted to override Hutchinson's veto, but the law has been blocked by a federal court thanks to the ACLU. This was a Republican governor vetoing a bill to protect children from sterilization and mutilation. His reasoning was that the bill "went too far in interfering with parents and physicians." He elaborated, "I do hope my veto will cause my Republican colleagues across the country to resist the temptation to put the state in the middle of every decision made by parents and health care professionals." But who said anything about putting the state in the middle of every decision made by parents and healthcare professionals? (He didn't seem to have any trouble involving the state in decisions made by healthcare professionals when he signed a near-total abortion ban that same year.) And why was Hutchinson encouraging other Republicans *elsewhere* to block measures to protect children?

In May 2023, Louisiana Republican senator Fred Mills made headlines when he cast a tie-breaking vote *against* advancing a bill to protect minors out of committee. The bill would have prohibited the administration of puberty blockers, cross-sex hormones, and surgeries on minors in Louisiana. Four Republican committee members voted to pass it out of committee and four Democratic lawmakers voted against it. Mills was the sole Republican to side with the Democrats and the bill died. Some of the top donors to his 2022 campaign committee included Pfizer, Humana, the Pharmaceutical Care Management Association, the Pharmaceutical Research and Manufacturers Association of America, and the Bayer Corporation—all drug companies and associations.

In June 2023, Joe Lombardo, the Republican governor of Nevada, signed a bill requiring medical insurers in the state to cover "gender-affirming care," including for minors. The bill he signed explicitly refers insurers to the WPATH Standards of Care for the purpose of determining when such care is "medically necessary." The WPATH Standards of Care, of course, contain extremely loose guidelines and essentially encourage healthcare providers to "affirm" a person's (including a child's) "gender" whenever the patient demands it. Former New Jersey governor and presidential candidate Republican Chris Christie has stated that he opposes bans on "gender-affirming care" for minors, saying that it should be a matter between children and their parents.

Again, it must be emphasized that most of the work being done at the state level to protect female-only sports and spaces and protect children from the abuse of "gender-affirming care" is being done by Republicans. Although I am not generally a fan of the Republican Party, I am extremely grateful to the Republican lawmakers who are willing to take these stands. But some Republicans are going in the *opposite* direction in part, at least, because they are paid by the industry. When I told Tucker Carlson in 2021 that having fully colonized the political left, the "gender identity" industry was coming for the political right, he referred to the right as "prime political real estate." I'm sad to say that I think we were both right.

As discussed in Chapter 5, conservative media is hardly any better than the Republicans who are caving to the industry. Conservative media outlets will at least publish stories about how men are invading women's sports, spaces, and prisons, and about how children's bodies are being harmed at the altar of "gender identity," but they generally do a terrible job of reporting on them. Take, for example, a February 2023 *Fox News* story about James Tubbs. Tubbs was arrested for and eventually pleaded guilty to child molestation in connection with a 2014 incident in which he attacked a ten-year-old girl in a Denny's bathroom stall. After he was arrested, he demanded to be known as Hannah and referred to using "she/her" pronouns. Tubbs was later charged with murder and robbery in connection with a different incident. *Fox News* ran the headline "LA DA Gascon suspends prosecutor for misgendering and 'deadnaming' trans child molester accused of murder" in a story that referred to Tubbs as Hannah and as "she/her" throughout. This is *Fox News*, which is widely regarded to be a conservative news outlet, reporting about a man who has been convicted of child abuse, charged with murder, and who is claiming to be a woman to access women's detention facilities, referring to him as "she" and "her." Other conservative outlets do the same thing. The right, including conservative media, just props up the edifice of "trans" when they use language that denies the material reality of sex; they're not the main perpetrators, but I view them as accomplices in betraying women and girls.

The Church

I am not religious, and this section should not be interpreted as an endorsement (or not) of any religion. It is, rather an exploration of ways in which some churches and denominations have been complicit in the abolition of sex.

I know a woman—a mom, lesbian, Democrat, and Christian—in her fifties. After a long and successful career as a teacher, she quit her job, went to divinity school, and became an ordained minister at her church. Later, her church made all the bathrooms "gender neutral" and started telling church members to use everyone's "preferred pronouns." She left the church in protest. In 2023, a video emerged of what appeared to be communion during a church service. As she invites the congregation to participate, the pastor says, "I invite everybody to rise, in body or spirit, and let us confess our faith today in the words of the sparkle creed [everyone says together], 'I believe in the non-binary God, whose pronouns are plural. I believe in Jesus Christ, their child, who wore a fabulous tunic and had two dads, and saw everyone as a sibling child of God. I believe in the rainbow spirit who shatters our image of one white light and refracts it into a rainbow of gorgeous diversity. I believe in the Church of Everyday Saints, as numerous creative and resilient as patches on the AIDS quilt, whose feet are grounded in mud, and whose eyes gaze at the stars in wonder. I believe in the calling to each of us that love is love is love. So beloved, let us love. I believe in the glorious God. Help my unbelief. Amen." This almost makes it seem as though "trans" *itself is a religion* (many people think that it is, and I cannot say I disagree).

Kaeley Triller is a Christian, conservative, anti-abortion Trump voter. She and I disagree on just about everything under the sun, but we have worked together in the past to push back against the enshrinement of "gender identity" in the law. In 2017, she co-founded an organization called Hands Across the Aisle: Women in Coalition with lesbian radical feminist Miriam Ben-Shalom. Hands Across the Aisle states on its website that its mission is to "table our ideological differences to stand in solidarity against gender identity legislation, which we have come to recognize as the erasure of our hard-won civil rights."

In July 2022, Triller published a piece in *The Christian Post* imploring Christian conservative men to "please stop screwing up the trans issue." Her main point in that article was to take men like Matt Walsh to task for talking down to and dismissing feminists like J.K. Rowling (and me, among others). She accurately notes that women who vote Republican owe feminism a debt for securing their right to do so. But she makes another very important point, which is that the Christian church in the U.S. has not done its due diligence in ridding society of the scourge of "gender identity." After she was fired from her job at the local YMCA in 2016 for refusing to write a policy of allowing men into the women's locker room based on their woman identity, she got active in politics. She stated, "I remember being dumbfounded as a Christian, as a mother, and, especially as a rape survivor, about the implications of such an absurdly misogynistic public policy, and I was even more dismayed to discover that literally none of the professing Christian men in my upline at the Y would take a stand alongside me.... A few friends and I ran a statewide initiative to repeal Washington state's gender inclusive locker room policies. One of our volunteers called no fewer than 400 churches to solicit their help. Only seven said yes. Even after we told them that men were raping women in women's prisons and shelters, that men were stealing women's hard-fought athletic opportunities, and that children were being sterilized in the name of inclusivity."

The Evangelical Lutheran Church of America (ELCA) has a social statement titled "Human Sexuality: Gift and Trust," which proclaims: "We recognize the complex and varied situations people have relative to human sexuality: being in relationships, being single, being a friend, living in a young or aging body, being male or female, being young or old, or having different sexual orientations and gender identities" and that "in ways that are still not fully understood, we develop strong gender identities at a very early age." It admonishes church leaders to "work toward greater understanding of sexual orientation and gender identity." As for a definition of "gender identity," the statement states simply that "gender identity indicates a person's own sense of identification with a gender (male or female) regardless of physiological characteristics."

In 2018, the General Assembly of the Presbyterian Church USA voted to "affirm and celebrate the 'full dignity and humanity' and gifts of people of all gender identities and sexual orientations." In 2022, it changed the way it collects demographic information from members to include a "nonbinary/genderqueer category." In a press release announcing the change, its manager of denominational roles and statistics stated, "We'll have the same categories, we're just not defining them any longer, which may upset people. The information will be there—we're just removing the definitions. For instance, we've always asked how many female members there are in the church. We're now asking how many men, women and nonbinary/genderqueer members there are. We've never asked that question so we don't know how many people will fill it out."

An organization called the Covenant Network of Presbyterians calls itself "a broad-based, national group of clergy and lay leaders working for a church that is simultaneously faithful, just, and whole." However, it appears to be exclusively devoted to abolishing sex in matters pertaining to the church. Its 2020 "Call to Covenant Community" states: "Confident in God's hopeful future and grateful for the ever-widening welcome of the Presbyterian Church (U.S.A.), the Covenant Network of Presbyterians seeks an equity still not fully realized for LGBTQIA+ people in church and society, by engaging the church to invite all of God's children into safe and welcoming congregational spaces of affirmation, healing, dignity and purpose; educating the church to expand our welcome of LGBTQIA+ people, to affirm their gifts for ordained office, and to uphold marriage equality for all; and equipping the church to bear witness to justice through advocacy and activism at the international, national and local church levels; speaking a prophetic word in anxious and divided times; and standing with others in fighting hate and oppression against any of God's children. The Covenant Network of Presbyterians calls the church to bear a unified witness to generous hospitality and faithful justice." Its Resources page contains a resource called "Becoming a Welcoming Church," which advises church leaders to "use people's correct pronouns" and promote "LGBTQIA+ Inclusive Prayers."

In 2009, the Episcopal Church sent a delegation of a group called TransEpiscopal to its General Convention in Anaheim, California. That year, the Convention expressed support for laws that protect discrimination based on "gender identity" and in 2012, it added "gender identity and expression" to its official nondiscrimination provision. In 2020, it began permitting members to change their name and "gender" on church records and in 2022, the Church's House of Deputies adopted Resolution D066 on "trans-gender care," affirming the church's support for "gender-affirming care" of any type and for any age—including children.

In 2023, a group of parents affiliated with the group Parents with Inconvenient Truths About Trans (PITT) published a "Letter to our Clergy." These parents had been present for hearings in Texas on whether Texas was going to join the ranks of states protecting children from medical harm and were there to urge Texas lawmakers to do just that. They reported that they watched bill opponents emerge. "They were the usual suspects, the LGBTQI+ community that believes that gender nonconformity should be medicalized through 'gender affirming care,' not just accepted, nurtured and celebrated. From their midst emerged a less expected crowd: clergy from some of the mainstream faith communities in America, Episcopal and Methodist among them, with their white collars on, rainbows and trans colors affixed to their garments." They said that "The believers among us could not help asking ourselves: how can it be that our trusted faith leaders are here advocating for medical interventions that will turn questioning, confused, gay, lesbian, and gender non-conforming children into lifelong medical patients with uncertain outcomes?" They implored the clergy to consider the possibility that what they were doing was harming children. They said that the presence of clergy members in opposition to a bill to protect children "shook their faith." They ended the letter with some passages from scripture and signed it "Believers in crisis." These are parents, medical professionals, and "detransitioners," all people of faith, whose faith in their own leaders was being shattered by the leaders' support for legislation whose purpose is to harm children. I do not share their faith, but my heart sure goes out to them.

Not all religious institutions have been captured though.

For example, the Catholic Church in the U.S. does not have an official position regarding "gender identity," although Pope Francis has made some statements critical of it. In August 2021, the Catholic Diocese of Arlington (Virginia) published "A Catechesis on the Human Person and Gender Ideology." I do not pretend to understand all the language in it, nor do I agree with many of its principles. But it does note that, "In the past decade our culture has seen growing acceptance of transgender ideology—that is, the claim that a person's biological sex and personal identity have no necessary connection and could in fact contradict each other. According to this view, 'human identity' is self-defined and 'becomes the choice of the individual. Consequently, our culture is experiencing a rapid rise in the number of persons claiming an identity contrary to their biological sex. Attempts to accommodate such claims already have resulted in tremendous upheavals in our social, legal, and medical systems.... To affirm someone in an identity at odds with biological sex or to affirm a person's desired 'transition' is to mislead that person. It involves speaking and interacting with that person in an untruthful manner. Although the law of gradualness might prompt us to discern the best time to communicate the fullness of truth, in no circumstances can we confirm a person in error." My personal worldview does not accept the idea that the body is a "gift from God" and I have no idea what the law of gradualness is, but I appreciate the Diocese's stance on this.

The Archdiocese of Washington (D.C.), however, appears to be going in a different direction. In June 2023, the Holy Trinity Catholic Church in Georgetown (which just happens to be where President Biden attends services) held a "LGBTQIA+ Pride Mass." In a statement on its website, the parish stated, "This Wednesday at our regularly-scheduled 5:30 p.m. Mass, our parish will celebrate our 3rd annual LGBTQIA+ Pride Mass. This celebration is an expression of our parish's mission statement *TO ACCOMPANY ONE ANOTHER IN CHRIST, CELEBRATE GOD'S LOVE, AND TRANSFORM LIVES.*" It continued, "Our LGBTQIA+ ministry is a response to the Holy Father's call to go out to the margins. Our celebration of Pride is not celebrating personal vanity, but the human dignity of a group of people who have been for too long the objects of violence, bullying and harassment. Our parish reaches out to LGBTQIA+ people as it reaches out to all Catholics in our area." When asked whether it supported this, the Archdiocese refused to comment.

The point here is that even many churches, some institutions that ought to be able to stand up to an industry that evangelizes that sex doesn't exist are, for the most part, not doing that. Christians purport to hold the view that God made men and women in his image. I don't happen to share that view, but one would think that this very basic tenet of Christianity would be upheld by churches themselves.

Everyone Else Who Went Along

There are countless millions of people, all over the U.S. and across the political spectrum, who have been going along with this while it has been happening, some by actively promoting it and others by remaining silent. By "remaining silent," I am not referring to women (or men) who speak out against it anonymously. I understand why many women (and men) do this. In today's society, speaking out in favor of the material reality of sex gets you labeled "transphobic," racist, or fascist. It can get you fired from your job (especially if you are a woman) and/or physically threatened or injured. I completely understand the reluctance of many women to speak out using their real names.

In 2023, *The Free Press* released a podcast called "The Witch Trials of J.K. Rowling." In episode 3 of that podcast, J.K. Rowling said, "I have had direct threats of violence and people coming to my house where my kids live and I've had my address posted online. I've had what the police regard as credible threats. The pushback is often 'You are wealthy. You can afford security. You haven't been silenced.' All of that is true, but that misses the point. The attempt to intimidate and silence me is meant to serve as a warning to other women. And I say that because I have seen it used that way. I have seen other women, and other women have told me they have been told 'Look what happened to J.K. Rowling—watch yourself.'" She's right, of course. So I understand why some women are too intimidated to speak out.

But what about the un-cancellable Americans? Where is Tina Fey? Where is Meryl Streep? Where is Queen Latifa? Where are these women while women's rights are being eroded and children are being harmed? I'm sure they can see what has happened to J.K. Rowling and don't want it to happen to them. Fair enough. But are they really going to leave it to relatively unknown people like me to fight this battle to the death? I'm prepared to die on this hill if I have to, but excuse me, ladies, those of us who have been fighting this war for the last decade could use a little help from those of you with platforms and influence.

I have seen first-hand how this pernicious ideology destroys people's minds. I have lost friends over it. I was once visiting an old friend (whom I have known since we were children) in her home and lightly broached the topic. She said, "I don't want to talk about it." I said, "No problem, but can you tell me why you don't want to talk about it?" She responded, "I DON'T WANT TO TALK ABOUT IT." I reiterated, "Okay, it's really no problem, I'm just curious why." That's when she put her hands over her ears, shook her head, and screamed, again, "I DON'T WANT TO TALK ABOUT IT!!!" Because I was at her home and wanted to be polite, I let it go at that point, but the exchange struck me. Over the next few months, she and I tried to have casual phone calls and email messages, but it fell flat, and now she won't return my messages.

At some point, and I don't know when, but the day is coming, everyone who has been complicit in abolishing sex are going to have to ask themselves: "Did I really support the housing of male violent rapists and murderers in prisons with women? Did I really support men being permitted to take medals, honors, and championships from female athletes? Did I really support children being permitted to sterilize themselves and get surgeries that permanently altered their otherwise healthy bodies? Did I deny that sex is real? Did I think that human beings can change sex? Did I really go along with the idea that women who fight for women's sex-based rights were hateful bigots who needed to be told to shut the f*ck up and threatened with violence? Did I really participate in the destruction of the very nature of humanity and of material reality itself?" Good luck.

PART 4

THE RESISTANCE

This is the essence of all sciences—that you should know who you will be when the Day of Reckoning arrives.
–Rumi

CHAPTER 8

THE DEMOCRAT DEFECTORS

This chapter is the shortest in the book. That's because of the paucity of powerful people on the U.S. left who have taken a stand against the abolition of sex. Some of those who have done so felt the need to leave the Democratic Party in the process. I can't say that I blame them.

The strongest public resistance to "gender identity" in the U.K. is coming from feminists on the political left. Perhaps the most famous prominent leftist to speak out is J.K. Rowling, who made headlines in December 2019 when she posted:

> Dress however you please.
> Call yourself whatever you like.
> Sleep with any consenting adult who'll have you.
> Live your best life in peace and security.
> But force women out of their jobs for stating that sex is real?
> #IStandWithMaya #ThisIsNotADrill

The Maya she was referring to is Maya Forstater, who had essentially lost her job at an international development think tank for insisting that sex is real. Forstater would go on to sue the think tank. She initially lost her suit when a British court ruled that a belief in the material reality of sex is "not worthy of respect in a democratic society." That ruling was overturned because, as any thinking person knows, a belief in the material reality of sex is in fact worthy of respect in a democratic society. She ended up co-founding an organization called Sex Matters, which lobbies for clarity on sex in law and institutions; publishes research, guidance, and analysis; supports and mobilizes people to speak up about the material reality of sex; and holds organizations accountable. I don't know anything about her party affiliation in the U.K., but I do know that she calls herself a feminist and that she knows what a woman is.

In the summer of 2020, Rowling published an essay about the reasons why she speaks out on topics related to sex and gender, where she said: "We're living through the most misogynistic period I've experienced. Back in the 80s, I imagined that my future daughters, should I have any, would have it far better than I ever did, but between the backlash against feminism and a porn-saturated online culture, I believe things have got significantly worse for girls. Never have I seen women denigrated and dehumanized to the extent they are now. From the leader of the free world's long history of sexual assault accusations and his proud boast of 'grabbing them by the pussy,' to the incel ('involuntarily celibate') movement that rages against women who won't give them sex, to the trans activists who declare that TERFs need punching and re-educating, men across the political spectrum seem to agree: women are asking for trouble. Everywhere, women are being told to shut up and sit down, or else." Since then, her support for women and girls (both online and materially) has only increased.

In the States, we don't have anyone on the political left with Rowling's stature standing up for women and girls. Bette Midler and Macy Gray are the only two prominent women in the U.S. who have even tried, and both of them backed down after receiving backlash. In July 2022, Midler posted, "WOMEN OF THE WORLD! We are being stripped of our rights over our bodies, our lives and even of our name! They don't call us 'women' anymore; they call us 'birthing people' or 'menstruators,' and even 'people with vaginas'! Don't let them erase you! Every human on earth owes you!" For this, she was accused of "enforcing a rigid gender binary." A drag queen (man) called "Panti Bliss" responded, "Don't fall for the anti-trans panic fake nonsense. No one is erasing women." Midler explained that she had not intended to be "transphobic," and that she has "fought for marginalized people" for "as long as [she could] remember." That same month, singer Macy Gray went on Piers Morgan's show "Uncensored" and said, "I will say this and everyone's gonna hate me, but as a woman, just because you go change your parts, doesn't make you a woman, sorry. I know that for a fact." Faced with backlash, she went on to say she has "nothing but love for the LGBTQ+ and transgender community" and has "been a supporter since day one." To the best of my knowledge, neither has put her head above the parapet ever since. Neither has anyone else of any prominence.

We do have a few brave souls on the left who are speaking out. Figuring out exactly what they think about "gender identity" is not always easy, but some information is publicly available. None of this should be read as support for any particular politician; it is an analysis of where some Democrats (and former Democrats) may stand on the topic of "gender identity."

Tulsi Gabbard was a Democratic U.S. representative from Hawaii who ran in the 2020 Democratic presidential primary. In 2019, Gabbard (along with every other Democratic House member) co-sponsored the Equality Act. However, in December 2020, just days before leaving office, she joined Republican Representative Markwayne Mullin to introduce the Protect Women's Sports Act. That bill would have made it a violation of Title IX "for a recipient of Federal funds who operates, sponsors, or facilitates athletic programs or activities to permit a person whose biological sex at birth is male to participate in an athletic program or activity that is designated for women or girls."

The bill caused quite a stir, with media outlets reporting on it in very different ways. The *New York Post* somewhat neutrally announced, "Tulsi Gabbard Introduces Bill to 'Protect Women's Sports' Based on Biological Sex." The conservative-leaning *National Review* celebrated with "Tulsi Gabbard Stands Up for Women's Sports." *TIME* lamented,

"Tulsi Gabbard Introduces Bill That Would Ban Trans Women and Girls from Female Sports." *Refinery29* ominously reported, "For Her Final Act, Tulsi Gabbard Is Promoting a Bill that Threatens Trans Women in Sports" and labeled the bill "transphobic." Gabbard herself posted, "My 'Protect Women's Sports Act' is based on science. It safeguards equality & ensures a level playing field for girls & women competing in sports. It upholds Title IX's original intent which was based on the general biological distinction between men & women athletes based on sex." The bill did not advance, although various versions of similar bills have been floating around in Congress for a few years now.

In October 2022, she announced that she was leaving the Democratic Party for a variety of reasons, and stated, "We have an administration in the White House, and woke politicians in Washington, a Supreme Court justice who are unable and unwilling to define what a woman is. How is it controversial to define what a woman is? It is the height of hypocrisy for those who claim to be feminists, who claim to be champions for women over decades...to deny that there is such a thing as a woman. Those who deny the biological differences between a man and a woman are not only erasing women as a category of people; they're denying the existence of objective reality, and the 'truth' becomes whatever those in power want it to be."

Gabbard also spoke at a meeting of the Conservative Political Action Coalition (CPAC) in March 2023. To be clear, I do not like anything about CPAC and never have. For years, it would meet annually in the neighborhood where I live in Washington D.C., and I hated seeing my (very liberal) neighborhood overrun by a bunch of anti-abortion conservatives marching down the street yelling "HUMAN RIGHTS START AT CONCEPTION." CPAC believes that "the Constitution of the United States is the best political charter yet created by men for governing themselves." Unlike ACLU lawyer Chase Strangio,[14] I am a huge fan of the

[14] In 2019, Strangio talked with political commentator Chris Hayes on Hayes's podcast and stated, "I am a civil rights and constitutional lawyer who fundamentally doesn't believe in the Constitution and the legal system."

U.S. Constitution. It is true that it was men who created it, but that's only because the women of the day were shut out of the process completely.

In any event, this is what Gabbard had to say at CPAC in 2023: "We just celebrated International Women's Day last week. I was scrolling through social media, seeing, you know, what are people saying about it? And you saw a lot of nice flowery words coming from a lot of people in Washington, celebrating women, and all that women have accomplished over the years, and all these great and inspiring examples of women leaders throughout our time. We know the hypocrisy there. You ask them, 'What is a woman?' and they can't answer the question. And one of the people they chose to honor in the White House on International Women's Day was not a woman at all. It was a biological male. There are two major points here. Number one is there is no greater expression of hatred and hostility towards women than to try to erase our existence as a category of people and to minimize us to being a construct of anyone's imagination. And the second thing that doesn't get talked about often enough as we are looking at this insanity is that by rejecting the objective truth that there is such a thing as a woman, they are rejecting the existence of objective truth as a whole. And when we remove those boundaries of what is actually true and false, not 'my truth' or 'your truth' or 'their truth,' or whatever it is, but that there is such a thing as objective truth, then we remove all the boundaries of our society and we end up in a position, which we're seeing right now, where what is declared as true is based on whatever those in power say that it is. And we've seen again how this changes over time." Needless to say, I agree with her completely.

I wish that Gabbard had not left the party, although I completely understand her reasons for doing so. She is absolutely right that Democratic Party leadership is both erasing women as a category of people and denying the existence of objective reality. It is hard to remain a member of a party that is doing this, as many rank-and-file Democrats know. I have met Gabbard in person and, whatever I might think about anything she has to say about any other topic, I trust her commitment to this one.

When she was running for president in 2020 (before *Roe v. Wade* was overturned), this is what she had to say on the topic of abortion: "The very real possibility of *Roe v. Wade* being overturned terrifies me. I am sick of women's bodies being used as pawns so politicians can score cheap political points at the expense of their freedom and safety. I am wholly committed to abortion remaining safe, legal and rare. We must commit to defending a woman's right to choose. I also support sensible codifying of *Roe v. Wade* preventing third-trimester abortion except when there are grave or life-threatening health consequences for the mother." I don't like the types of limits that she would impose on women's right to access abortion, but I understand them and think that they are not unreasonable. I don't know anything about whether Gabbard has future presidential aspirations, but I strongly suspect that if she runs as an Independent in 2024, she'll garner a lot of votes from Democrats and Republicans alike, especially if the other options are Joe Biden and Donald Trump.

In September 2023, it was announced that the Kansas Health Department will no longer allow people to change the sex markers on their birth certificates. The department is overseen by a woman named Janet Stanek and although I do not know anything about her political affiliation, I know that she was appointed by Democratic governor Laura Kelly, so this happened under Kelly's watch. Kansas is an interesting state to watch—Kelly has vetoed several bills that would be good for women and girls (or prevent harms to children), but the legislature has managed to override many of them (with the help of a handful of Democrats). I'm not entirely sure what to make of all this, but I'll be paying close attention.

A tiny handful of state Democratic lawmakers have taken a stand. In Louisiana, five Senate Democrats voted to pass the state's Fairness in Women's Sports Act in 2022. They were: Regina Barrow, Katrina Jackson, Jay Luneau, Gary Smith, and Gregory Tarver. Seven House Democrats and one Independent did the same. They were: Roy Adams, Delisha Boyd, Ken Brass, Robert Carter, Mack Cormier, Cazerrick Johnson, Jeremy LaCombe, and Francis Thompson. Eight Democrats sat out the vote rather than either throw Louisiana women and girls under the bus or stand up for them. The bill passed in both houses and became law when the state's Democratic governor failed to veto it. The most important vote on that bill was in the Senate, to bring the bill back to the floor for a final vote. Only one Democrat voted to bring it back, Katrina Jackson. In Pennsylvania, a lone Democrat took a stand in 2022 in voting to pass that state's Protect Women's Sports Act. The bill passed in both houses, but Democratic governor Tom Wolf vetoed it and there were not enough votes in the legislature to override the veto. Three North Carolina Democrats followed suit in 2023 and later that year, two North Carolina Democrats even voted to override their own party governor's veto of the bill. In June 2023, the Louisiana legislature voted to pass a bill to ban "gender-affirming care" for minors. Three Senate Democrats and eight House Democrats voted to pass it. The Democratic governor vetoed the bill, but then both houses voted to override the veto. One Democratic state senator who voted to override the veto was none other than Katrina Jackson.

In March 2021, South Carolina Democratic Representative Cezar McKnight introduced the Vulnerable Child Compassion and Protection Act, which would bar doctors from prescribing medication or performing procedures designed to obscure the reality of sex or to delay puberty for anyone under age eighteen. Representative McKnight represented a largely rural, heavily Democratic area where two-thirds of residents are black. McKnight told reporters that he had received an outpouring of support from constituents. The bill was pronounced dead in May 2022, and one month later, he was defeated in the Democratic primary House race by Democrat Roger Kirby. McKnight had also been a vocal supporter of South Carolina's Save Women's Sports bill, but Kirby had spoken out against it.

In April 2023, former state representative and Democrat from Detroit Cynthia Johnson took to social media to engage in what some local media outlets referred to as a "transphobic rant." In this "rant," she referred to the use of opposite-sex pronouns as "bullshit," and said what most Democrats are afraid to say: "All that extra stuff that they're adding on, do you [sic] that's okay but don't lie to us about who you are. If you were born male but you don't feel that body is the one that you want to be in, it doesn't make you a female it just makes you want to be in a different body." Johnson also has a son who is gay, and she talks openly about how proud she is of him. Being accused of going on a "transphobic rant" in local media really irritated her, and later, she had this to say: "Yes, I said my son is gay. MY SON. THE PERSON WHO I AM SO PROUD OF! So despite the Trump like propaganda to shut me down for speaking up for the babies and the mothers and the fathers and those who are in the community, and I am a part of the community, because my son is in the community, you will never win despite having been indoctrinated and/or being the indoctrinator. Furthermore, fuck you! Let me emphasize it...FUCK. YOU! Only truth accompanied by proof and not by a person who we have no idea about the background or the biases that the person may or may not have but still allowed to make intentional false reports. PROBLEMATIC ON SO MANY LEVELS!... Finally, the question must be asked: WHAT THE FUCK IS THE REAL AGENDA?" Indeed, Representative Johnson, what is the real agenda indeed?

Also in April 2023, Kansas Democratic representative Marvin Robinson voted to override the state governor's veto of a bill to protect female-only sports. He was the only Democrat to do so and his vote decided the matter—without it, the legislature would not have had the votes needed to override. Later that same month, he also voted to override the governor's veto of the state Women's Bill of Rights (a modified version of the federal bill discussed in Chapter 7), which defines sex biologically throughout state law. Robinson stated, "I thought the definition of a woman was the cradle and portal of life. I found out that's not what the definition is to the people of the Democratic Party."

In May 2023, Texas Democratic representative Shawn Thierry voted in support of a bill to ban "gender-affirming care" for minors, explaining that she had thoroughly researched the issue and decided that the best way to protect children suffering from depression and "gender dysphoria" was to ban such "care." She said, "As they navigate through the challenging journey of finding the best version of themselves,... I absolutely believe we raise the age to 18 for children to receive GnRH analogs, cross-sex hormones, and to undergo potential irreversible body altering surgeries." This is a woman who had done her research. In response, her local Democratic group voted to censure her (though the vote was thirteen to seven, meaning that seven local Democrats either agreed with her or disagreed but didn't think that censure was appropriate).

In June 2023, a North Carolina Democratic senator named Val Applewhite was the only senate Democrat who voted to pass the state's Fairness in Women's Sports Act (which passed). In response, she received messages that she described as "frightening." When asked for specifics, she said, "The one that kind of captures it all was that I was a 'transphobic cisgendered whore.' I don't want to go through the rest of them." In discussing her vote, she made some very interesting comments. She said, for example, "I'm telling you, people are afraid to speak out publicly.... Even the coaches and parents that I spoke to, they don't want to say it publicly. That's not good when we are afraid to have public discourse over issues." She compared it to a debate the state had recently had about some proposed abortion restrictions, saying that as contentious as that debate was, this one was "just different."

Katrina Jackson, Cesar McKnight, Cynthia Johnson, Marvin Robinson, Shawn Thierry, and Val Applewhite are all black. Thierry has spoken movingly about her own emergency C-section and about her state's failure to address the maternal mortality crisis among black women. She said, "It's easy to dismiss Black women's lives."

I was starting a new job back in 2018 and had to attend an all-day orientation session. The session covered numerous topics, including a local law and an agency policy that prohibited discrimination on the basis of "gender identity." The trainer for that section was a man who, in my view, clearly did not agree with the law or the policy. While sporting a very stereotypically male hairstyle and wearing clothing stereotypically associated with men (including pants, shoes, and a button-down shirt) he got up in front of the attendees and announced, "Local law and agency policy dictate that I am permitted to use the women's bathroom looking exactly as I look now." He was making a true statement. A black woman in the back of the room stood up and said "OH HELL NO!"

I live in Washington D.C., a city whose population includes a large proportion of church-going black women (and men). These voters have historically voted Democrat because they have viewed the Democratic Party as most likely to protect their interests. I was once walking down the street, a few steps behind an elderly black woman who was dressed the way that elderly black women often dress—very classically, in a skirt suit, handbag, and tidy hat. While she was crossing the street, a tall white man (a "transwoman") wearing a pink bikini and a long blond wig zipped around the corner on a scooter and nearly ran her down. I could see from her face that she was appropriately appalled.

I have a friend who is also a black woman and a TERF. I have asked her before what black women really think about this stuff and she has told me things like, "Kara, Black women know a thing or two about forced sterilization and we are NOT going to go along with this." Polling supports this. According to a 2023 poll commissioned by Women's Declaration International USA, 84 percent of Black voters agree that women are female. In my view, it is going to be black Democratic legislators (especially women) who are going to lead the party back to sanity. Or at least, they are not going to go down without a fight. White Democrats in office have a thing or two to learn from them.

CHAPTER 9

THE JUDGES

In *The Abolition of Sex*, I addressed a series of cases that had made their way through the federal judiciary and that, for the most part, obliterated the material reality of sex and single-sex spaces and sports, to the detriment of women and girls. There have been more similar rulings in the years since. However, more recently, there have been several cases that take the opposite approach—these cases affirm that sex is real and can be protected as a coherent category consistent with federal law and the U.S. Constitution.

Adams v. School Board of St. Johns County

The case of *Adams v. School Board of St. Johns County* had been pending before the federal judiciary for about five and half years when, on December 30, 2022, the Eleventh Circuit Court of Appeals issued an *en banc* (full court) ruling that schools may, under both the Constitution and Title IX, maintain sex-specific bathrooms and refuse to allow students to use the bathrooms assigned to members of the opposite sex based on the students' "gender identity." Most people predicted that it was headed to the Supreme Court. If it had ended up there, that would have given the Supreme Court an opportunity to revisit *Bostock v. Clayton County*, where it ruled that employment discrimination based on sexual orientation or "transgender status" constitutes unlawful sex discrimination, without telling us what it might have meant by "transgender status." It would also have given the Court an opportunity to answer a question, explicitly left open in *Bostock*, about whether its reasoning applies outside of the employment context. But it didn't get there.

Adams's complaint was filed on June 28, 2017. The first sentence of the complaint reads, "Drew Adams ('Drew' or 'Plaintiff') is a 16-year-old boy who attends Allen D. Nease High School ('Nease High School') in Ponte Vedra, Florida." Adams, however, is female. Thus, the entire case begins with a lie; specifically, the lie that a female person can be a boy. The complaint alleged that the school refused Adams access to the boys' bathrooms. This is true. The school had engaged in an exhaustive examination of how best to accommodate the needs of all students (considering both sex and "gender identity") and ended up with a policy of maintaining three sets of bathrooms: one for boys only, one for girls only, and one set of single-stall locked bathrooms that anyone could use. Adams was given a choice: use either the girls-only restrooms (because of her female sex) or the single-stall ones that anyone could use (regardless of sex). But Adams was refused access to the boys' restrooms, which had open, undivided urinals. Adams then used the boys' restrooms in violation of the policy and several male students and their parents complained. The parties agreed that these complaints had been lodged with the school administration.

Adams alleged that the school's policy violated both Title IX and the Equal Protection Clause of the 14th Amendment. Title IX is a landmark federal law that makes it unlawful for any educational institution that receives federal funding (which is virtually all of them) to discriminate on the basis of sex, but it also allows such educational institutions to maintain single-sex facilities. The Equal Protection Clause of the 14th Amendment essentially says that no government entity is allowed to "deny to any person within its jurisdiction the equal protection of the laws." It was added to the Constitution in the mid-nineteenth century and was generally intended to remedy centuries of unequal protection of the laws on the basis of race. The Supreme Court eventually ruled in 1971 that women count in the category "persons" and that we are entitled to equal protection too. It was later decided that even though women are entitled to equal protection of the laws, it is permissible for government entities to discriminate between the sexes under certain circumstances.

Adams's complaint was signed by three private attorneys and three attorneys with the Lambda Legal Defense Fund, another traditionally progressive organization that works very hard to dismantle legal protections for women and girls at the altar of "gender identity." About a year after the filing of the complaint, the District Court sided with Adams. The District Court's opinion begins: "The parents of St. Johns County, along with teachers and administrators of the St. Johns County School District, have a solemn obligation to guard the well-being of the children in their charge. As recent events from around the country have tragically demonstrated, this is a very challenging job. Recognizing the difficulty of this task and that local school boards, answerable to the citizens of their community, are best situated to set school policy, federal courts are reluctant to interfere.... Everyone agrees that boys should use the boys' restroom at Nease and that girls should use the girls' restroom. The parties disagree over whether Drew Adams is a boy."

By "as recent events from around the country have tragically demonstrated," I assume that the court is referring specifically but obliquely to the tragic shooting at Stoneman Douglas High School in Parkland, Florida, which is about a five-hour drive from Ponte Vedra, where this litigation took place. That shooting had occurred a few months before the decision was issued. Why the court felt the need to invoke this horrific stain on America's history in the context of a case about whether sex is real is not particularly a mystery. I think the court did this to invoke a sense of sympathy for high school children. I'm sure that Americans across the political spectrum have tremendous sympathy for the kids who endured that shooting. But the shooting should not have anything to do with the question of whether sex is real. In any event, the court never explained why it thought that the question of whether Drew Adams is a boy (she isn't) was a legal matter to be resolved by the federal judiciary.

Judge Timothy Corrigan ruled that the school was in violation of both Title IX and the Equal Protection Clause by refusing to allow Adams to use the boys' restroom. The decision contains this language: "Adams has encountered no problems using men's restrooms in public places, and there were no reports of problems from any boys or boys' parents during the six weeks of his freshman year when Adams used the boys' restrooms at Nease." But this is simply outright not true because, as mentioned, the parties had agreed at the outset of the litigation that complaints had been lodged with school administrators.

The school board then appealed to the Eleventh Circuit and things got interesting. The appeal went before a three-judge panel consisting of Chief Judge William Pryor, Judge Beverly Martin, and Judge Jill Pryor (I have no idea whether William Pryor and Jill Pryor are related). In August 2020, about two years after the District Court ruled in favor of Adams, the panel issued a ruling affirming the District Court's decision. The majority decision begins, "Drew Adams is a young man and recent graduate of Nease High School in Florida's St. Johns County School District." It ended up agreeing with the District Court that refusing Adams access to the boys' restroom violated Title IX and the Equal Protection Clause.

Judge William Pryor dissented from that opinion, writing: "Not long ago, a suit challenging the lawfulness of separating bathrooms on the basis of sex would have been unthinkable. This practice has long been the common-sense example of an acceptable classification on the basis of sex. And for good reason: it protects well-established privacy interests in using the bathroom away from the opposite sex. Although the Supreme Court recently considered the relationship between transgender status and sex in the context of claims of employment discrimination under Title VII, it declined to consider the permissibility of sex-separated bathrooms." He would have ruled that the school's policy violates neither Title IX nor the Equal Protection Clause. His dissenting opinion concluded: "The majority transforms an appeal that it should have resolved with straightforward applications of [applicable law] into something unrecognizable.... [T]here is nothing unlawful, under either the Constitution or federal law, about a policy that separates bathrooms for schoolchildren on the basis of sex. I dissent." On the same day that the panel decision was issued, something very strange happened—a judge (not named) withheld the ruling.

The case stayed with the same panel, and on July 14, 2021 (nearly a full year after the first panel opinion issued), the court issued a new decision *again* affirming the District Court's judgment, but this time ignoring the Title IX claim and simply ruling that the district's policy was unconstitutional because "the School District assigns students to sex-specific bathrooms in an arbitrary manner." This was a majority of a three-judge panel of a federal appeals court saying that dividing bathrooms based on sex is "arbitrary." To do that, it engaged in some impressive gymnastics to argue that sex isn't real. But if the majority spent an entire year hoping to get Judge William Pryor to go along with this, they didn't fare very well. He dissented again, reiterating his view that separating restrooms by sex is just fine.

That was July 2021. The school board then sought *en banc* (full court) review of that decision. The *en banc* decision was authored by Judge Barbara Lagoa, and the legal outcomes are inarguably great for everyone in that they confirm the material reality of sex and allow for the provision of single-sex bathrooms in schools that receive Title IX funding. The ruling begins simply: "This case involves the unremarkable—and nearly universal—practice of separating school bathrooms based on biological sex. This appeal requires us to determine whether separating the use of male and female bathrooms in the public schools based on a student's biological sex violates (1) the Equal Protection Clause of the Fourteenth Amendment and (2) Title IX of the Education Amendments Act of 1972. We hold that it does not—separating school bathrooms based on biological sex passes constitutional muster and comports with Title IX." At no point did the court refer to Adams using "he/him" pronouns, which I take to be significant. The court's Equal Protection analysis properly centered on the legal framework courts use to examine government laws and policies that discriminate based on sex. The school's policy indisputably discriminated based on sex: boys in one bathroom, girls in the other (with a third set for anyone regardless of sex). The question then became whether such discrimination was constitutional and the court ruled that it was. The entire analysis is really very simple, legally and factually.

There was also an important question of whether the school's bathroom policy "discriminates against transgender students" and the court found that it didn't because the entire policy is framed as pertaining exclusively to sex. Again, boys in one bathroom, girls in the other (with a set of bathrooms that anyone can use regardless of sex). Probably most people would find this arrangement to be totally acceptable. If girls are comfortable using a single-stall locked bathroom that boys are also permitted to use, there should be nothing against that. None of that has anything to do with anyone's "gender identity."

The court then went on to ask whether the word "sex" is ambiguous in Title IX (which the District Court had found). To do that, it looked to numerous dictionary definitions that existed at the time of Title IX's enactment and quoted them. The definitions the court quoted were all very clear and grounded in basic biology. The ruling concluded by pointing to an analogous situation: "Think of a biological female student, who does not identify as transgender and who sued her school under Title IX to gain access to the male bathroom. Regardless of whether preventing the female student from using the male bathroom would constitute separation on the basis of sex—and it plainly would—the carve-out for bathrooms under Title IX would provide the school a safe harbor. In other words, because Title IX explicitly provides for separate bathrooms on the basis of sex, the student's claim would fail. So, too, must Adams's claim, because the carve-out for bathrooms provides the School Board a safe harbor for the same reasons."

When we think about all of this in those terms, everything becomes clear. A girl who demanded access to the boys' bathroom just for the hell of it would probably be denied, as would, presumably, a boy who demanded access to the girls' bathroom just for the hell of it. The only thing that distinguishes Adams from any other girl, and the only reason this case even exists, is the magical use of the word "transgender." Adams and her attorneys at Lambda Legal had until Friday, March 31, 2023, to seek review before the Supreme Court. They did not do so, strongly suggesting that Lambda Legal knows it is on very shaky legal ground. The Eleventh Circuit's *en banc* decision stands, and in Alabama, Florida, and Georgia, schools may legally maintain single-sex bathrooms.

Green v. Miss U.S.A.

In November 2022, a three-judge panel of the Ninth Circuit Court of Appeals ruled that a beauty pageant can exclude men who claim to be women from competing. The pageant restricts competition to "natural-born females." A man named Anita Green applied to compete and was denied, so he got mad and sued the pageant. He lost at the District Court level and appealed to the Ninth Circuit.

I am categorically opposed to beauty pageants, but this case isn't fundamentally about beauty pageants. It is about celebrating women-only spaces and freedom of speech. The Ninth Circuit panel ruled that Green, who "self-identifies as an openly transgender female," sued the Miss United States of America beauty pageant, alleging that the pageant's "natural-born female" eligibility requirement violated state law. It is interesting that the court used the phrase "self-identifies." This appears to be an implicit acknowledgment that "trans" is just an identity, and that it isn't real in any material sense. The court didn't say that explicitly, but I can't really think of a way that the court would disagree, given its deliberate choice to use the phrase. Judges (particularly federal appellate judges) choose their words carefully. I have read other judicial opinions (including out of the Ninth Circuit) that say things like "plaintiff is a transgender woman." The phrase "self-identifies" reads very differently.

The ruling made another great point, which is that if the pageant were required to include Green based on his "female gender identity," it would also have to include anyone who claims to identify into any of the other categories of eligibility requirements. For example, the pageant includes only women between the ages of eighteen and twenty-eight. If it can be required to include Green, it would logically also be required to include an eighty-year-old. Again, I think all these images of what constitutes an "ideal" woman are preposterous and misogynistic, and I don't think the pageant should exist at all. But it does, and the point the court was making was that one can no more "identify into" the category woman than one can identify into an age category in which one doesn't belong.

This is all very good news for those of us fighting to maintain the category "women" as exclusively for adult human females. This ruling agrees with us, and confirms that we can say this out loud, consistent with our First Amendment rights. The Ninth Circuit panel's decision stands and groups like Miss USA have a First Amendment right to exclude men. This is a solid win for women and girls.

Neese v. Becerra

Susan Neese and James Hurley, both physicians, sued HHS because of HHS's interpretation of sex to include "gender identity." HHS had decided in May 2021 that it was going to interpret sex to include "gender identity" under the Affordable Care Act (ACA), which means that medical professionals who receive federal funding under the ACA aren't allowed to discriminate against people based on their "gender identities." What that means in practice is that medical professionals aren't allowed to provide sex-specific medical care to people who claim to be members of the opposite sex. All this was done in accordance with Biden's lie that *Bostock* means that "gender identity" is a protected category for all purposes. Title IX is relevant in this case too, because the ACA refers to Title IX in its non-discrimination provision, meaning that sex discrimination is prohibited in the provision of healthcare.

Dr. Neese treats adults with "gender dysphoria" but sometimes refuses to refer patients for hormones or surgery if she feels that is not appropriate, and she refuses to refer minors for hormones or surgery under all circumstances. Dr. Hurley insists on providing sex-specific care, regardless of "gender identity." For example, he has a male patient who claims to be a woman. Dr. Hurley was concerned that his patient might have prostate cancer and sought to refer him to an oncologist for cancer screening, but the patient refused because he insisted that he is a woman and therefore does not have a prostate. Dr. Neese argued that if she is not permitted to discriminate on the basis of "gender identity," then she is prohibited from refusing to prescribe hormones and/or surgery for patients for whom she thinks such treatments are inappropriate. Dr. Hurley argued that if he is unable to provide sex-specific treatment when medically appropriate, he is prohibited from treating his patient's prostate cancer because the patient claims to have a woman "gender identity."

The gist of this ruling was that *Bostock* itself does not apply to HHS decisions. That's great on its own, but the ruling went even further—not only does the *Bostock* decision *itself* not apply, but its *reasoning* doesn't apply either (the Biden administration's claim has consistently been that it does). In determining whether "gender identity" is a protected category under Title IX, the court did something that *should not be*, but in light of contemporary circumstances *is* extraordinary—it ruled that for Title IX purposes at least, sex is binary.

The decision contains some very helpful language about physiological differences between the sexes and about how those differences should not be used to justify discriminatory treatment against women and girls, which is very good news for those of us who care about women's sports. It also notes that Congress has enacted hate-crime laws that enhance penalties for crimes committed because of a person's sexual orientation or "gender identity" (quotes mine), suggesting that if Congress wanted to amend Title IX to define sex as including "gender identity," it could do so. This is also good, as it suggests that members of Congress know that eliminating women's sports is deeply unpopular among the general public. In short, there is a lot in this ruling for defenders of the sex-based rights of women and girls to be very happy about.

The Biden administration appealed the case and as of writing, the matter is pending before the Fifth Circuit, where WDI USA filed a friend-of-the-court brief.

B.P.J. v. West Virginia State Board of Education

This is, in my view, one of the more interesting cases making its way through the federal judiciary addressing sex and gender because it involves a plot twist at the end. On January 5, 2023, a federal district court announced a decision in this case. It began with: "West Virginia passed a law that defines 'girl' and 'woman,' for the purpose of secondary school sports, as biologically female. Under the law, all biological males, including those who identify as transgender girls, are ineligible for participation on girls' sports teams. B.P.J., a transgender girl who wants to play girls' sports, challenges the law. The question before the court is whether the legislature's chosen definition of 'girl' and 'woman' in this context is constitutionally permissible. I find that it is."

Before delving into the details of the decision, I want to say a few things about B.P.J. B.P.J. ("Becky," according to the ACLU, which represents him) is a boy. He has been on puberty-blocking hormones since the age of nine, with his mother's consent. This, despite the fact that there is not a single long-term study to demonstrate the safety or efficacy of puberty blockers. What *is* known is that even temporary use of puberty blockers has been associated with depression, osteoporosis, mood disorders, seizures, cognitive impairment, and, when combined with cross-sex hormones, sterility. Nearly 100 percent of children who are given puberty blockers for treating so-called "gender dysphoria" eventually go on to take cross-sex hormones, meaning that B.P.J. will probably eventually become sterile. Finally, when administered in young boys, puberty blockers impair the development of a healthy adult penis, making eventual vaginoplasty impossible at best, and dangerous at worst. In other words, B.P.J. is not likely ever to have anything resembling a healthy sexual or reproductive life. So, while I celebrate this legal outcome as a win for women and girls and for the material reality of sex, I feel absolutely dreadful for this young man as a person.

The law in question is a West Virginia law titled the "Save Women's Sports Bill" (SWS). It was introduced in March 2021 and enacted by both chambers of the legislature in April 2021. It was signed by the governor in April 2021 and codified into law on May 20, 2021. Six days later, the ACLU was ready with its complaint on behalf of B.P.J., before the law had even become effective (it went into effect in July).

B.P.J. wanted to compete on the girls' cross-country and track teams but the school said no, based on the SWS law and on his male sex. B.P.J. and his mother then sued the school, arguing that the school's refusal to let him compete on the girls' teams violated both Title IX and the Equal Protection Clause of the 14th Amendment. As previously discussed, Title IX is a federal law that makes it unlawful for any educational institution that receives federal funding (which is virtually all of them) to discriminate based on sex, but it also allows such educational institutions to maintain single-sex living facilities. Title IX's regulations also permit schools to maintain single-sex housing, toilet, locker room, and shower facilities so long as the facilities provided to one sex are comparable to those provided to the other sex.

The case was assigned to Judge Joseph Goodwin in the District Court for the Southern District of West Virginia, who ruled in late July of 2021 (the same month in which the law went into effect) that B.P.J. was entitled to have the law blocked for him (but not statewide). Judge Goodwin clearly hates the SWS law. Toward the beginning of his 2021 decision, he stated, "At this point, I have been provided with scant evidence that this law addresses any problem at all, let alone an important problem." He refers to B.P.J. as a girl consistently throughout the opinion.

I said this about the case in my book *The Abolition of Sex*: "But this is silly. Even assuming that B.P.J. does, in fact, 'transcend conventional expectations,' the only way that that fact magically turns B.P.J. into a girl is if the material reality of sex is irrelevant. It ought to be fine for kids to look and behave in ways that defy society's expectations of what girls and boys are supposed to do without suggesting that such defiance turns kids into the opposite sex." In any event, B.P.J. initially won at the district court level, at least with respect to B.P.J. himself.

But then in January 2023, the same judge *dissolved his own injunction, denied summary judgment to B.P.J., and granted summary judgment on behalf of all the state defendants*. A summary judgement is a court order ruling that a trial is not necessary because there are no factual issues to be tried. That put an end to the litigation at the district court level. Judge Goodwin clearly still hated the SWS law. In his new grant of summary judgment, he said sneeringly with respect to the law's legislative findings: "The law, which was clearly carefully crafted with litigation such as this in mind, begins with the following legislative findings": and then went on to list the findings, which are aligned with the material reality of sex and cite pertinent federal caselaw. (In the judge's defense: Having participated in a coalition of advocacy organizations that lobbied heavily for this law, he was completely right that it was written very carefully with "litigation such as this in mind." I'm glad to see that tactic worked exactly as intended!)

Judge Goodwin stated that he would "not get into the business of defining what it means to be a 'girl' or 'woman.' The courts have no business creating such definitions, and I would be hard-pressed to find many other contexts where one's sex and gender are relevant legislative considerations. But I am forced to consider whether the state's chosen definition passes constitutional muster in this one discrete context." It mystifies me that Judge Goodwin claimed to be "hard-pressed" to find many other contexts where one's sex and gender are relevant legislative considerations. The 19th Amendment provides one quite obvious example of sex being a "relevant legislative consideration." It's right there: "Amendment XIX: The right of citizens of the United States to vote shall not be denied or abridged by the United States or by any state on account of sex. Congress shall have power to enforce this article by appropriate legislation." If Judge Goodwin was "hard-pressed" to find examples of sex being a relevant legislative consideration, it is only because he was irritated at having to decide whether a law that defines sex according to biology is legal.

In the end, Judge Goodwin ruled that sex is real because, really, he had no choice but to do so. He said, "It is beyond dispute that, barring rare genetic mutations not at issue here, a person either has male sex chromosomes or female sex chromosomes. Gender, on the other hand, refers to 'a set of socially constructed roles, behaviors, activities, and attributes that a given society considers appropriate.'... I recognize that being transgender is natural and is not a choice. But one's sex is also natural, and it dictates physical characteristics that are relevant to athletics." If I am reading this right, the judge was saying that there are people who do not conform to sex stereotypes, which is absolutely true, and also that not conforming to sex stereotypes is different from "gender identity," and also that "gender identity" is a deeply held belief that one is the opposite sex. Whatever one thinks of the idea that someone who has a "deeply held belief that one is the opposite sex" "is transgender" and/or how that matter should be addressed, the judge was also saying here that sex is real. I think it irritated him to have to do so. You can tell from reading the entire ruling that this judge was *really* irritated at having to rule in favor of the state over the ACLU because he could not get out of acknowledging that sex is real.

And here comes the plot twist: Judge Goodwin was appointed to the federal judiciary by President Bill Clinton in 1995. I suspect he is naturally inclined toward the arguments put forth by the ACLU and toward the idea that it is important to protect fairness for historically marginalized groups of people, including, as far as he is concerned, "transgender people." To the best of my knowledge, this was the first time that a federal judge who was appointed by a Democratic president has issued a ruling in support of the material reality of sex and against the lies put forth by the ACLU. He didn't want to do it, but he did it anyway. Judge Goodwin's contempt for the SWS law is clear throughout both the 2021 opinion and the one from January 2023. He has fully accepted the idea that a boy who claims to be a girl can be a girl based on his "gender identity." And yet even he knows that sex is real. He did his job: consider the undisputed facts, apply the pertinent standards, and issue a judgment on the law. I'm glad that he did so. In February 2023, the Fourth Circuit Court of Appeals re-issued the injunction pending appeal, but the Supreme Court later vacated that decision, and B.P.J. can compete with the girls for now. In the meantime, the

Fourth Circuit has to decide what to do with Judge Goodwin's conclusion that sex is real and WDI USA has filed a friend-of-the-court brief arguing that it should affirm Judge Goodwin's welcome decision.

L. W. v. Skrmetti

In early 2023, the Tennessee legislature enacted Senate Bill 1, which prohibits the administration of puberty blockers, wrong-sex hormones, and "gender-affirming" surgeries on minors. It took effect in March of that year. Almost immediately, a group of minors (along with their parents and doctors) sued the state, arguing that the law violates their rights under the Due Process and Equal Protection Clauses of the 14th Amendment. They were represented by the ACLU, the ACLU of Tennessee, Lambda Legal, and a few prominent law firms. They won their case at the District Court level, and the District Court blocked the law from taking effect statewide. The U.S. Department of Justice intervened in the case, claiming that "every person has a gender identity."

The state filed an emergency appeal to the Sixth Circuit Court of Appeals and asked that court to lift the District Court's decision. The Sixth Circuit did lift the opinion, which left the law in effect. Then the Sixth Circuit did something that is extremely unusual in my experience—it issued an expedited briefing schedule and committed itself to issuing a final opinion by the end of September. Federal Courts of Appeals don't usually do this. They like to take their time and, as frustrating as that can be for litigants who are anxiously awaiting their decisions, that's probably a good thing in general. We should want federal courts to take their time when deciding important matters. But when the Sixth Circuit expedited this case, it showed they were taking it very seriously; the court understood the stakes. In its decision lifting the District Court's ruling, it also said that Tennessee was likely to succeed on the merits of the case—that's fancy legal jargon for "this law is probably constitutional." That signaled very good news for those of us who care about the material reality of sex and want to protect kids.

WDI USA quickly put together a friend of the court brief to file by the deadline the court imposed for filing such things. We made three arguments: (1) Sex is grounded in material reality, whereas "gender" (including linguistic derivatives like "gender identity," "transgender," and "cisgender") is grounded in regressive sexist stereotypes; (2) The word "transgender" is a linguistic sleight of hand that cannot be protected legally as a quasi-suspect class under Equal Protection analysis because it has no coherent meaning; and (3) Children have an international human right to grow into adulthood and to be protected from the physical and psychological harms that result from blocking puberty and/or administering opposite-sex hormones. We quoted HRC's *own definitions* at length in making the case that "trans" is not a coherent category of people. We also quoted Stonewall, which is basically the U.K.'s version of HRC. We asked the court to permanently lift the District Court's decision and leave the law in place.

The Sixth Circuit's final decision, issued at the end of September 2023, is *great* for proponents of the material reality of sex. The court said that "trans" is not immutable, not "definitively ascertainable at birth," and "describes a huge variety of identities and expressions." It noted that the existence of "detransitioners" proves that "trans" is not immutable. Finally, it noted that "trans" is not a "politically powerless group." This is crucial. "Trans" proponents are always going on about how it's "the most marginalized community." This is nonsense, and the court accurately noted that the plaintiffs had the backing of the president and the Department of Justice, twenty states, the major medical associations (like WPATH, the AAP, and the Endocrine Society), and several large law firms. The court said, "These are not the hallmarks of a skewed or unfair political process." And the court skewered WPATH in the process. This is a big deal.

To be clear, other courts have ruled differently. Federal courts have blocked similar laws in Montana and Texas, and most likely in other states as well. But the Sixth Circuit's decision provides reason to hope that the federal judiciary will ultimately come out on the side of material reality when it comes to the topic of preserving children's bodies in the sex that they are.

Parents Defending Education v. Linn Mar

This case concerns a policy that had been adopted by the Linn Mar School District in Iowa setting forth regulations for the District that "address the needs of transgender students, gender-expansive students, nonbinary, gender nonconforming students, and students questioning their gender to ensure a safe, affirming, and healthy school environment where every student can learn effectively." The policy provides that a student has "the right to be addressed by a name and pronoun that corresponds to their gender identity" and that "[a]n intentional and/or persistent refusal by staff or students to respect a student's gender identity is a violation of school board policies," including "anti-bullying" and "anti-harassment" policies. The policy defines "gender identity" as "[a] person's deeply-held sense or psychological knowledge of their own gender." A student who violates the policy "shall be disciplined by appropriate measures, which may include suspension and expulsion." In other words, the policy provided that refusing to "respect a student's gender identity" constitutes bullying and harassment under District policy.

The group Parents Defending Education sued. They had two sets of arguments—one group of parents were concerned that their autistic (or otherwise disabled) children might suddenly announce that they "are trans" without the parents' knowledge and the other group of parents do not believe in "gender identity" and worried that the policy compelled their children's speech, in violation of the First Amendment. The parents lost at the district court level and appealed to the Eighth Circuit Court of Appeals.

In the meantime, Iowa enacted a law that prohibits a school district from knowingly giving false or misleading information to parents regarding their children's "gender identity." So the court decided that the former group of parents' concerns had been addressed by the legislature and that their complaints were now moot. But the group *did* end up prevailing on the First Amendment issue. One of the parents said that her son wants to state his belief that biological sex is immutable, that he shouldn't have to go along with another student's claimed "gender identity," that he should be able to say that boys should not be allowed to compete in girls' sports, and that he should be able to express discomfort about sharing bathrooms with teachers or students of the opposite sex. But because of the policy, her son remains silent in school in order to avoid violating the policy.

The court decided in September 2023 that this student's proposed activity is probably proscribed by the policy and that there was a credible threat of enforcement, meaning that the policy chilled his speech. It also ruled that the parents were entitled to have the policy blocked because they're likely to win on First Amendment grounds. In other words, the court ruled that public school students have the right to think (and to say out loud) that they don't believe in "gender identity." It told the District Court to block the policy from taking effect. This is a big win for material reality.

* * * * *

There are plenty of other cases making their way through the federal judiciary that concern the topic of "gender identity" and the Supreme Court will eventually have to contend with the fallout from its *Bostock* ruling. But these stand out to me as examples of court decisions that affirm the material reality of sex. A lot of people will say that I should not like any of these rulings because most judges who made them were appointed by Donald Trump. To them, I say this: Look, I don't like Donald Trump any more than you do. I have never voted for him and will never do so. I don't like the fact that the electoral college went in his direction in 2016 and that he was able to appoint judges to the federal judiciary. I have no doubt that his appointees (including on the Supreme Court) will continue to obliterate abortion rights, and I don't like that fact at all. But here's the thing: It is not my fault that he was elected and there's nothing I can do about it. The judges who issued these rulings are holding that sex is real and that it sometimes matters. They are good rulings that, for the most part, do not compromise on language. They will help us move toward an acknowledgement that women and girls constitute a coherent sex class and that we matter. I'll take it.

CHAPTER 10

THE TERFS

I was once at a conference in Toronto in 2018. Conference attendees included mainly political conservatives, concerned parents of kids who were starting to "identify as transgender," and a few medical professionals who had studied the impacts of puberty blockers on young bodies. During a break between panels, I was casually chatting at a table with a few attendees, including one woman whom I would characterize as a moderate-to-conservative journalist. After I introduced myself, she said, "Oh, you're a TERF." I smiled and said, "Yeah, basically." After a brief pause, she looked directly at me from across the table and said, "It's going to be the TERFs who save us all."

Life as an American TERF can be a bit odd. The reason that it is odd is that we are never really quite sure how much is popularly understood about "trans," especially among mainstream liberals. We constantly read on social media and in feminist news sources about male rapists and murderers being housed in women's prisons because they "are trans"; about men being allowed to participate in women's sports on the basis that they "are trans"; and about children being sterilized and put under the knife because they "are trans." TERFs know all about the relationships between "trans" and pornography. We know that all our society's institutions, including the government, the media, academia, civic institutions, and corporate America, have all been captured by the lie of "trans." And yet we go about our days, doing our jobs, raising our kids, grocery shopping, having our cars repaired, paying our bills, and checking the mail, knowing about all of these things. Yet we also know that there is virtually no coverage of any of this in any mainstream media outlets because the media is hell-bent on pretending that these phenomena are not occurring. And so we never really know: "*Do ordinary Americans know about any of this? And if they do, why does no one ever say anything?*"

We TERFs know that countless parents are bereft about their children being lost to what they view as the cult of "trans." We know that countless young adults are waking up to the reality that they, sometimes with parental consent, allowed themselves to be sterilized and often castrated because some mental and physical health practitioners persuaded them that they "are trans." We know that young women are dehydrating themselves in order not to have to use the restroom at school, knowing that boys will be present on the basis that they "are trans." We know that there is a very dark undercurrent at play, highly pornographic and predatory, that is capturing our society's children. We know that "gender identity" is a lie that obscures the reality of sex.

We do not hail from the political right. Radical feminists come from the left and typically have very traditional liberal values, including full equality of opportunity for women and minorities to participate in all aspects of political and economic life, education, sports, and culture. We tend to support universal access to health care, adequate housing for everyone, nutrition, and other social services. We are committed to values that support liberty and justice, as well as democracy and responsive government. We are committed to protecting and advancing the interests of women and girls as a sex class. It is mystifying for many of us to watch all of society's institutions, including many that we used to trust, cave to an industry-fueled men's rights movement that denies basic biology and erases women and girls.

Being a TERF is also dangerous. In March 2021, a man named Matt Thompson (who goes by "they/them" pronouns and describes himself as being "genderfuck") wrote a paper in connection with his studies in gender and sexuality at the London School of Economics and Political Science (LSE). He presented it at a conference in April that year for a course on Transnational Sexual Politics. The paper was titled, "Trans* Endemics: Embodying Viral and Monstrous Threat in Times of Pandemic."[15] In it, he said: "TERFs see transness as an endemic threat to feminism, a 'social contagion', the frontier on which they're going to defeat patriarchy. They don their JK Rowling masks and shout bloody murder about 'female erasure'. They see trans* people and gender studies departments as brainwashing the population against the sanctity of biological sex. Actually, on this last point, they're not too far from right." The paper concluded: "If TERFs think trans* is an endemic threat to feminism, let us be the threat to feminism. We are the endemic, the viral, the toxic onslaught of ideology that attacks the very core of what you hold dear. We go unnoticed, right up until the moment they scream for mercy. Am I a threat to you? Do I send chills down your spine? Picture this: I hold a knife to your throat and spit my transness into your ear. Does that turn you on? Are you scared? I sure fucking hope so." These people mean business. They do not, for the most part, threaten conservatives in this way (though that is starting to change). They threaten us in this way because we are women, because they know they can get away with it (no one at LSE seemed to think the paper was problematic), and because they know that we present a genuine political threat to the enshrinement of "gender identity" in law and throughout society. And, of course, one of the greatest ironies of the contemporary women's rights movement is that we are not even allowed to talk about it.

For TERFs, the issue comes down to this: Women as a class have always been oppressed by men as a class (regardless of the benign behaviors of any individual men) *on the basis of sex*, and we are all quite angry about it. There is a reason that suffragists had to fight for the right to vote

---

[15] Some people put an asterisk after the word "trans." They do this, they say, to denote that "trans" is an umbrella term that covers a variety of identities. It's a bit like the inclusion of the + symbol after LGBT (or LGBTQ or LGBTQI or LGBTQIA or whatever the acronym is these days).

after being denied the franchise for centuries and that countless men and institutions fought hard to stop them. There is a reason that all over the world, men beat, rape, torture, and murder women and girls at astronomical rates. There is a reason that lesbians are routinely targeted for harassment or worse. There is a reason that men used to burn women for allegedly engaging in witchcraft. It was not on the basis of "identity"—no one bothered to ask women which pronouns they preferred before burning them. It was on the basis of sex. And now, the entire "gender identity" movement denies that sex even exists or that it might matter.

The prevailing narrative is that being "pro-trans" or "trans-inclusive" is a leftist position. But it's not. All "gender identity" and "transgender" issues are an embrace of politically regressive, sexist, homophobic stereotypes. It is anti-speech and incredibly authoritarian. It is the most politically regressive idea the Democrats have embraced in my lifetime. TERFs see right through all of it. We aim to win, and if that means calling out our own political tribe for the atrocities it has committed at the altar of "gender identity," then that's what we'll do.

The Second Wave of feminism in the sixties, seventies, and eighties created feminist theory, ethics, and strategy based on grassroots in-person discussions. And it worked, to a great extent. They won women's rights to divorce their husbands in places where that right didn't exist, to open bank accounts and own credit cards, and to prosecute their husbands for rape. All over the country, rape crisis centers and domestic violence shelters opened to care for women who were fleeing male violence. And, of course, American feminists won the right to abortion in 1973 when the Supreme Court decided *Roe v. Wade*. All that work was done on behalf of all women, regardless of political party or orientation. No one asks a woman for her political affiliation when she shows up at a domestic violence shelter, bloodied and bruised. Sadly, many second-wave feminists later retreated into academia and made much less progress in the movement to secure women's liberty. The movement largely disbanded, as many women assumed that all the work had been done. But we are back.

Political conservatives often like to take credit for making progress in the movement to stop the abolition of sex, and much of that credit is deserved. Politically conservative groups (especially women's groups) *have* made much progress in efforts to push back against the Democratic Party's insistence on shredding women's rights at the altar of "gender identity." As discussed above, several Republican congressmen and women have introduced important legislation to advance the cause.

But in the end, I think there are several reasons why conservatives are not ultimately going to win the fight against "gender identity." I also think the "trans" movement agrees with me, which is why it is so hell-bent on silencing TERFs. The "trans" movement pushes back on conservatives, but they do not actively work to silence them in the media or in government. I think the "trans" movement is banking on the idea that they have a decent shot at beating the conservatives, but no shot at beating the TERFs, and I think they are right.

First, I think that conservatives severely underestimated the country's support for same-sex marriage and allowed themselves to be viewed as homophobic bigots, and that characterization has stuck. I don't think that conservatives are going to be able to shake that off. To be clear, I do not think that all conservatives are actually homophobic. I think there are many who *do* support same-sex marriage. I also think that it is possible to be against same-sex marriage without actually hating gay men or lesbians. I don't happen to agree with Christians who think that marriage is a sacrament that exists solely between one man and one woman, but I think it is possible to have that religious view without wanting gay men or lesbians to be electrocuted, jailed, or converted. I personally know many Republicans who do think that marriage is a sacrament that exists solely between one man and one woman and who also think that gay men and lesbians are entirely deserving of civil and human rights on the basis of sexual orientation in realms outside of marriage. In my experience, for example, most do not think that anyone should be fired from a job due to her or his sexual orientation. But still, the right's opposition to same-sex marriage painted them as religious zealots who hate gay people and that characterization now makes it politically challenging for them to succeed in fighting back against "gender identity."

A second reason is that the players on the political right who are fighting the abolition of sex are doing so because of their own version of devotion to gender. They don't like "gender identity," but they *do* have an affinity for stereotypical sex roles and stereotypes. Ultimately, the Christian right views women and men as having been created by God as male and female, in his image, and they advance very traditionalist arguments about what this should mean for men's and women's places in society. This is not universally true among the political right. Many conservatives (especially conservative women) do think that women have roles to play in civil society, including getting an education and working outside the home. But many don't. They think that women exist solely to have babies and serve men. From a feminist perspective, that's a disaster for women and girls. *The Daily Wire* premiered Catholic conservative Matt Walsh's film *What Is a Woman?* in 2022. The film did a good job of exposing the absurdity of the fact that plenty of people don't seem to know what a woman is and bringing attention to the industry that is harming children. However, the film was also a celebration of sex stereotypes, with girls being love-bombed with pink and glitter and boys being love-bombed with blue and trucks. I think the film was generally successful, but I don't think that a film produced by *The Daily Wire* and starring a Catholic conservative man is going to reach the segment of society that needs to be reached if we are going to beat the "gender identity" industry—moderates and liberals. TERFs, who are ourselves progressives and liberals, can do a much better job of that.

Third, most Americans across the political spectrum, including many Republicans, think that "trans" is an extension of "gay" because a massive industry succeeded in getting the T attached to the LGB acronym. Getting the T included was an ingenious political strategy. Becoming popularly known as a component of a legitimate civil rights struggle allowed "gender identity" to make a tremendous amount of traction. That's probably because "We demand rights for LGBT people!" is a much more persuasive rallying cry than "We demand that all of civil society pretend that sex isn't real!" Many Republican lawmakers are afraid to push back on the Democrats because if "trans" is an extension of "gay," then push-back appears to be homophobic. For these reasons, I think the strongest constituency in the fight to protect the sex-based rights of women and girls and to stop the abolition of sex is the TERFs—the leftist feminists (especially lesbians) who sincerely care about the liberation of women and girls from male dominance.

TERFs can also criticize "gender identity" before Democratic lawmakers in a way that conservatives can't. On Monday, June 6, 2022, I went to Harrisburg, Pennsylvania for a June 7 lobby day. I was there to lobby to support the Protect Women's Sports Act. The state assembly had already passed the bill, and now it was before the state senate. WDI USA had discussed internally how involved we wanted to be in efforts to get the senate to pass the bill. We knew that even if the bill passed, the Democratic governor was likely to veto it, and that we probably would not be able to amass enough votes to override a gubernatorial veto. We reasoned that it didn't matter. If most lawmakers voted to pass the bill in Pennsylvania—the home of the Big Ten Penn State Nittany Lions—that would be a massive victory in and of itself. If we could get even one Democrat to vote yes on the bill, that would be icing on the cake. A woman with Concerned Women for America (a conservative women's group) had arranged a series of meetings, some with Republicans, others with Democrats. In the meantime, the WDI USA state legislative action team was mobilizing a team to attend the lobby day.

I got up at five in the morning the next day and headed to the Capitol, armed with ten copies of my book, *The Abolition of Sex*, and a stack of fliers. Other women brought more copies of the book. There were twenty Democrats in the Pennsylvania Senate at the time and our goal was to deliver one copy to each senate Democratic office. We did that, and I also spoke at a press conference, making sure to emphasize that I was a Democrat in support of the bill and asking my fellow Democrats to join me.

I had four meetings with Democratic offices—one with a senator and three with staff. Two of these meetings revealed the moral and intellectual bankruptcy of Democratic support for "gender identity." Democrats who support "gender identity" simply wither in the presence of TERFs. As I sat down to talk with the senator, I began by explaining that I am a lifelong Democrat and an abortion rights supporter, thanked her for her leadership on protecting abortion rights, and then posed a question: "If women have a right to choose, where do those rights end? If women have a right to choose abortion, do women also have a right to choose not to compete in athletics against men?" She wasn't quite sure what to do with that question. She said, "Let me make one thing straight: I believe that trans women are women." My response was to note that I am very worried about the health of the Democratic Party, in part because we claim to be the party of science, yet we throw biology out the window when we say things like "Trans women are women." She wasn't quite sure what to do with that either.

At one point, she said something about boys and girls playing sports together at young ages and I politely interrupted to ask if I could ask a clarifying question and she said yes. I then asked, "Can you please explain what you mean by the words boys and girls?" At that point, all the color went out of her face, and she just stared at me. I sat there calmly, while she removed her glasses and placed them on her notepad. Then she just looked at me blankly. Her staffer was sitting on the sofa directly behind me, and she piped in with a bunch of postmodern gobbledygook about "gender identity." Toward the end of the meeting, I simply said this: "I hear from rank-and-file Democrats every day. They are tired of what party leadership is doing and even more tired of being ignored. They tell me that they have left the party, plan to leave the party, or will never vote for a Democrat again *because of this issue*." She thanked us for our time and we left.

Later that day, I met with a Democratic staffer who was even more hostile to me than the senator had been. I gave her the same basic opening that I had given to the senator, thanking her for her boss's support for abortion rights and asking if women have the right to choose abortion, do we also have the right to choose not to compete against men in athletics. She huffily asked, "What harm does having trans women compete on women's teams do to cis women?" I could have taken that opportunity to break down the TERF opposition to terms like "trans women" and "cis women." But since I knew that it was already a lost cause, I took a different tack. I rattled off a bunch of information and statistics about Title IX—its history, its author, its impacts on the lives of women and girls, and its implementing regulations that permit sex segregation under certain circumstances. She didn't like that at all. She later demanded to know why I approve of having girls be forced to undergo intrusive vaginal examinations to compete in girls' sports. I asked her what aspects of the Pennsylvania bill would require such a thing. She could point to none. She continued with this line of questioning, furiously underlining random things on her notepad. She demanded to know exactly how doctors are supposed to verify the sex of their patients without conducting a genital exam. I calmly responded, "Doctors know the sex of their patients. Why are you even talking about genital exams? No one else is." She didn't like that at all either. By the end of the meeting, she was visibly angry. She was physically shaking and kept furiously shaking her head in exasperation. She had absolutely no idea what to do with me. We thanked her for her time and left.

I met with another Democratic staffer who was much more receptive. I made it clear that I'm a Democrat and that I supported the bill. He seemed genuinely curious about this. Because the WDI USA state legislative team had done its homework, I knew that his boss (a woman) served on a state commission on women's health. I pointed that out to him and emphasized that the phrase "women's health" *must* mean something. In that moment, the look on his face strongly suggested that he got it.

In the end, one Democrat voted for the bill and I had the chance to meet with her staffer. He said right off the bat, "Let me cut to the chase: My boss is going to vote for this bill. She has done the analysis. She is an athlete. She understands the importance of this issue." It was a brief meeting. I told him that I could make available many Pennsylvania Democrats who would support her and hopefully help persuade some of her colleagues to join her in voting to override the eventual gubernatorial veto. He was very open to that suggestion and gave me his card. The bill passed later that day. So, we accomplished what we set out to do: The bill passed and at least one (one counts as "at least one") Democrat voted for it. As predicted, the governor did end up vetoing it and the legislature did not have the votes to override the veto.

WDI USA has received a lot of criticism for working with the American political right. There are several Facebook groups that are dedicated exclusively to complaining about feminist individuals and groups like WoLF and WDI USA who have chosen to work across the political aisle to achieve change. That's extremely politically naïve. There is absolutely nothing wrong with cross-partisan organizing. Groups do it all the time. It is the only way anyone ever gets anything done. In addition, the members of those groups do absolutely nothing to make any progress toward protecting the sex-based rights of women and girls. All they ever do is write long and tedious blog posts that almost no one reads and chat with each other on Facebook about how the right wing is evil. I fail to see how feminists will make any positive political change if we all just dropped our advocacy and spent all our time writing blog posts that would go ignored and chatting among ourselves on Facebook.

By December 2022, the Equality Act appeared to be dead, although it came back in 2023. As discussed in Chapter 1, this insidious bill would have redefined sex to include the nebulous, vacuous, and meaningless concept of "gender identity," in ways that would have been disastrous for women and girls. President Biden had promised to get it enacted within 100 one hundred days of taking office if he won the 2020 presidential election. Not only did he fail to do that, but he failed to get it passed *at all*. We believe this is due in part to the tireless work of the volunteers at WDI USA. As explained, WDI USA spent a lot of time and energy in early 2021 explaining to Senate Majority Leader Charles Schumer why enshrining "gender identity" in the law is harmful to women and girls, and in January of 2022, WDI USA sent a copy of *The Abolition of Sex: How the "Transgender" Agenda Harms Women and Girls* to every single member of Congress. We think the apparent death of the Equality Act is at least in part because of the relentless work of TERFs.

What we need to stop the abolition of sex is a broad-based grassroots global movement and I cannot say it better than Hannah Berrelli, U.K. feminist, *Reduxx* author, and founder of Lesbian Labour, when she says: "If speaking in small meetings with women who already agree with you, disappearing into academia, and refusing to do any action that reaches out to non-academic working class women was an effective political strategy, we wouldn't be in the position we are in today. For over thirty years the priority of radical feminists has been getting their books published by tiny academic presses, and doing retreats in the woods. Now we have a generation of girls who believe that if they aren't sufficiently feminine, they should have organs chopped off. They created this situation with their ineptitude, incompetence, and ultimately favouring lifestyle politics over mass political action. We tried [that] way. It was a catastrophic and devastating failure. Enough." Berrelli is British, but this analysis holds true in the U.S. as well. We *do* need a mass political movement that reaches women and girls (and men and boys) of all educational levels, all economic classes, all races, all religions, and all political affiliations. TERFs are leading the way.

WDI is an absolutely amazing global organization dedicated to protecting the sex-based rights of women and girls. It is an all-volunteer organization with volunteers all over the world. Its most active volunteers meet virtually on a weekly basis. Every Saturday, it puts on a women-only webinar to talk about all sorts of topics related to protecting the sex-based rights of women and girls. Women gather to talk about abolishing the prostitution industry, stopping female genital mutilation, radical feminist theory, lesbian organizing, and, of course, developments (positive and negative) in getting "gender identity" eliminated from law and society. The webinar has a chat function and the chat is always lively. Participating can be moving, exciting, infuriating, and/or fun, depending on the topic being discussed. Regardless of anything else, it is always inspiring and invigorating. I would encourage more American liberal and progressive women to join us. Get involved. Read the Declaration on Women's Sex-Based Rights, sign it if you agree, and then apply to volunteer with us. We need all hands on deck—moms, non-moms, accountants, web designers, truck drivers, construction workers, electricians, librarians, plumbers, doctors, and lawyers. All women are welcome.

Feminist author Eliza Mondegreen does hard work that most of the rest of us don't want to do—she combs Reddit pages for clues into what's going on in the minds of the people who are caught up in "gender identity," who think they "are trans." Not long ago, she posted a piece called "Leaving Is the Hardest Part," about the process of waking up to the truth. She quoted one young woman (who thinks she's a man) as saying: "I've kept falling into the rabbit hole of terfs and radfems on Tumblr and I hate them, I really do. I hate how they hate me despite never having met me and I hate the awful things they say and I hate their bigotry. But I look at the posts, I see their unflattering pictures of trans women and the asks they get saying 'suck my girlcock' and **there's this voice in the back of my head that says *what if they're right?*...** And a part of me that I don't like says *TERFs were right all along. You felt pressured into staying trans and they were right about it. They were right that trans people just perpetuate stereotypes and that this all was a fad for privilege westerners*" (emphasis in original).

That poor young woman is right. TERFs *are* right. We *have* known all along. It is, as my Canadian conservative journalist friend told me during that 2018 conference in Toronto, going to be the TERFs who save us all. Democrat party leaders, let this serve as your reckoning. It is time to come clean. No lying, no gaslighting, no pretending that you didn't know. There is no hiding from this. You knew. You knew the entire time. It is time to make things right by America's women and girls.

AFTERWORD

A CAUTIONARY TALE AND A POLICY PRESCRIPTION FOR DEMOCRATIC PARTY LEADERSHIP

Democratic Party leadership: You must change course, and you must do so immediately. You should do this because it is the right thing to do, but you should also do it for the health of the party. You only need to look at some of our allies across the pond and down under to understand why. Women all over the world are rejecting their left-of-center parties for refusing to represent our interests and for sacrificing women and children at the altar of "gender identity." Google "Nicola Sturgeon gender recognition" if you want to understand what happens to politicians who ignore of a bunch of angry Scottish feminists. At the end of this section, I'll suggest some policy changes that you should start making immediately, but first I would like to offer a cautionary tale.

All was quiet on the sex and gender front in the U.K. Until, that is, it wasn't. Until women, including lesbians (and many gay men), collectively said NO to "gender identity." When feminists started to complain, some leaders of the major left-leaning U.K. political parties started getting scared, and rightly so. These women and gay rights activists had had it and weren't going to take it anymore.

In 2004, the U.K. Parliament enacted a bill called the Gender Recognition Act (GRA), which is still on the books (for now—there have been numerous calls for repeal). This is the law in England, Wales, Scotland, and Northern Ireland. It basically makes it possible for anyone to obtain legal recognition of their preferred "gender" by complying with some minimal requirements, including that the person is "living in their acquired gender." It established the legal fiction that it is possible for people to be the sex that they are not. People who meet the requirements can obtain a Gender Recognition Certificate (GRC). Pretty much no one paid much attention to this law and very few people took advantage of it to obtain a GRC. As of 2018 (fourteen years after the law was enacted), fewer than 5,000 people had one. Fast forward to 2018, when essentially all hell broke loose.

In July 2018, the U.K. government launched a consultation into the Reform of the Gender Recognition Act for England and Wales (Scottish "reform," discussed below, would come later). The stated purpose of this so-called reform was to "make the process of obtaining new birth certificates less intrusive and bureaucratic for transgender people." What was actually being proposed was the elimination of *any* requirements for receiving a GRC. Women in the U.K. were, quite understandably, outraged. In my view, the original GRA is ridiculous in that there is no such thing as "living in a gender." Every single one of us is either female or male. To the extent that there is such a thing as "living in a gender," this just points to conformity with opposite-sex stereotypes, and in my view, no man should be able to be legally considered a woman, even if he really thinks he is one and even if he wears dresses and high heels. I mean, if a man wants to wear dresses and high heels, sure, go for it. Men like David Bowie pulled off non-conformity with sex stereotypes quite effectively for a very long time, and no one thought he wasn't a man. But still, this was different. This was the U.K. government suggesting that perhaps anyone should be able to be legally considered the opposite sex based on his or her say-so.

By then, discontent among feminists within the Labour Party due to tensions between women's rights and "gender identity" had been brewing for a while. In January 2018, a leftist feminist named Venice Allan was suspended from the Labour Party for alleged "transphobia." Allan said at the time, "If stating that males are men means that Labour don't want me, quite frankly I hope they chuck me out." Rather than wait for them to "chuck her out," Allan left, stating that Labour was no longer a safe place for women. Allan wasn't alone.

The U.K. government eventually decided in 2020 not to adopt the proposed "reforms" to the GRA, thanks in large part to the feminists who complained about it. That was a major win for U.K. women, but tensions between feminists and the Labour Party did not subside. In late September 2021, the U.K. Labour Party met for its annual conference. When asked by a news reporter, "Is it transphobic to say that only women have a cervix?" Labour leader Keir Starmer said that that is something that "should not be said." Doubling down, Labour member David Lammy later said that the statement "only women have a cervix" may not be "transphobic, but it is not accurate." Lammy would go on to refer to feminists as "dinosaurs" who want to "hoard rights." Needless to say, none of this went over well with feminist members of the Labour Party, who started mocking Lammy by wandering around London wearing dinosaur costumes.

The hashtag #LabourLosingWomen has frequently trended on X over the course of the past several years, and an actual account called @LabourLosingWomen appeared in 2021with the bio: "For Labour members and voters who won't support them whilst they continue to ignore the concerns of women." By January 2023, things had gotten so bad for the Labour Party that the hashtag #NeverLabour was trending on X, often accompanied by quips like this:

> Labour has a little Keir
> His words are sweet n cosy.
> He'll listen to your worriment
> Unless your name is Rosie.
> In fact, if you're a female,
> This party ain't for you.

They'll squirm at saying what you are
You have a willy too!
#NeverLabour

Rosie is a reference to Rosie Duffield, a Labour Member of Parliament who publicly bucks her party's leadership to take a strong stand for women's rights. Finally, Starmer started to backpedal, although at first, he couldn't quite bring himself to do it completely. Asked to clarify his stance on "trans," he stated that 99.9 percent of women "of course haven't got a penis," prompting conservative PM Rishi Sunak to respond that, in fact, 100 percent of women do not have penises. By then, thanks to the Labour Party, one of the hottest topics in the U.K. had become the precise percentage of women who have penises (some, according to Starmer).

None of this went over well with women in the U.K. Feminist (and former *Guardian* correspondent) Suzanne Moore published a piece in *The Telegraph* titled, "Keir Starmer's Mishandling of the Trans Debate Is an Open Goal for the Tories: Women's Right to Single-Sex Spaces Either Matters to the Labour Leadership or It Doesn't—They Cannot Have It Both Ways." One British X user posted: "Hi, @Keir_Starmer, I voted for Labour for the first time aged 18, & have voted for you on numerous occasions since then. HOWEVER, I can guarantee you I will not be voting Labour again until you stop pretending that women can have penises. Do you want my vote?" In July 2023, it was reported that the Labour Party had lost over 10,000 members in just two months.

While all of this was happening, the Gender Identity Development Service (GIDS) at Tavistock and Portman NHS Foundation Trust in London (the only provider of "gender identity services" for children and young adults in the U.K.) was starting to crumble (though many in the U.K. still worry that not enough is being done to end its barbaric practices). In 2022, it was announced that it would close and be replaced with regional centers that focused more on mental health services. In 2023, a BBC journalist named Hannah Barnes published the book *Time to Think: The Inside Story of the Collapse of the Tavistock's Gender Service for Children*, in which former clinicians at GIDS spoke about their regret for having prescribed puberty blockers and wrong-sex hormones to kids under sixteen and compared such prescriptions to the doping of athletes representing East Germany in the sixties and seventies. At first, she had trouble finding anyone to publish her findings. Of the twenty-two publishers who received her book proposal, ten did not respond at all.

It is not just Labour either. The U.K. Green Party is having similar problems. Emma Bateman was, until recently, the co-chair of Green Party Women. Her X bio reads: "We are @TheGreenParty women. Supporting women in politics. Championing ecofeminism. Internationalist. Working for a world that is feminist, just & green." In December 2020, the party chose a man (who claims to be a woman) named Kathryn Bristow as Bateman's co-chair of Green Party Women. In March 2022, Bateman announced that she was taking legal action against the Green Party, and on January 19, 2023, she announced that the party had expelled her for standing up for women's sex-based rights.

For all these reasons, countless women have left the party over the past few years. Some of their reasons are: "The Green Party does not support women so I cannot support the Green Party. Having a man or other 'non women' representing the concerns of women and girls is a backwards step. It is men silencing women by taking up our spaces. We got fed up with men speaking on behalf of women's rights over 100 years ago. —Former grassroots activist." Another reads, "I have left the party over its stance on women's rights. You can't even discuss it without being accused of transphobia. It's a terrible situation which I believe is driven by a powerful lobby intent on driving an agenda which is anti-gay and anti-women. —Ex-Green woman." These are clearly very left-wing feminist women. And they have had it with their party's total embrace of "gender identity" at the expense of women and girls.

Discontent within the party continues to brew. In 2023, women in the party announced the "Green Women's Declaration," stating, "This Declaration has been initiated by members of the Green Party of England and Wales (GPEW) who believe in the right to advocate for women as a sex.

Women's rights, based on the reality of biological sex, have been eroded within the GPEW, as elsewhere in society. We believe the consequences of this disregard for the protected characteristic of sex are extremely damaging for women and girls, especially lesbians, mothers and those who are disabled. There now exists a chilling atmosphere of censure and fear within the Party, which affects not only free speech but also free thought."

And then the Liberal Democrats got into the mix. Back in 2021, England and Wales were grappling with an epidemic of violence against women and girls (a situation that has not abated), and the government set out to do something about it. After the vicious murder of Sarah Everard (who was kidnapped, raped, and strangled to death, burned, and left in a nearby pond) by police officer Wayne Couzens, a report was commissioned. That report revealed that in a single year, an estimated 1.6 million women were victims of domestic abuse, 618,000 women were victims of sexual assault, and 892,000 women were victims of stalking in England and Wales.

Even so, Sir Ed Davey, the leader of the Liberal Democrat Party, maintained that housing male prisoners in women's prisons, domestic violence shelters, and rape crisis centers was a good idea. In September 2021, he appeared on a BBC radio program to discuss that very report. When asked if there should be *any* spaces in society in which women could be free from men who claim to have a woman identity, his answer was "No." At a party conference in March 2023, conference organizers scheduled a session to discuss women's representation on internal party committees. But when a vote was taken on whether to go forward with the session, Davey went out of his way to vote against having the session. After women in the party complained about this suppression of their voices, Councillor Sean MacLeod (another party officer) posted, simply, "Fuck the TERFs." In May 2023, Davey appeared on a call-in show called *Leading Britain's Conversations.* When asked "Can a woman have a penis?" his answer was, "Quite clearly," prompting U.K. feminist and journalist Jo Bartosch to quip, "With these few words, Davey surely shredded his reputation among rational human beings." Democrats in positions of leadership, please rest assured that rational Democrats feel the same way about you every time you deny the material reality of sex.

Wales entered the fray in a very public way in February 2023 when it announced its "LGBTQ+ Action Plan for Wales." The plan was essentially a proposal to "make it simpler for someone to legally change their gender." Feminists and gay rights activists understand that this is code for allowing men who claim to have a woman identity to get legal recognition to be the opposite sex by simply ignoring the material reality of sex. They aren't having it. As of writing, this is all happening under the leadership of First Minister (and Labour Leader) Mark Drakeford. The Wales Women's Rights Network said the Welsh government was being "tone deaf to events in Scotland" (discussed below) and that it was another government "prepared to trample over women's rights." A gay-rights advocacy organization called LGB Alliance Cymru put out a statement opposing the plan ("LGB" refers to lesbian, gay, and bisexual and Cymru is the Welsh word for Wales—the group is part of a larger group simply called the LGB Alliance, of which the U.S. has a chapter).

In late 2022, it was reported that the Scottish Parliament at Holyrood was pursuing something called the "Gender Recognition Reform" (GRR) bill. All this was being done with the support of the First Minister, Nicola Sturgeon, leader of the Scottish National Party (SNP). I do not know the details of that bill, other than the fact that it was very similar to the 2018 proposed GRA "reforms" in England and Wales—it would usher in "gender self-ID" by allowing anyone to be legally recognized as the opposite sex on the basis of his or her say-so alone. Feminists fought hard to stop it. For days, countless women and plenty of men—including members of the SNP itself—protested outside of Holyrood wearing suffrage banners and carrying signs that read Woman = Adult Human Female. The vast majority (77 percent) of Scots, women and men, opposed the "reforms." Holyrood went ahead and voted for the bill anyway in December 2022.

By February 2023, it was being reported that 95 percent opposed it. By March 2023, the SNP had lost over 30,000 members and Sturgeon was forced to resign.

Joanna Cherry is a Scottish MP, barrister, and a member of the SNP. She is also a lesbian and an outspoken champion for the sex-based rights of women and girls. In the spring of 2023, she was scheduled to talk at the Edinburgh Festival Fringe as part of a series called "In Conversation." However, some staff at the venue decided that her stances on women's rights made them "uncomfortable," so the venue cancelled the booking. Plenty of Scottish lawyers seemed to think that her cancelation violated the U.K.'s 2010 Equality Act. I don't know whether the move was unlawful, but I do think it is reprehensible. U.K. journalist Joan Smith lamented, "This is a cross-party issue, affected elected representatives from other Left-of-centre parties, so where is the outrage from the Labour and Lib Dem leaders in Scotland and the rest of the UK? Even Kier Starmer, who has so signally failed to stand up for one of his own MPs, Rosie Duffield, must by now be aware of what's going on—and that the law is being broken." In August 2023, Robin Harper, the U.K.'s first Green parliamentarian, quit the Scottish Green party, stating that the party had "lost the plot" over this issue (among others).

By mid-2023, the U.K. government could no longer ignore the issue and a session was held in Parliament to debate the meaning of the word "sex" under U.K. law. Prime Minister (and the head of the Conservative Party) Rishi Sunak announced that he would change the law to explicitly protect single-sex spaces for women, saying that "biological sex is fundamentally important." Miriam Cates, a Tory MP, introduced a bill in Parliament to give parents the legal right to see materials used in sex education lessons and prohibit schools from using externally produced teaching resources not available for public scrutiny—a perfectly sensible policy that most parents across the political spectrum can probably support. Unfortunately, it appears that the Labour Party is simply letting the Tory Party be the party of sense and reason, much like the Democrats are doing stateside. Finally, by August 2023, Starmer was forced to backpedal and acknowledged that a woman is an adult human female and said that Labour would work to protect female-only spaces (although many still question the party's sincerity and its commitment to doing so).

The same topic has been roiling the left in Australia for several years now. In 2020, the Australian Labor Party and premier Daniel Andrews announced the Change or Suppression (Conversion) Practices Prohibition bill in the state of Victoria. This purported to be a bill criminalizing gay conversion therapy, but concerns were raised that it would have the additional effect of criminalizing healthcare practitioners who did not automatically agree to "affirm" a minor's "gender identity." It was signed in 2021 and went into effect in February 2022.

Speaking in a private Facebook group a few months later, a Green Party councilor (himself a gay man) raised concerns about the law, expressing worry that "many others in my age bracket who experienced gender dysphoria when puberty hit before discovering that they were lesbians much later...all genuinely worry that girls in a similar situation today are being told they are trans. I don't think women who raise concerns about those consequences are hateful." He added that these matters should be able to be discussed openly and publicly. His comments were leaked and he was immediately labeled "trans-exclusionary." A group of 300 rank-and-file Green Party members from across Australia sent a letter to the head of the Victoria Greens, demanding "new standards to resolve significant concerns about trans-exclusionary influences on the party." This was a gay man with influence in the party, speaking up for lesbians and for open public debate, and he was immediately denounced.

Andrews, the Labor leader who had announced and signed the law, later called Kellie-Jay Keen's "Let Women Speak" event in Australia "hateful" and conflated Keen's event with Nazis, even though it was obvious that no one attending Keen's event had anything to do with Nazis. Leaders of the Green Party backed up Labor, but not all members of the Green Party were having it. Helen Lewers, a long-time Green Party activist, quit the party, stating that "the issues most Greens members are passionate about (the environment, biodiversity, climate change, refugees, etc.) can hardly be discussed any more. The agenda is almost constantly interrupted by TRAs [trans rights activists].... The Party has been all but taken over by an active faction comprised of a bunch of women's rights-hating transwomen and their allies." By August 2023, at least one prominent Australian physician in "gender medicine" had acknowledged that the evidence to support "gender-affirming care" is "of low quality" and admitted that there are legitimate questions to be asked about the reversibility of puberty blockers.

In May 2023, Raquel Rosario Sánchez, a feminist from the Dominican Republic, published a piece in *The Telegraph* titled, "The Left Betrayed Women in Spain—Now They Face a Reckoning: The government approved a controversial trans law that saw feminist groups and opposition parties united in condemnation." In February, the government (a coalition of left-leaning parties) had passed a law that allows anyone to be legally recognized as the opposite sex. Three months later, voters kicked them out, ushering in a new conservative government. Sánchez states that "Upon winning the 2018 election, Pedro Sánchez hailed his coalition as 'the most progressive' in Spanish history. If only. No feminist I know relishes the prospect of an emboldened hard-right intent on crushing reproductive rights or male violence legislation. But that does not mean a hard-Left obsessed with putting male rapists in female prisons or abolishing the female categories in sporting competitions get a free pass." I could not agree more, and the Democrats in power should take note of Sánchez's warning. All over the world, left-of-center parties have lost the plot, and that includes the U.S. Democrats.

Meanwhile, plenty of countries are moving toward banning so-called "gender-affirming care" for minors. In 2020, the Finnish Health Authority, after conducting a systematic review of the evidence that found the evidence for "gender-affirming care" to be "inconclusive," issued guidelines backing psychotherapy instead of puberty blockers and cross-sex hormones as the first line of treatment. Sweden decided in February 2022 to halt hormone therapy for minors except in "very rare cases." In 2023, one of Australia's biggest medical insurers decided to stop covering private practitioners prescribing puberty blockers and cross-sex hormones to adolescents. Also in 2023, NHS England confirmed that it would only give puberty blockers to minors "as part of clinical research." Denmark followed suit in 2023. But Democrats in the U.S. just continue to push the idea, against all evidence, that poisoning children with hormones that cause sterilization and other long-term health problems is a good idea.

One of the reasons why the U.S. is going in a different direction from these other countries, according to political scientist Leor Sapir, is that the other countries are following the principles of evidence-based medicine, while the U.S. is not. Systematic reviews are the highest quality of evidence that associations should be relying on when developing policies, practices, and guidelines. WPATH, the AAP, and the Endocrine Society (discussed in Chapter 6) have all put out guidelines that do not rely on *any* systematic reviews. They don't even claim that their policies and statements rely on systematic reviews. England has broken from WPATH, and the director of Belgium's Center for Evidence-Based Medicine has said that he would "toss [WPATH's guidelines] in the bin." Yet other U.S. medical groups routinely cite WPATH, the AAP, and the Endocrine Society when assuring the public about "gender-affirming care." That's how they get away with creating an illusion around "settled science," although, in fact, none exists. President Biden and other Democrats in positions of leadership and our society's traditionally progressive organizations do the same thing.

I have met many of the feminist women who are campaigning against "gender identity" all over the world. They are fierce, outspoken feminists, and they all have their political roots in traditional leftist politics. It remains to be seen whether any left-leaning party leaders in the U.K. or elsewhere will survive their steadfast refusal to engage in any good-faith discussions with feminists within their own parties about how "gender identity," by denying the material reality of sex, affects women's lives. Democrats in positions of leadership are unlikely to fare any better unless they take steps to make amends.

So, what is to be done?

Democrats in position of leadership must immediately clarify that women and girls exist as a distinct class of human beings and that we are worthy of human and civil rights protection on the basis of sex. They should state unequivocally that a woman is an adult human female (and it would help if they would state the obvious fact that zero women have penises, whatever their friends in the U.K. Labour Party have to say on the matter). They should publicly commit themselves to protecting women's sports and spaces for women and girls and state that men do not belong in women's spaces regardless of any identity they may claim to have. Candidates for the presidency should state these things on the record (Robert F. Kennedy Jr. has taken a strong stance for women's sports and I would like to see him go even further by insisting that no men are female and no women are male).

I know it will be very difficult for Democrats to do these things. It will be very difficult for them to walk back positions that they have insisted on pushing on the American public at least since 2016. It would be much easier for them to simply and quietly stop talking about it and hope the issue goes away. It is not going away. Too many women have been raped in prisons by men who claim to have woman identities; too many women and girls have lost opportunities in athletics; too many women and girls have been exposed to male genitalia in bathrooms, locker rooms, and spas; too many children have been sterilized and had their bodies irreparably harmed—all because of policies that they have been pushing—for them to be able to get away with that. And they can do it if they want to. In August 2023, an Irish Senator from the Labour Party named Gerard Craughwell who had voted for the GRA said, simply, "I was wrong."

Democrats, I know it's hard, but you can do it too.

In the U.K., there is a Labour Women's Declaration and a Green Women's Declaration (in addition to the more general Declaration on Women's Sex-Based Rights, which WDI promotes). Both take strong stances in support of the sex-based rights of women and girls. I would be very pleased to see a Democrat Women's Declaration and happy to work with any female Democrat member of Congress to draft one.

Beyond that, there are several steps that Democrats in positions of leadership must take in order to restore credibility with voters of both sexes. First, the president should rescind Executive Order 13988, the Preventing and Combating Discrimination on the Basis of Gender Identity or Sexual

Orientation. It was an absolute slap in the face to American women and girls when he signed it on the first day of taking office. I have never liked Joe Biden, and I will never forgive him for his treatment of Professor Anita Hill during the confirmation hearings of Supreme Court Justice Clarence Thomas. Nonetheless, I voted for him in 2020 for the sole purpose of joining the millions of Americans who were desperate to get the lunatic p*ssy grabber out of the Oval Office. I now regret that decision; I wish I simply hadn't voted and I have no intention of voting in the 2024 presidential election unless the Democrats get a grip.

Once he has rescinded that order, he needs to rescind every subsequent order, memo, and/or directive that followed in its wake from the Departments of Health and Human Services, Housing and Urban Development, Justice, Education, and every other federal agency that has been complicit in his nefarious agenda of abolishing sex as a meaningful category and throwing women and girls to the wolves. Since multiple federal courts have already ruled that those orders, memos, and directives are either procedurally or substantively flawed (or both) anyway, the Biden administration would save us all a lot of time by simply rescinding them.

The administration also needs to concede loss in the case of *Neese v. Becerra*, where a federal judge ruled that doctors are permitted to provide sex-specific medical care where such care is called for (readers may recall that in that case, one of the plaintiff doctors alleged that a male patient refused treatment for possible prostate cancer on the ground that he identifies as a woman and therefore cannot have a prostate). Finally, the president should withdraw the Justice Department's legal complaint against the state of Tennessee in the case of *L.W. v. Skrmetti*, where it argues, incomprehensibly, that a perfectly sensible state law "denies necessary medical care to youth based solely on who they are," in violation of the Equal Protection Clause of the U.S. Constitution. The state law in question is designed to protect the health and welfare of minors. Its aim is to protect children from the harms that come to them when they are given puberty blockers, wrong-sex hormones, and medically unnecessary surgery. The Justice Department says in the first line of the section on factual allegations that "every person has a gender identity." This is a lie and the president knows it. Every single person on the face of the planet—all eight billion of us—is either female or male, regardless of any claimed identity. The vast majority of Americans do not go along with the absurdity of "gender identity," so it would be good if the administration would stop telling the obnoxious lie that we all have one.

I know that the vice president knows what a woman is. I was in the audience during the 2017 symposium "Women Unshackled: Policy Solutions to Address the Growth of Female Incarceration" when she was a U.S. senator. I remember listening to her speak movingly about the plight of incarcerated women. She talked about the Dignity for Incarcerated Women Act, which would mandate that female inmates receive free menstrual products, outlaw shackling and solitary confinement for pregnant women, and provide that the location of a mother's children would factor into her placement in the federal prison system. After the event, she told reporters many of these solutions were "pretty obvious." She argued that "this is something that should not be thought of as even bipartisan—this should be a nonpartisan issue." I agree with her completely. Neither should the dignity of women and girls or the material reality of sex be partisan issues. At exactly what point did she forget what all these words mean?

I was also in the audience during the 2012 Women in the World conference at Lincoln Center in New York City, where the vice president appeared on a panel with her sister, Maya Harris. At the time, she was the Attorney General of California and Maya was the Vice President for Democracy, Rights and Justice at the Ford Foundation (as discussed earlier, in 2017 she joined the board of the Arcus Foundation, which promotes the abolition of sex globally). I distinctly recall her and Maya discussing the importance of teenage girls having access to menstrual products in schools. For a moment, she appeared to be uncomfortable discussing the topic, but then she settled in and said something along the lines of, "Oh, it's okay, we're all women here, right?" Indeed. The cavalier way with which the vice president has dismissed the legitimate concerns of women and girls has been nothing short of appalling and she owes American women and girls an apology. She needs to reverse course and encourage her boss to do so as well. While she's at it, she might have a word with the First Lady. Jill Biden knows what a woman is too, regardless of what she might have to say on the topic publicly, and regardless of her affinity for men like Sarah (Tim) McBride, who insist they are women and that we all have to go along with their charade.

Beyond the administration, the U.S. Congress needs to either (a) bin the Equality Act forever, or (b) remove all references to "gender identity" from it. I strongly suspect that a majority of members of both chambers (on both sides of the aisle) would support a bill that protects lesbian, gay, and bisexual people based on sexual orientation without obscuring the material reality of sex by defining it out of existence. Remember, twelve Republican senators voted to pass the Respect for Marriage Act, enshrining marriage equality in U.S. law in case the Supreme Court votes to overturn *Obergefell v. Hodges*. If they voted for that, they're likely to vote for an Equality Act that protects sexual orientation without enshrining "gender identity" in the law. I suspect that Senate Majority Leader Charles Schumer and former House Speaker Nancy Pelosi would support that too, even though the president continues to blather on about the current Equality Act during his State of the Union Addresses. It is time for them, and for all Congressional Democrats, to say so.

Congress should also pass the Women's Bill of Rights, the Protection of Women and Girls in Sports Act of 2023, and Iowa Senator Joni Ernst's resolution to establish a National Women's Sports Week. Then, Congress should eliminate all references to "gender identity" from every piece of legislation that includes them. That includes the Infrastructure Act of 2022 and the Violence Against Women Act. I realize that Congressional Democrats are unlikely to initiate these moves, but I would ask them to encourage their Republican colleagues to do so behind the scenes and then support their efforts publicly.

There is a lot of work to be done at the state level too. In state houses across the country, Democrats have been working hard to obscure the material reality of sex and throw women and girls under the bus. They do this by opposing bills to protect female-only sports and spaces, supporting bills to redefine sex to include "gender identity" and/or allow men access to women's spaces and prisons, and championing bills to sterilize children by denying their sex. As discussed in Chapter 8, a few Democratic state lawmakers are bucking the trend, and I applaud them. The more state Democrats come out for material reality and for women and girls, the more cover they give others to do so as well.

Democrats in power: You have done wrong by American women and girls and you know it. You have betrayed us and it is time to come clean. It is time for the abolition of sex to end. The year 2024 is right around the corner and you need to right this ship. In August 2023, the Republican National Committee adopted a resolution to "protect children from unsafe sex trait modification and experimentation." The resolution states that "sex-trait modification procedures" (including puberty blockers, wrong-sex hormones, and "gender-affirming" surgeries) are "permanent, risky, and experimental," with potential harms including infertility, low bone density, and heart disease. The stated aim of its sponsor is to incorporate this resolution into the 2024 Republican Party platform. *You* have allowed the Republican Party to become the party of sanity and child-safeguarding. *You* have allowed the Republican Party to become the party of women's rights. *You* have lost the trust of millions of rank-and-file Democrats. To regain trust among Democratic voters of both sexes, you need to hold yourselves accountable and publicly concede defeat on this issue. 2024 depends on it. Good luck.

APPENDIX

ARCUS "SOCIAL JUSTICE" GRANTS (2022)

Recipient	Amount	Purpose	Location
Borealis Philanthropy	$750,000	One year of funding to the Fund for Trans Generations (FTG) for grants, technical assistance, and mentorship to dozens of grassroots U.S. organizations working to build a future in which trans, gender nonconforming, and nonbinary people can live freely and without fear.	Minneapolis, MN
Borealis Philanthropy	$50,000	One year of funding to the Emerging LGBTQ Leaders of Color (ELLC) Fund to support LGBTQ and BIPOC organizations advancing reproductive justice in the U.S. following the overturning of *Roe v. Wade*, which had established that the constitutional right to privacy protects the choice to have an abortion.	Minneapolis, MN

Borealis Philanthropy	$475,000	One year of support for the Emerging LGBTQ Leaders of Color (ELLC) Fund to resource the leadership and visibility of LGBTQ young people of color within and across social justice movements in the U.S.	Minneapolis, MN
California Rural Legal Assistance	$250,000	Two years of funding to support legal representation of LGBTQ California residents who experience discrimination and harassment in the workplace, as well as training to ensure service providers can best understand and address the needs of these communities.	Oakland, CA
Equality Federation Institute	$200,000	One year of funding for the National LGBTQ Movement Convening to develop long- and short-term plans for securing equality and justice in the U.S.	Portland, OR
Equality Florida	$250,000	Two years of support to advance safety and protections for LGBTQ communities across the U.S. state of Florida, including support for organizational safety and security needs.	St. Petersburg, FL

Equality Foundation of Georgia	$250,000	Two years of support to advance fairness, safety, and opportunity for LGBTQ communities and allies throughout the U.S. state of Georgia, including support for organizational safety and security needs.	Atlanta, GA
Equality New Mexico Foundation	$100,000	One year of funding to expand and diversify the movement for LGBTQ rights throughout New Mexico, with a focus on partnering with local activists and leaders to increase public understanding of harmful laws and policies.	Albuquerque, NM
Equality North Carolina Foundation	$250,000	Two years of support to build a powerful LGBTQ+ community across the U.S. state of North Carolina, and to advance safety and protections, including support for organizational safety and security needs.	Durham, NC
Freedom Center for Social Justice	$200,000	Two years of support to advance the cause of justice, equality, and protections for LGBTQ people and others most impacted by structural inequities, centering those who are BIPOC, elder, and/or youth in the U.S. state of North Carolina.	Charlotte, NC

Groundswell Fund	$300,000	Two years of funding for the Black Trans Fund for grantmaking, technical assistance, and capacity building support to U.S.-based groups organized by and for Black trans communities.	San Francisco, CA
Highlander Research and Education Center	$100,000	One year of funding to catalyze grassroots community organizing and movement-building in support of economic, racial, and climate justice, and to map faith-led efforts for social justice in the U.S. South and Appalachian region.	New Market, TN
JASMYN	$150,000	Two years of support to promote increased safety for LGBTQ youth and adults in the Jacksonville, Florida, area in the U.S.	Jacksonville, FL
Many Voices	$50,000	One year of funding for work to open dialogue and advance understanding between and among LGBTQ people and Black communities of faith in the southern U.S., with an emphasis on engaging faith leaders in the movement for LGBTQ social justice.	Durham, NC

Mijente	$150,000	One year of funding to advance protections and safety for Latinx and immigrant LGBTQ communities in Arizona, Georgia, and North Carolina via grassroots coalition-building and leadership training.	Phoenix, AZ
National LGBTQ Task Force	$200,000	Two years of funding to support initiatives to advance LGBTQ rights in the southern United States, with a focus on empowering LGBTQ communities to build power through voter education and uplifting faith-based movements for equality and justice.	Washington, D.C.
New York City Gay and Lesbian Anti-Violence Project	$300,000	Two years of funding to support an expanding nationwide network of organizations and service providers working to address and prevent violence, discrimination, and hate crimes against LGBTQ communities and HIV-affected people.	New York, NY
Power California	$250,000	Two years of funding to mobilize a growing and diverse base of LGBTQ people of color in California's Central Valley, empowering community members to advocate for housing rights, climate justice, and healthcare equity.	Oakland, CA

Proteus Fund	$400,000	One year of funding for the Rights, Faith, and Democracy Collaborative Fund to combat harmful religious exemption policies and to advocate for LGBTQ protections in the U.S. states of Georgia and New Mexico.	Amherst, MA
Public Religion Research Institute	$300,000	Two years of funding to support research into the role of religion and values in U.S. public life, monitoring shifts in attitudes on LGBTQ rights, reproductive justice, racial justice, and faith via high-quality public opinion polling.	Washington, DC
Santa Fe Dreamers Project	$200,000	Two years of funding to secure the safety and liberty of trans and queer migrants before, during, and after their journey through the U.S. immigration system via advocacy, legal representation, and support services.	Santa Fe, NM
Soulforce	$100,000	One year of support to equip U.S. Southern LGBTQI movement organizations and queer Latinx communities with tools and approaches to counteract harmful anti-LGBTQ and white Christian supremacist messaging and organizing.	Abilene, TX

Southern Vision Alliance	$200,000	Two years of support to build a powerful cross-issue membership base and resource frontline LGBTQIA-led organizations across North Carolina and the U.S. South.	Durham, NC
Spark	$200,000	Two years of support to build the leadership, power, and advocacy skills of queer and trans young people of color in the U.S. state of Georgia.	Atlanta, GA
The Source LGBT+ Center	$175,000	One year of support to address increased safety and security needs, as well as provide spaces within communities of LGBT+ people in California's Central Valley to learn, grow, belong, transform, question, and support.	Visalia, CA
Third Wave Fund	$200,000	One year of funding to provide grantmaking and technical assistance to small and emerging organizations throughout the U.S. Southeast and Southwest working to expand the movement for justice within rural and suburban communities of color.	Brooklyn, NY
Transform Network	$100,000	One year of support to resource, train, and mobilize faith and LGBTQ+ communities across North Carolina and the U.S. South through grantmaking and capacity building activities.	Asheville, NC

Transforming Hearts Collective	$50,000	One year of funding to provide faith leaders throughout the U.S. South with resources to advocate for trans justice and inclusion both within their faith communities and in the public square.	Durham, NC
Transgender Law Center	$225,000	One year of funding for the Border Butterflies Project to provide support to LGBTQ migrants at the U.S./Mexico border while advocating reform of harmful immigration policies.	Oakland, CA
Transgender Legal Defense and Education Fund	$200,000	Two years of support to advance safety and legal protections for trans and nonbinary people in the United States.	New York, NY

ACKNOWLEDGMENTS

First, this book would not have been possible without the tireless efforts of countless women (and plenty of men) who work hard every day to expose the harms of "gender identity." They do this despite receiving very little recognition for their work, and almost no money. They do it in service to the movement to protect the sex-based rights of women and girls and to stop the abolition of sex. They do it knowing that they are providing an indispensable service because of the mainstream media's role in perpetuating the lies. Without them, I would not have been able to track the countless examples of men and boys invading women's and girls' spaces or the insidious industry that is fueling this entire movement. I can't name them all here, but they include, and are not limited to: Jennifer Bilek at *The 11th Hour Blog*; Genevieve Gluck (who co-founded the feminist magazine *Reduxx* and writes at *Women's Voices*); Parents with Inconvenient Truths about Trans (PITT); Eliza Mondegreen on Substack; Graham Linehan at The Glinner Report (along with his sidekick who goes by JL and does incredible work reporting "This Week in the War on Women" and the "Good News Supplement"); and Colin Wright and his co-writers at *Reality's Last Stand*.

Second, a special thanks goes to WDI—the leading global organization working to protect women's sex-based rights. WDI is doing herculean work to protect the sex-based rights of women and girls and stop the abolition of sex globally. I want to especially acknowledge the women who currently serve on the board of the U.S. chapter—Megan Rose, Lauren Levey, Irene Lawrence, Lorraine Nowlin, and Katherine Kinney. None of this would have been possible without them.

Third, I want to acknowledge the members of a private Facebook chat that has over the years variously been called "Terves and TDs," "Terves and TDs—The Return," and "GIIR." Most readers will have no idea what I'm talking about, but you know who you are. Thank you for helping me preserve my sanity with much-needed humor.

Finally, thanks as always to my partner in crime Jeff, a registered Democrat who regularly sends email messages to Democratic politicians telling them exactly what he thinks of "gender identity" and its assault on women and girls as a sex class and on children, and refuses to give them any more money until they get a grip.

ABOUT THE AUTHOR

Author Photo Credit: Tina Glass

Kara Dansky is a lawyer, feminist, public speaker, and author of *The Abolition of Sex: How the "Transgender" Agenda Harms Women and Girls*. She serves as the president of the US chapter of Women's Declaration International and previously served on the board of the Women's Liberation Front. She started her law and policy career as a public defender and went on to serve as, among other things, executive director of the Stanford Criminal Justice Center, senior counsel at the ACLU's Center for Justice, and general counsel at the District of Columbia Sentencing Commission. Dansky got her JD from the University of Pennsylvania Law School and her BA from Johns Hopkins University.

Printed in Great Britain
by Amazon

39323277R10205